WHY "A" STUDENTS WORK FOR "C" STUDENTS

and "B" STUDENTS work for the government

WHY "A" STUDENTS WORK FOR "C" STUDENTS

and "B" STUDENTS work for the government

Published by Plata Publishing, LLC

Plata Publishing, LLC
4330 N. Civic Center Plaza
Suite 100
Scottsdale, AZ 85251
(480) 998-6971

Visit our websites: PlataPublishing.com and RichDad.com
Printed in the United States of America
042013

First Edition: April 2013
ISBN: 978-1-61268-076-7

Cover photo credit: Christopher Barr

"Everyone is born a genius, but the process of life de-geniuses them."

– R. Buckminster Fuller

Dedication

To parents... a child's first and most important teachers

"When I was five years old
my mother always told me
that happiness was the key to life.

"When I went to school, they asked me
what I wanted to be when I grew up.
I wrote down 'happy.'

"They told me
I didn't understand the assignment,
and I told them
they didn't understand life."

– John Lennon

Contents

Introduction *Awaken Your Child's Financial Genius* 1

Part One *Are Schools Preparing Your Child for the Real World?* 11

Introduction to Part One 13

Chapter One
Lesson #1: An Educational Crisis 15

Chapter Two
Lesson #2: The Fairy Tale Is Over 31

Chapter Three
Lesson #3: Prepare Your Child for the Worst 47

Chapter Four
Lesson #4: Windows of Learning 75

Chapter Five
Lesson #5: Why Valedictorians Fail 107

Chapter Six
Lesson #6: Why Rich People Go Broke 117

Chapter Seven
Lesson #7: Why Geniuses Are Generous 149

Chapter Eight
Lesson #8: The Entitlement Mentality 171

Part Two *Another Point of View* 199

Introduction to Part Two 201

Chapter Nine
Another Point of View on Intelligence 209

Chapter Ten
Another Point of View on Report Cards 217

Chapter Eleven
Another Point of View on Greed 235

Contents

Chapter Twelve
Another Point of View on Debt 255

Chapter Thirteen
Another Point of View on Taxes 269

Chapter Fourteen
Another Point of View on Words 283

Chapter Fifteen
Another Point of View on God and Money 307

Part Three Give Your Child an Unfair Advantage 319

Introduction to Part Three 321

Chapter Sixteen
The 10 Unfair Advantages of a Financial Education 327

Part Four Graduate School for Capitalists 349

Introduction to Part Four 351

Chapter Seventeen
Be the Fed 357

Chapter Eighteen
How I Print My Own Money 363

Final Thoughts 379

Epilogue 391

Meet the Lannon Family 393

Meet the McElroy Family 395

Bonus Sections 401
Rich Dad Poor Dad for Teens
Rich Dad's Escape the Rat Race

Glossary 445

Resources 453

Introduction

AWAKEN YOUR CHILD'S FINANCIAL GENIUS

"Everybody is a genius.
But if you judge a fish by its ability to climb a tree,
it will live its whole life believing that it is stupid."

– Albert Einstein

INTRODUCTION

Whenever I think about writing a new book I ask myself: Why am I writing this book?

For me, the answer has always been simple, and always the same. I have always wondered why money is not a subject taught in school. Day after day, our teachers drummed this into our heads:

"Go to school to get a job. If you don't go to school, you won't get a good job."

Why Go to School?

This caused me to ask my teachers, "Isn't the reason for getting a job to make money? If money is the objective for getting a job, why not get right to the point and just teach us about money?"

My question was never answered.

The Emperor Has No Clothes

The Emperor's New Clothes is a Danish fairy tale written by Hans Christian Andersen, published in 1837.

The Plot:
Once upon a time, there lived an emperor who cared only about his clothes and about showing them off. One day two con men came to him and said that they could make him the finest suit of clothes from the most beautiful cloth. This cloth, they said, was very special. The cloth was invisible to the stupid and the low-born.

Being a bit nervous about whether he himself would be able to see the cloth the emperor first sent two of his trusted advisors to see this special material. There was, of course, no cloth at all, but neither would admit that they could not see it and so they praised it.

As word of this special cloth spread, all the townspeople were now interested to learn how stupid their neighbors were.

The emperor then allowed himself to be dressed by the con men in his special new suit, made of this special cloth, for the procession through town. Although he knew he was naked, he never admitted it for fear that he was too unfit and stupid to see that he was wearing nothing. He too was afraid that the townspeople would think that he was stupid.

Of course, all the townspeople wildly praised the magnificent clothes of the emperor, themselves afraid to admit that they could not see the clothes, until a small child said: "But he has nothing on!"

The child's parents gasped and attempted to silence the child, but the child would not be silenced. As he twisted and turned, pulling his parents hands from his mouth, he continued to say, "The emperor is naked!" Soon, a few of his classmates were giggling and joined in.

After awhile adults joined their children and began to whisper, "The kids are right! The old guy has nothing on. He's a fool and he expects us to be foolish with him."

What Americans Really Want

In his 2009 book, *What Americans Really Want…Really*, Dr. Frank Luntz, a respected pollster who measures the heartbeat of America, asked this survey question:

If you had to choose, would you prefer to be a business owner or CEO of a Fortune 500 Company?

Those questioned responded with the following:

80% The owner of a business that employs 100 or more people.

14% The CEO of a Fortune 500 Company that employs more than 10,000 people.

6% Don't know/refused to answer.

In other words, Americans today want to be *entrepreneurs.*

The problem is that our school system is training our kids to be *employees.*

This is why schoolteachers and many parents continue to say, "Go to school to get a good, high-paying job." Few parents or teachers are saying, "Go to school to learn to *create* good, high-paying jobs."

There is a tremendous difference between the skill sets of an employee and the skill sets of an entrepreneur. The skills required to be an entrepreneur are not taught in most schools.

Dr. Luntz found that over 70% of full-time, corporate employees are considering or have considered starting their own businesses. Many people dream of becoming entrepreneurs, but few will take the leap of faith. The lack of financial education is the primary reason why most people will remain employees. Without a financial education, most employees are terrified of losing their job, not having a steady paycheck, or simply failing.

Financial education and the transformation it delivers are essential for entrepreneurs.

Forget MBAs

Dr. Luntz goes on to state:

"So how to equip a generation of Americans for success in entrepreneurship? Forget about MBAs. Most business schools teach you how to be successful in a big corporation rather than start your own company. But starting something from scratch and nurturing it as it grows is where our country has been at its strongest and most innovative."

Killing the American Dream

Americans have always wanted to be entrepreneurs.

People immigrated to America—some enduring unimaginable hardships—attracted by the promise of the American Dream. Millions left the oppression of the kings and queens of Europe and the tyranny of communist dictators in other parts of the world, just for a shot at the American Dream. *Their* American Dream.

The American Dream is just as Dr. Luntz describes: *"Starting something from scratch and nurturing it as it grows is where our country has been at its strongest and most innovative."*

Our schools seem to have forgotten about the American Dream. The problem is that our educational system trains students to be "A" students—*academics*—or "B" students—*bureaucrats*. Our schools *do not* train our young people to be "C" students: *capitalists*. Furthermore, it's these "C" students who so often follow an entrepreneurial path, carrying the torch of capitalism and creating new jobs.

Ask entrepreneurs today and many will tell you that bureaucracies are actively destroying the entrepreneurial spirit of capitalism.

They will also say many young graduates do not have the skills required for today's work environment. In fact, many have a "bad attitude" towards capitalists.

Hatred of Capitalists

In 2008, The Kaufman Foundation, a leading entrepreneurial think tank in America, commissioned Dr. Luntz to find out what Americans thought about capitalism. His survey found:

> "It's hard to tell which has become the stronger emotion: *respect* for entrepreneurs or *hatred* toward CEOs."

In November of 2012, Hostess Brands, the maker of iconic baked goods including Twinkies and Wonder Bread, shut its doors and filed for bankruptcy protection. The CEO of Hostess claimed the company forced to shut down due to union demands for higher wages and benefits.

Making matters worse, it's not just the 18,000+ workers who were affected. When the company closed, 18,000 families felt the impact as well. If there is an average of four people in a family, the number of lives impacted jumps to 72,000. This ripple effect spreads from each family, affecting schools and businesses such as dentists, grocery stores, dry cleaners, retailers, auto repair shops, even churches, and the rest of the community.

It was later disclosed that the CEO of Hostess Brands and his team of merry men and women paid themselves millions in severance bonuses.

Small wonder that Americans now *hate* CEOs. Many are graduates of our finest business schools and it begs the question: Is this what our business schools teach?

Unfortunately, it is.

Many of our brightest students go on to business schools, graduating with MBAs, and begin to climb the corporate ladder as *employees*, not *entrepreneurs*. The most ambitious become CEOs and executives of big business.

CEOs Are Not Capitalists

Later in this book I'll write about the fact that most CEOs are not capitalists. Most CEOs and corporate executives fall into a category called *managerial capitalists*, employees who work for *real* entrepreneurs—entrepreneurs like Steve Jobs, Thomas Edison, Walt Disney, Mark Zuckerberg, and others—but who have no personal financial stake or investment in the business.

Interestingly enough, Edison and Disney did not complete high school. Jobs and Zuckerberg never graduated college.

Most "A" students, graduates from our finest schools, become "*managerial capitalists*"—employees—rather than "*true capitalists*." It is these managerial capitalists, typically "A" students who land high-paying jobs, who give capitalism a bad name.

Managerial Capitalists Are Scary

In his book, *What Americans Really Want…Really*, Dr. Luntz states:

> *…"in today's world, 'capitalists' frighten people and 'capitalism' is short hand for CEOs taking tens of millions of dollars on the same day their pens wipe out 10,000 jobs."*

Tragically, many people do not understand the difference between *managerial capitalists* and true *capitalists*.

Just think of the CEOs who were paid huge bonuses, while millions lost their jobs, their homes, and their retirement nest eggs. Is this what our schools teach our best and brightest young people?

Again, the answer is "Yes." Our schools give capitalism a bad name, because what they teach is not true capitalism.

Unfortunately, most parents are proud when little Johnny or Susie graduates at the top of their class and is hired by a Fortune 500 firm earning a six-figure salary at the age of 26 and begins climbing the ladder. Most parents do not care that their child has been trained to be a managerial capitalist, rather than a true capitalist, an entrepreneur like Steve Jobs or Thomas Edison. Today we have a global crisis because:

- Schools are more focused on greed not generosity.
- Schools are about "How much money can I make?" versus "How much money can I make serving others?"
- Schools are about *finding* a high-paying job rather than *creating* high-paying jobs.
- Schools are about *climbing* the corporate ladder rather than *how to create* companies and corporate ladders.
- Schools are about *job security* rather than *financial freedom*, which is why most employees live in fear of "losing their job."
- Schools teach little to nothing about money, which is why millions of people now believe in entitlement programs, like Social Security and Medicare in the United States. And millions take jobs in government or military service, not to serve their country but for the retirement and medical benefits.

The New Depression

In 2007, the world awoke to the New Depression. There are many reasons for this modern-day depression. A few of them are:

1. Governments printing money.
2. Trillions of dollars of debt, both personal and governmental.
3. Underfunded entitlement programs such as Social Security and Medicare in the United States and a growing entitlement mentality all over the world.

4. High youth unemployment and student loan debt that can damage a student's "credit worthiness."

5. Globalization, including workers in emerging countries working for less and causing jobs to be exported, leading to lower wages at home.

These are the problems your child will face.

The Emperor Has No Clothes!

So the question parents should ask is: Are schools preparing my child for the real world?

The answer is "No."

And so the plot thickens…As Hans Christian Anderson warned us in 1837 in his tale of the Emperor:

> *Soon the whisper spread from person to person until everyone in the crowd began shouting, "The emperor has no clothes."*
>
> *The emperor heard it, of course, and although he knew they were correct, that he was stark naked in front of the town, he held his head high and finished the procession.*

It seems to me that the school system cannot admit they are not preparing children for the real world. That would be admitting to failure—and we all know what failure means in the school system.

It means the school thinks your child is not smart—but it really only means that your child isn't doing what the school tells them to do.

Without financial education, your child will leave school naked. He or she might be an "A" student…but they will be parading through life like the emperor. As the tale goes:

> *"Although he knew he was naked, he never admitted it for fear that he was too unfit and stupid to see that he was wearing nothing. He too was afraid that the townspeople would think that he was stupid."*

Since our schools will never admit that they are not preparing your child for the real world, it is up to parents—a child's first and most important teachers—to give children the financial education required for the real world, a world that runs on money.

Part One

Are Schools Preparing Your Child for the Real World?

Modern-Day Version of
The Adventures of Tom Sawyer

Mark Twain, 1876

Part One
INTRODUCTION

School is a great experience for some children. For others, school is the worst experience of their lives.

Every child has a genius. Unfortunately, their genius may not be recognized by the educational system. Their genius may even be crushed.

Thomas Edison, one of the great geniuses of modern times, was labeled "addled" by his first teacher. Addled means "mixed up or confused." He never finished school, and instead became an inventor and an entrepreneur. The company he founded, known today as General Electric, creates products that have changed the world. A few of Edison's early projects were the phonograph, the motion picture camera, and the electric light bulb.

Albert Einstein also failed to impress his teachers. From elementary school through college, his teachers thought he was lazy, sloppy, and insubordinate. Most of his teachers said, "He will not amount to anything." Yet Einstein became one of the most influential scientists in history.

Genius is an acronym for "Geni-in-us"—the genie or magician in each of us.

All parents have met the genius in their child. Most parents know that a child's true genius is found in their dreams. We see glimpses of it from an early age...the ideas and things that delight them, fascinate them, and challenge them.

Protecting and nurturing the genius in your child is a parent's most important job.

This book is written as a guide to help you develop child's financial genius.

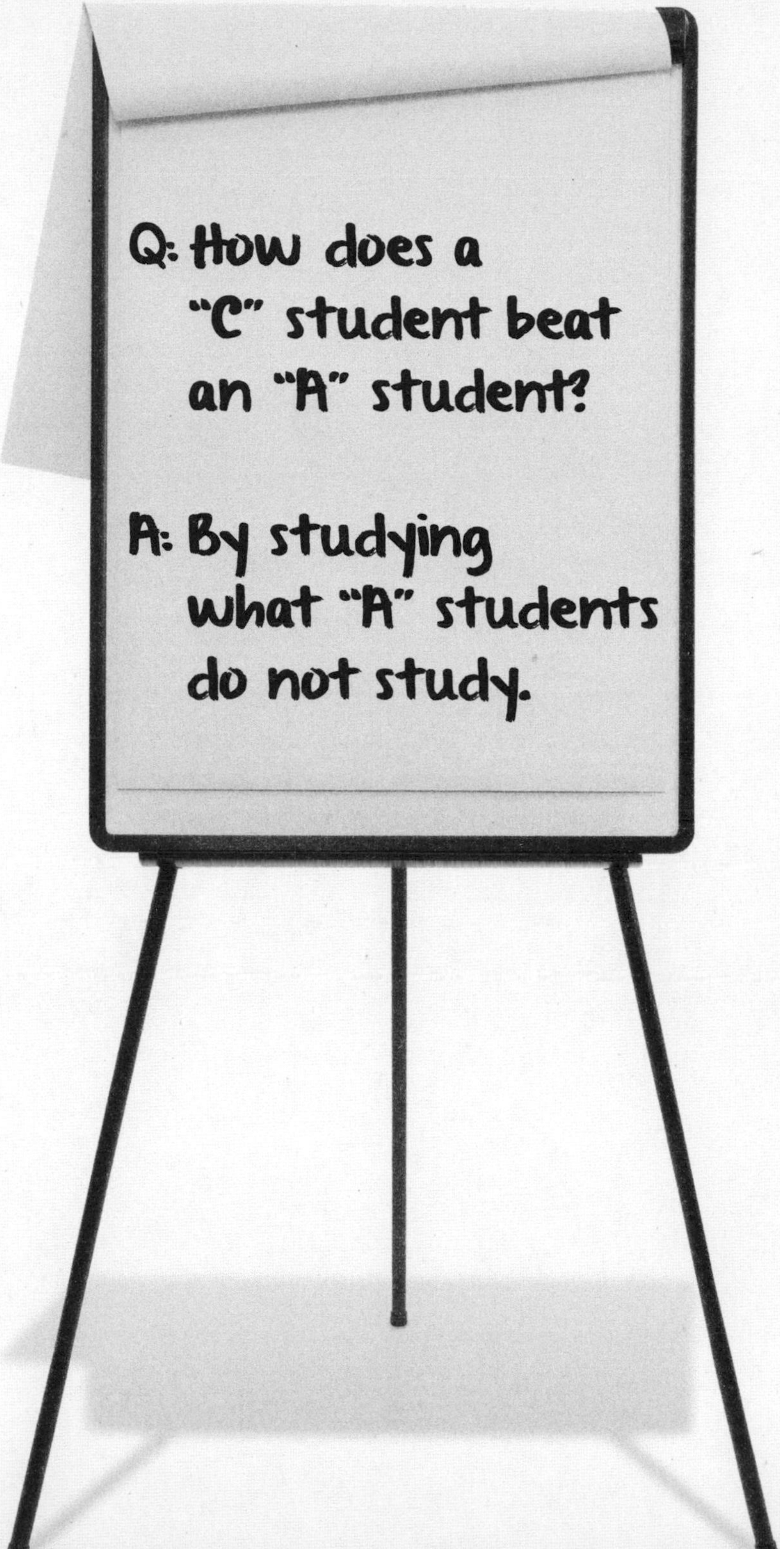

Q: How does a "C" student beat an "A" student?

A: By studying what "A" students do not study.

Part One | Chapter One

LESSON #1: AN EDUCATIONAL CRISIS

The 2012 U.S. Presidential campaign between President Barack Obama and former Massachusetts Governor Mitt Romney brought to light the difference in their levels of financial education.

While both are highly educated men, one candidate was financially sophisticated…the other less so.

Obama vs. Romney

During the campaign, President Obama disclosed that he paid 20.5% in taxes on approximately $3 million in income. Mitt Romney paid 14% on $21 million in income.

This gap in income and taxes angered many voters, especially the poor, middle class, and younger voters. Rather than ask why and how Romney made more money and paid a lower percentage in taxes, many voters just got angry. Most failed to ask, "How did Romney do that?" Or "How did he earn $21 million and pay 14% in taxes?" Or "How is that legal?" Or "Who is smarter when it comes to money…President Obama or candidate Romney?"

In his second term as President, Mr. Obama seems determined to and already has raised taxes on the rich—rather than teach kids about money and capitalism, which is how and why the rich get rich and stay rich and often pay less in taxes. Rather than teach kids to fish, it seems President Obama prefers to give kids fish.

This book is about teaching kids to fish.

What Does It Take to Become Rich?

Many people believe the rich are crooks, and some are. Yet there are far more rich people who are honest, hard working people…and are not crooks. They achieved the American Dream the old-fashioned way—through education, hard work, budgeting wisely, building businesses, creating jobs, and paying their taxes…as little as, legally, possible. They also acquired this wealth by studying subjects not taught in our schools.

This difference in education is reflected in President Obama and Mitt Romney.

Both men went to great schools. President Obama is a graduate of Columbia University and Harvard Law School. Mitt Romney is a graduate of Harvard Business School and Harvard Law School.

The primary difference between President Obama and Romney is that President came from a poor family and the former governor comes from a rich family.

Their story is similar to the ones found in *Rich Dad Poor Dad*. The lesson of financial education is taught at home…not in school.

This book is written for parents who want to give their child a financial headstart, at home, studying subjects most students—even "A" students—never study.

Making the Case

The "business" of education is one of the biggest industries in the world, impacting the lives of nearly every person on the planet in one way or another. In the United States public elementary and secondary schools alone—which employ 3.3 million full time teachers—$571 billion will be spent for the 2012-2013 school year. That's only in the United States, a country where approximately five million students entered high school in the 2010-2011 school year. Globally that number grows exponentially. I often ask myself how many of these kids finished high school…and how many dropped out? How many went on to college or university…and how many actually graduated? The staggering statistics on the college loan debt they're saddled with have made headlines around the world. And how many went on for an advanced degree—at even greater cost—in the hope of proportionately higher salaries when they joined the global workforce?

Not only are hundreds of billions of dollars spent on elementary through university education, but the military also spends billions of dollars to train young men and women to serve their country. Corporate training of employees is another billion-dollar industry as are the trade-schools that teach future technicians to repair and maintain our cars, refrigerators, electrical systems, and computers.

But financial education, at least in the established, formal arenas of school systems and curricula, is largely ignored. I've asked myself again and again: Why is that?

- Could the lack of financial education be one of the reasons behind our financial crisis?
- How much of the subprime mortgage crash was caused by a lack of financial education?
- How many of the millions of families who lost their homes lost them, in part, due to a lack of financial education?
- Could the lack of financial education be the reason why so many people are dependent upon government programs like Social Security, Medicare, military and public service pensions—pensions which are bankrupting cities, states, and entire countries?
- Is the United States—like countries around the world—heading for bankruptcy because millions of Americans need the government to take care of them socially, medically, and financially?
- Is our escalating national debt a reflection of our corporate and political leaders' lack of financial education?
- Is the United States decaying into the same economic demise countries such as Greece, Italy, France, Japan, England, and Spain are facing?

Welfare for the Rich

We all know there are welfare programs for the poor, but what about welfare for the rich?

- Why do our leaders—the President, Congress, and other political bureaucrats—vote themselves giant pensions and generous benefit packages while the number of families on public assistance goes up? Are our leaders as financially needy as those who rely on the government to meet their most basic needs?
- What would happen if we had leaders who knew how to create wealth rather than just knowing how to spend other people's (the taxpayers') money?
- Why do CEOs grant themselves massive pay increases, stock options, and perks at the same time they lay off workers? Are CEOs greedy due to a lack of financial education, or did they go to school to learn to be greedy?
- Did the bankers who lost billions have an adequate financial education?
- Why were millions of employees laid off, and thousands of small businesses closed, while the bankers who caused the crash were paid multi-million dollar bonuses?
- Why do teachers' unions and government bureaucrats determine what our children learn? What about asking the kids and their parents what they need to learn?
- Why are many of America's highest paid workers no longer from the private sector? Why are so many well-paid employees, so called public servants, some of the highest paid workers in America today? Why are firefighters and police officers retiring with millions in lifetime benefits? What has happened to government service?
- Who caused this financial crisis?

Today's financial crises were not caused by poor, uneducated people. Behind the chaos are some of the most well-educated people in the world, people such as Federal Reserve Chairman Ben Bernanke, a former Stanford and Princeton professor, a student of the Great Depression, but, unfortunately, someone without much financial education or real life business experience.

This book is about education. But not the education taught in our schools.

An Educational Crisis

We are not in a financial crisis. We are in an educational crisis. This crisis begins when our children enter school, spending years—sometimes decades—learning nothing about money and being taught by people who know little about money.

For some reason, our schools have a quasi-religious view about money.

Schools seems to believe:

"For the love of money is the root of all evil."
– Timothy 6:10

Schools ignore the passage that reads:

"My people perish from a lack of knowledge."
– Hosea 4:6

People are perishing economically due to a lack of financial education in our schools.

Lao Tzu, the Chinese founder of Taoism in the 5th Century BC, stated:

"If you give a man a fish, you feed him for a day.
If you teach a man to fish you feed him for a lifetime."

Unfortunately, rather than teach people to fish, we are teaching kids the Robin Hood philosophy of economics:

"Take from the rich and give to the poor."

That's also known as socialism.

Ultimately, all that this generosity does is create more poor people.

On November 2, 2012 a headline in *The Weekly Standard* stated:

"Food stamp rolls grow 75 times faster than jobs."

As expected, the Republicans blame President Obama for this crisis and the Democrats state that Republicans are to blame.

This book is not about politics. It is about education, and about how the lack of financial education is the true cause of financial crisis.

Lag Times

Most schoolteachers are great people. The problem is that most teachers, and parents, are products of the same educational system.

Many teachers are frustrated. Many teachers are pushing for change. Unfortunately, the education industry seems to be an industry that has one of the slowest rates of change.

Different industries have different lag times. One definition of *lag time* is the time delay between a new idea being proposed and its adoption. For example, I've been told that in the world of technology, lag time is around 18 months, the time between a new idea and that idea taking the form of a new product. That's why competition can become so fierce in bringing a new product to market...and why new companies soon find themselves out of business because someone else can deliver new products or technology faster, better and cheaper.

Lag times in the Agrarian Age were measured in hundreds of years. Lag times in the Industrial Age were measured in fifty-year increments. Lag time in the Information Age is measured in half-years.

I've heard that the auto industry has a lag time of 25 years. This means the new ideas you see on cars today were conceived 25 years ago...ideas such as hybrid cars. And that the business of government has a lag time of approximately 35 years.

The reason many teachers and parents are frustrated is because, among all industry sectors, the educational industry has the second-longest lag time—50 years.

The only slower industry is the construction industry, with a lag time of 60 years.

Notice that the automobile, government, construction, and educational sectors all have strong labor unions…and labor unions are products of the Industrial Age.

The Future of Education

The lag time in education means that children starting school today will be grandparents before the educational system adopts the changes this book offers.

By teaching your kids the lessons in this book, you are giving your child a financial headstart. If lag times hold, it will take until the year 2065 before the ideas in this book enter most classrooms. I don't believe we can afford to wait.

This book is written for parents, parents who know that it's up to them—not the school system—to prepare their child for the real world. And that world is a fast-paced, ever-changing, Information-Age world… a world unlike any of us have ever experienced.

This book is also written for parents who know their children face larger financial challenges, the financial garbage heaps previous generations have left behind.

This book is written for parents who want to understand why President Obama earns $3 million and pays 20.5% in taxes while Mitt Romney earns $21 million and pays 14%.

Once a parent knows and understands the differences in what the two men know, they can pass that knowledge on to their children.

My Story

I have been an advocate for financial education for most of my adult life.

In 1973, I returned home to Hawaii from the Vietnam War and found my dad, the man I call my poor dad, unemployed. He had been the Superintendent of Education for the State of Hawaii. His problems began when he ran for Lt. Governor as a Republican against his boss, a Democrat. In losing the election, he also lost his job.

My dad committed professional suicide by running for Lt. Governor. He risked his "job security" because he was a man of principle. Once he reached the top of the school system's ladder, as head of the Department of Education, he was outraged at the corruption he found in Hawaii's government, a government *Forbes* magazine has since called "The People's Republic of Hawaii." That same article stated, "The state taxes everything that moves. Fidel Castro would feel right at home here."

President Obama grew up in Hawaii. He is the first U.S. President from Hawaii. The *Forbes* article may explain why the President has the views he has on government, business, and taxes.

The End of Empires

I am not a Republican or a Democrat. And I do not blame President Obama for the crisis we face. This crisis has been brewing for decades and similar crises have occurred throughout history. Financial ignorance and political corruption have brought down empires for centuries. The same financial ignorance and corruption threatens to bring down America.

Economics of War

Empires also end when empires fight too many wars in far away places. In doing that America is proving we've failed to learn from history.

While in junior high school, I listened to President Eisenhower's warning to the nation about the threat of the "military-industrial complex." I was in my early teens, and his warning meant little to me. Returning from Vietnam in 1973, I understood the President's warning. We were not fighting for the freedom of the

Military-Industrial Complex

On January 17, 1961, President Dwight Eisenhower gave the nation a dire warning about what he described as a threat to democratic government. He called it the military-industrial complex, a formidable union of defense contractors and the armed forces. Eisenhower, a retired five-star WWII Army general who led the allies on D-Day, made the remarks in his farewell speech from the White House.

Vietnamese people. We were fighting for money. We had been lied to by the elites. We had no business fighting in Vietnam, apart from the issue that war is big business. When I returned from Vietnam, I knew it was time to stop blindly following orders. I knew it was time to start thinking for myself.

I do not criticize my fellow sailors and soldiers. Most of the young men and women I met in the service were great people dedicated to their country. Our problem was that we were fighting wars to make the military-industrial complex richer. Anytime the military-industrial complex needs more money, they simply start another war.

We are making the same mistakes, in my opinion, when it comes to printing money.

The Roman Empire crumbled when the Romans began destroying their own money, fighting wars in far away lands, and raising taxes on its workers.

The United States is repeating the mistakes of the past, proving the old saying:

"Those who fail to learn from history are doomed to repeat it."

Studying Subjects "A" Students Don't Study

In 1973, I informed my dad I was leaving the military service. He was disappointed because he wanted me to stay in the military for the retirement and medical benefits. Counting my time at the military academy, I had 10 years accrued toward retirement. I only had 10 more to go.

When I nixed that idea, my poor dad suggested I fly for the airlines, as many of my fellow Marine pilots were doing. When I told him I was through flying, he finally suggested I go back to school, get my Masters Degree, possibly my PhD, and climb the corporate ladder.

I loved my dad dearly, but he was suggesting I do what he had done, follow in his footsteps...proving, once again, that we repeat mistakes if we do not learn from them.

And while I loved my dad, I did not want to make the same mistakes he had made.

If I had followed my poor dad's advice, I might be like him today… a highly educated but poor 60+-year-old, hoping my savings, pension, Social Security, and Medicare would take care of me.

In 1973, I decided to follow in my rich dad's footsteps. I began by studying subjects my poor dad had never studied.

This book is about the subjects I studied and the courses most people do not study, including "A" students. Because there is a big pay-off for studying subjects "A" students do not study.

In 1997, the book *Rich Dad Poor Dad* was self-published because every publisher we offered it to turned it down. As you might expect, most publishers are "A" students, like my poor dad. Most publishers me sent rejection letters stating, "We are not interested in your book at this time." A few more honest publishers stated, "You do not know what you are writing about." Or, "Your ideas are ridiculous."

"Your House Is Not an Asset"

Rich Dad Poor Dad was harshly criticized due to statements such as "Your house is not an asset." Ten years later, in 2007, millions of homeowners all over the world found out the hard way that their home was *not* an asset. As property values plummeted all over the world, millions were pushed into bankruptcy experiencing first hand that their home could be a giant liability.

"Savers Are Losers"

I have also been harshly criticized for saying, "Savers are losers." Today, millions of people are aware that the central banks of the world, banks such as the Federal Reserve Bank in the United States, are printing trillions of dollars contributing to the destruction of the purchasing power of people's savings.

After the crash of 2007, banks lowered interest rates on savings. Before the crash, many savers lived off the interest on their savings. Today, millions of savers are living on their savings.

In the year 2000, the price of gold was less than $300 an ounce. Today, gold is over $1,500 an ounce, which is yet another reflection of the loss in the purchasing power of the dollar. At the same time, banks are paying less than 2% interest on savings while inflation runs at 5%... although the government claims there is no inflation. That is why "Savers are losers." It's simple math: $1,500 for an ounce of gold is greater than $300 an ounce. Inflation at 5% is greater than 2% interest on your savings. You do not need algebra or calculus to figure out that "savers are losers."

"Debt Is Good"

Most financial pundits recommend that people "Get out of debt." To me, that shows a lack of financial education.

The fact is that there is good debt as well as bad debt. Simply stated, "Good debt can make you richer and bad debt makes you poorer." Unfortunately, most people only know bad debt, the money they borrow to acquire liabilities versus assets.

Taxes Make the Rich Richer

Not only does good debt make you richer, good debt can also reduce what you pay in taxes. Learning to leverage good debt and understanding its ability to lower a person's taxes makes a good case for the importance of financial education.

Since taxes are the number one expense for most people, doesn't it seem odd that taxes are not a subject taught in most schools? In this book, you will learn who pays the least in taxes—and why. And this will offer another point of view on why President Obama paid taxes of 20.5% on $3 million of income and Mitt Romney paid taxes of 14% on $21 million.

Oprah Called

In the year 2000, *Rich Dad Poor Dad* made the *New York Times* Best Sellers list, the only self-published book on the list at the time. Then Oprah Winfrey called. I went on her television show and the *"Oprah effect"* took over.

Rich Dad Poor Dad has become the number one personal finance book of all time. It was on the *New York Times* Best Sellers list for over six years. To date, it has sold over 30 million copies world wide, has been published in 53 languages and is available in 109 countries.

The irony is, I failed English twice in high school. I failed because I could not write, could not spell, and because the teacher did not agree with what I was writing.

I mention all this not to brag or toot my own horn. People from around the world have told me that *Rich Dad Poor Dad* speaks to them, resonates with them. The book has struck a chord with people around the world who know that there are voids in their education—especially related to money. I've also been told that one of my gifts is the ability to take complex ideas and concepts and simplify them. That's what I did in *Rich Dad Poor Dad* and that's my goal in writing this book for parents.

An important part of this book is the Action Steps for Parents that you'll find at the end of every chapter. They were created to give you tips, tools, and resources in taking the first steps to teaching your child about money.

Closing Thoughts

President Obama and former governor Mitt Romney are very smart men. Both appear to be good men. Both men received the very best in formal education, yet one made $3 million and paid 20.5% in taxes while the other made $21 million and paid only 14% in taxes.

The difference it seems is not what they learned in school, but what they were taught at home. In many ways, the story of Romney versus Obama is similar to the story of rich dad versus poor dad.

This book is written for parents who want their child to have the type of education most people do not receive, not even "A" students.

Action Step for Parents

Turn your home into a place of active learning.

Kids learn most by doing. Unfortunately, in most schools kids are expected to learn by sitting at a desk then coming home to sit (again) and do home work.

Create a WEN, a "Wealth Education Night." Set aside one night a week or a month to be a time for active learning about money. Make it a family ritual. And make it fun.

Play games like *Monopoly*® or *CASHFLOW*® *For Kids* or *CASHFLOW 101*® and *202*® and use the time playing and having fun. In the process opportunities will present themselves to discuss age-appropriate, real-life money activities, challenges, and problems as they relate to the game. I encourage you to check out the Rich Dad online financial games and content for mobile devices.

That one night a week or month will serve as a foundation for a better life for your child, better family relationships, and a commitment to be a life-long learner.

Use this book for support and discussion material. Rich Dad also has a workbook and study guide, *Awaken Your Child's Financial Genius*, that delivers more focused content as well as games, activities, and exercises. The good thing about money is that there is a lot of information out in the world. All a person or family needs to do is dedicate the time to absorb it. And learn to tell the difference between *education* and a *sales pitch*.

My rich dad played *Monopoly* with his son and me at least once a week for years. He used fun lessons from the game to teach us lessons in real life. My poor dad only asked, "Have you done your homework?"

Give Your Child a Financial Headstart... without Giving Them Money.

Part One | Chapter Two

LESSON #2: THE FAIRY TALE IS OVER

There are many reasons why the role of parents in a child's life has taken on a new and critical dimension. Few would argue with the fact that times have changed...and that, today, change is a constant in our lives. In most cases, and in my opinion, most of us are not changing with the times. The financial advice we got from our parents is old and outdated—obsolete in today's world.

Making the Case

The Fairy Tale Is Over

Once upon a time, all a person had to do was go to school, get a job, work hard, and retire. Until a few years ago, the company you worked for took care of you when you retired...you received a paycheck and medical benefits for life. Today this is a fairy tale.

Once upon a time, all a person had to do was buy a house, and the house went up in value. Homeowners got rich in their sleep. Many people could sell their home, some even pocketing a small fortune to sustain them through retirement, downsize to a smaller house, and live happily ever after. Today this is a fairy tale.

Once upon a time, the United States was the richest country in the world. Today this is a fairy tale.

Once upon a time, the U.S. dollar was as good as gold. Today this is a fairy tale.

Once upon a time, all a person had to do was go to college and they were virtually assured of earning more money than those who did not graduate from college. Today this is a fairy tale.

In 2007, the subprime mortgage market collapsed, and the biggest financial disaster in history began. The fairytale is now a nightmare. And the nightmare is not over…yet.

Out of fear, millions of parents continue to advise their children, "Go to school and get a college degree so you can get a high-paying job." Panicked parents recite this mantra in spite of the fact that unemployment is high among young people, even those with college degrees. Many college graduates, unable to find work, go on to graduate school for advanced degrees. They then leave school even deeper in student-loan debt, still searching for that elusive high-paying job.

Education Gets More Expensive

As prices around the world collapsed, why did the cost of education go up?

- In 2006, home prices in the United States averaged $230,000. By 2011, home prices had fallen 26 percent, to an average of $170,000.

  As home prices fell, the price of a college education rose by 4.6 percent between 2006 and 2007 to an average of $22,218.

- On October 9, 2007, the Dow Jones Industrial Average hit an all-time high of 14,164. By March of 2009, the Dow had fallen over 50 percent to 6,469.

  As the stock market crashed between 2007 and 2008, college tuition rose by 5.9% to a new average of $23,712.

- In July of 2008, oil hit a peak of $147 a barrel and crashed to about $40 a barrel before recovering.

  As oil prices were falling between 2008 and 2009, college tuition rose 6.2 percent to $25,177.

  In 2011, college loan debt surpassed credit card debt for the first time—over $1 trillion in the United States alone.

Unforgivable Debt

Today, thousands of highly educated students leave school strapped with student loans, the worst possible debt of all. Student loans are the worst form of debt because student loans can never be forgiven, or discharged. With most other types of debt, like a home mortgage or credit card debt, a person can declare bankruptcy and the loans are wiped out. That's not the case with student loans. Even if a student dies, their parents are on the hook for repayment of the loan, if they were co-signers, as many are.

The Clock Is Ticking

Once a student graduates, the interest clock begins ticking and interest starts to accrue. Rather than get richer after leaving school, millions become poorer, going deeper in debt as interest on the original school loan starts to pile up.

A student loan can negatively affect the student for life. A student loan can affect the home a student buys (if they can afford one), the quality of life for their family (if they can afford a family), and their hopes for a secure retirement (if they are able to retire).

For many, a student loan will be the proverbial albatross around their neck...for life.

What's a College Education Worth?

For the first time in history, people are questioning the value of a college education. A few will even say that the ROI (Return On Investment) of a college education is not worth the investment.

Between 2006 and 2007, the median starting salary for college graduates in America was $30,000. Between 2009 and 2011 it had fallen to $27,000.

The Unemployment Crisis

Youth unemployment is an international crisis, a problem that has led to the "Arab Spring," "Occupy Wall Street," and other gatherings of unemployed youth.

In 2012, as the Presidential campaign heated up, both political candidates promised to bring jobs back to America. How can that happen when American factory workers earn between $125 to $200 a day, once benefits are factored in? Many workers in low-wage countries earn just $2 a day.

Future Shock

For the first time in America, many believe their children will not do better financially than their parents.

Even China is having problems with low-wage countries. It's estimated that there are dozens of countries in which workers' wages are even lower than those in China. You do not need to be a math professor to know that factories follow low-wage workers, and $2 a day is less than $200 a day.

On November 5, 2012, *Time* magazine published this piece by Peter Gumbel:

Why the U.S. Has a Worse Youth Unemployment Problem than Europe.

The latest unemployment statistics released this week on both sides of the Atlantic show that the number of jobless is continuing to rise in Europe far above the rate in the U.S., and the picture is especially bleak for young Europeans under the age of 25. In the 27 E.U. nations as a whole, the youth unemployment rate rose to 22.8% in September, up from 21.7% the previous year. In Greece and Spain, that proportion is over 50%. In the U.S., meanwhile, the unemployment rate was essentially unchanged in October, at 7.9%, the Bureau of Labor Statistics announced Nov. 2. And the U.S. rate of unemployment among young people under 25 was 16%.

But such statistics are rather misleading because they don't tell the whole story. They don't include the millions of youngsters who are not in the labor market because they are continuing with their education or are engaged in training programs. If you take those young people into account, the picture is still grim everywhere, but the U.S. actually comes off as having a worse youth unemployment problem than Europe.

Education is becoming more important than ever. Our schools provide the important function of training skilled workers to support the economy. For example, schools train doctors, accountants, lawyers, engineers, teachers, social workers, mechanics, construction workers, cooks, police officers, and military personnel, who are all essential to a civilized society.

Yet, as the global economy contracts, how many of these people, educated or uneducated, will find jobs? In April of 2012, less than 50 percent of America's graduating class was able to find meaningful employment. Many found jobs, but are underemployed.

The question is: What kind of education is important?

And why do we keep saying to our kids, "Go to school to get a high-paying job," when jobs keep migrating to lower-wage countries? Why become an accountant or attorney when technology makes it possible to hire accountants and attorneys in lower-wage countries? Why talk about job security when advances in technology make some jobs obsolete? And, just as important: Why is there so little, if any, financial education taught in our schools?

Top of the Food Chain

Most parents want their child to have a good education for a secure future. They want their child to make it to the top of the food chain. Most parents dread the thought of their child toiling at a menial job, underemployed, earning low wages, paying higher and higher taxes, and battling inflation all their lives.

Many parents hope a sound education will put their child at the top of the class or the leader of the pack—possibly a doctor, lawyer, or CEO.

The Sales Pitch

The sales pitch from the schools is:

"You must finish school."

"You must have a college degree."

"If you do not finish school, you will not be successful in life."

The following are 50 people who did not finish school, but that didn't let that stop them. They made it to the top.

1. George Washington	President of the United States
2. Abraham Lincoln	President of the United States
3. Harry Truman	President of the United States
4. Grover Cleveland	President of the United States
5. Zachary Taylor	President of the United States
6. Andrew Johnson	President of the United States
7. John Glenn	Astronaut, U.S. Senator
8. Barry Goldwater	U.S. Senator
9. Benjamin Franklin	U.S. Ambassador
10. Winston Churchill	Prime Minister of England
11. John Major	Prime Minister of England
12. Robert Frost	Poet
13. Florence Nightingale	Nurse
14. Buckminster Fuller	Futurist and Inventor
15. George Eastman	Founder of Eastman Kodak
16. Ray Kroc	Founder of McDonald's
17. Dave Thomas	Founder of Wendy's
18. Ralph Lauren	Fashion designer and Entrepreneur
19. Doris Lessing	Nobel Prize recipient in Literature
20. George Bernard Shaw	Playwright
21. Peter Jennings	News anchor for ABC
22. Christopher Columbus	Explorer
23. TD Jakes	Pastor
24. Joel Osteen	Pastor
25. John D. Rockefeller	Founder of Standard Oil
26. Karl Rove	Presidential advisor
27. Ted Turner	Founder of CNN
28. Quentin Tarantino	Movie director
29. Peter Jackson	Movie director *(Lord of the Rings)*
30. Mark Twain	Author

31. Leon Uris	Author
32. Carl Bernstein	Washington Post reporter
33. Carly Fiorina	CEO of Hewlett Packard
34. Charles Dickens	Author
35. Andrew Carnegie	Industrialist
36. William Faulkner	Nobel and Pulitzer Prize winner
37. Li Ka Shing	Wealthiest man in Asia
38. Richard Branson	Founder of Virgin Atlantic Airways and Virgin Records
39. Enzo Ferrari	Founder of Ferrari
40. Henry Ford	Founder of Ford Motor Company
41. J. Paul Getty	Founder of Getty Oil
42. Jack London	Author
43. Larry Ellison	Founder of Oracle
44. Tom Anderson	Founder of My Space
45. Mark Zuckerberg	Founder of Facebook
46. Steve Jobs	Founder of Apple
47. Steve Wozniak	Founder of Apple
48. Bill Gates	Founder of Microsoft
49. Paul Allen	Founder of Microsoft
50. Ringo Starr	Beatle

Stay in School

I'm not suggesting that kids should drop out of school, or that school is not important. Education is very important. The question is: What kind of education? And where will your child's education take them? Will your child's education prepare them for their future? Will a good education help your child's financial security in a world with less and less security?

This book is about the education not taught in schools. It's about putting your child on a path where they won't need a job or a government pension to feel secure. It's about getting to the top, rather than working for those at the top.

This book is about capitalism. It will explain why some of the greatest business leaders of our time never finished school. Notable examples are Steve Jobs, Bill Gates, and Mark Zuckerberg. In this book, you will find out what these entrepreneurs know—and why they left school.

The Future of Education

Once upon a time, all a child had to do was focus on two types of education. They were:

1. **Academic Education:** This education supports the general skills of learning how to read, write, and solve math problems. This is an extremely important education.

2. **Professional Education:** This education provides more specialized skills to earn a living. The top students, the "A" students, become doctors, accountants, engineers, lawyers, or business executives. Other schools at this level are trade schools for students who want to become mechanics, construction workers, cooks, nurses, secretaries, and computer programmers.

What was missing?

3. **Financial Education**: This is the level of education not found in our school system. *This is the education of the future*. Again, we advise kids to go to school to get a job and work for money, yet we teach then little or nothing about money.

   The statistics tell a sad and sobering story: While 90 percent of students want to learn more about money, 80 percent of teachers do not feel comfortable teaching the subject. Someday, financial education will be part of the curriculum of all schools, but not in the near future.

My Story

My financial education began when I was nine years old. It began with my rich dad. He was not my real dad, but my best friend's father. And he used the game of *Monopoly®* as an educational tool, and we would play the game for hours after school.

When I got home, my real dad, the one I call my poor dad, would ask, "What have you been doing all day?"

When I replied, "Playing *Monopoly*," he would say, "Stop wasting your time with that silly game. You should be at home studying, doing your homework. If you don't do your homework, you won't get good grades, you won't get into a good college, and you won't get a good job." Since I never achieved good grades—I was the eternal "C" student—my poor dad and I had this discussion on a regular basis.

My best friend Mike was rich dad's son. We went to a school for rich kids. The good news was: we were poor kids. (My Rich dad was not yet rich…and my poor dad was successful, but never rich.) This caused rich dad to step up our financial education by playing *Monopoly* with us on a regular basis. He wanted us to become smarter, and richer, than the rich kids.

One day he took his son and me on a "field trip." Rather than go to a museum or an art gallery, he took us to see his "green houses," his rental properties. That was when I realized that rich dad was playing *Monopoly*…in real life. "One day," he said, "these green houses will become my big red hotel."

When I returned home and told my dad that rich dad was playing *Monopoly* in real life, my dad laughed. He thought the idea was ridiculous. His advice was to stop wasting my time with games and do my homework.

At that time, my dad was the head of education for the Big Island of Hawaii. A few years later, he would reach the top of the state education system and become the Superintendent of Education for the entire state.

My poor dad was an "A" student, class valedictorian, and class president. He loved school. He graduated with a four-year degree from the University of Hawaii in only two years. He also attended Stanford University, the University of Chicago, and Northwestern University.

My rich dad never even finished the eighth grade, because his father died so he had to take over the family business. Although his formal education was limited, he would eventually become one of the richest men in Hawaii. When I was 19, rich dad purchased his "red hotel" right on Waikiki Beach. In 10 years, his "little green houses" had become a giant "red hotel."

At the time, I did not realize how profoundly the game of *Monopoly* and my rich dad's education would change the direction of my life. Rich dad was using a game—*Monopoly*—to train me to think like a capitalist.

My poor dad and my rich dad were polar opposites. Both were very good men, but they never did see eye to eye. Their differences erupted when I was about 10 years old. My poor dad was not happy when I told him I had accompanied my rich dad to collect rents from his tenants in his "green houses." My poor dad did not like the idea of me collecting rent. He was very upset. So was my mother. They thought it was a cruel lesson for a 10-year-old boy. To me, it was an eye-opening lesson about real life.

Later I would learn why my mom and dad were so upset. We were renters. They too had a landlord knocking on our door to collect the rent. A few years later, when I was in junior high, they finally saved enough money to buy a home.

My Unfair Advantage

A formal education was important to both dads. Both dads expected their sons to go on to college, and we did. Rich dad's son graduated from the University of Hawaii, running his father's business between classes.

My father did not have the money to pay for my college education. Once I graduated from high school, I knew I was on my own. That inspired me to apply to the military academies. Although my grades were horrible, my SAT scores were decent and I was a pretty good football player. I received two Congressional nominations—one to the U.S. Naval Academy at Annapolis in Maryland, and the other to the U.S. Merchant Marine Academy at Kings Point in New York. I accepted the appointment to Kings Point and graduated in 1969 with a Bachelor of Science degree.

Looking back, I can see how my time with rich dad gave me an unfair advantage in life, especially when it came to money. Between the ages of nine and 18, until I left for school in New York, I spent one or two days a week after school and two Saturdays every month working for free for rich dad. If you have read *Rich Dad Poor Dad*, you know how this disturbed my poor dad. My poor dad believed that my rich dad was exploiting us because he was not paying us. Being a member of the teachers union, I shouldn't have been surprised to hear my poor dad muttering about "child labor laws."

> ***Rich Dad Lesson***
>
> *"Games are better teachers than teachers."*

Rich dad never paid his son or me because he was training us to be capitalists. He did not pay us because he did not want to train us to be employees who worked for money. He was training us to be employers… entrepreneurs, capitalists who had OPT (Other People's Talents) and OPM (Other People's Money) working for them.

Obviously, rich dad's ideas about "work to learn, not to earn" angered my poor dad, who was more of a socialist than a capitalist.

Pictured on the following page is the Cone of Learning developed in 1969 by Dr. Edgar Dale, a professor of education. Dr. Dale (1900–1985) received his doctorate degree from the University of Chicago and taught for years at Ohio State University.

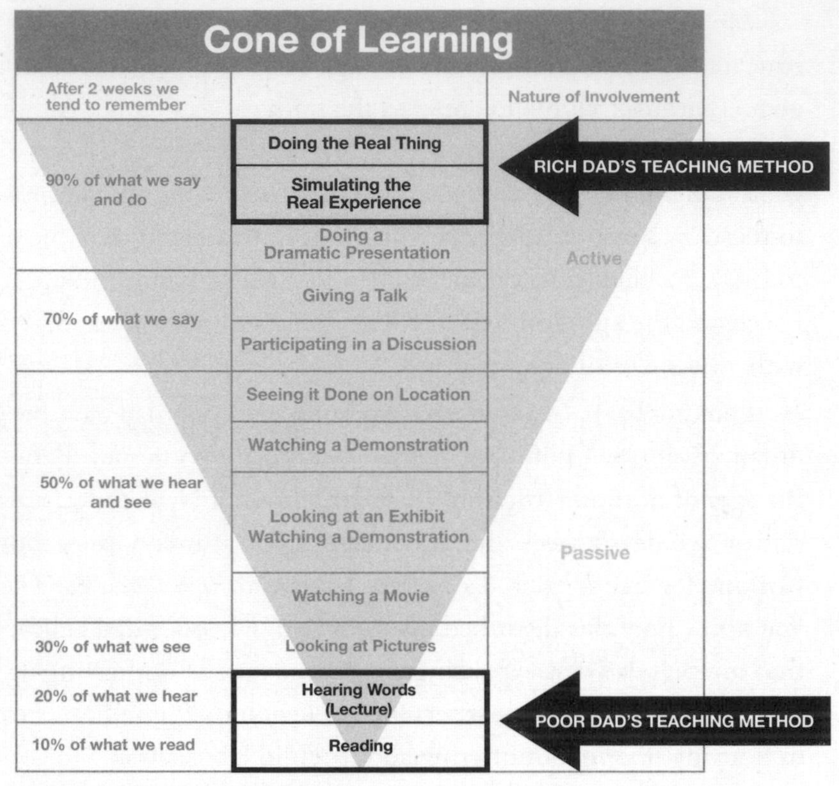

Reprinted with Permission. The original work has been modified.

According to Dr. Dale, my rich dad's use of *Monopoly* as a teaching tool, and then taking us to collect rent, was a very effective way of teaching his son and me about money.

Question: Does this mean that reading and lectures are not important?

Answer: No, at least not for me. The game of *Monopoly* inspired me to learn more. Today I read more, study more, and attend classes more because the game, the simulations of real life experiences, inspired me to want learn more.

Although I am a poor and slow reader, I plow through complex financial and business books few people would choose to read. I credit the game of *Monopoly* for giving me a solid foundation upon which to build my real-world education.

More importantly, I learned more, retained more, and *wanted to learn more* from the experience of *Monopoly* as a kid and applying what I was learning to collecting rent for rich dad. These lessons are locked in my brain. While I have a Bachelor of Science degree from a great school, I do not remember much of what I learned during those four years. For example, I remember taking three years of calculus, but I could not solve a math problem using calculus today. As the saying goes, "Use it or lose it." I would need calculus if I were a rocket scientist, but I do not need calculus to be rich. Elementary level math—addition, subtraction, multiplication, and division—will do.

Entrepreneurship

Dr. Frank Luntz's book, *What American's Really Want...Really* reported that those surveyed:

- 81% say universities and high schools should actively develop entrepreneurial skills in students
- 77% say the state and federal governments should encourage people to be entrepreneurs
- 70% say the success and health of our economy depend upon it

In 1984, my wife Kim and I founded a financial education company with offices in the United States, Australia, New Zealand, Singapore, Canada, and Malaysia. We taught investing and entrepreneurship using games and simulations. Learning was fun and exciting.

In 1994, we retired. Kim was 37, and I was 47. We retired on the passive income, the cash flow, that we received from our investments. Like rich dad, we were playing *Monopoly* in real life. And we still do today. And following the crash of 2007, our income (cash flow) went up as asset prices fell. Knowing how to do well even in a crash or in turbulent markets is an essential aspect of financial education.

In 1996, Kim and I founded The Rich Dad Company. The Rich Dad Company produces financial education products such as the board games *CASHFLOW® 101*, *CASHFLOW® 202*, and *CASHFLOW® for Kids*. Board games are great ways for families to learn together.

We also have an expanding line of electronic games for mobile devices and tablets. Our electronic products will be supported by on-line curriculum and assessment tools…so you can grade yourself, correct, learn, and improve.

In 1956, when Mike and I were nine years old, rich dad began teaching us financial and entrepreneurial skills using games and simulations. Rich dad was ahead of his time and that gave us an unfair advantage over our classmates.

Action Step for Parents

Take time to discuss money and the role it plays in life

Unfortunately, in many homes, there is little discussion or conversation about money. And when there is, it's often an argument.

As a young boy, I have painful memories of the fights between my mom and dad over money. No matter how much money my dad earned, we never had enough money. Rather than discuss money, my mom and dad—the two people I loved most—only fought about money. My rich dad, on the other hand, spent hours discussing real money problems. Today, I carry my rich dad's discussions into my own marriage. Rather than fight about money, Kim and I opening discuss our money problems.

Once you establish the ritual of your family Wealth Education Nights make it a time to discuss real life money problems when they occur in the course of everyday life. Talk about the problems and challenges, what caused them, and how you'll solve them.

Invest the time to make your home to be a place of *discussion* rather *arguments* about money.

Why Are Parents Important?

Part One | Chapter Three

LESSON #3: PREPARE YOUR CHILD FOR THE WORST

As a child's first and most important teachers, parents are the ones who provide the foundational building blocks of education. Parents celebrate a child's first words and teach them new ones, teach them to count and walk and read and ride a bike. As a child grows up, many parents become sounding boards, guides, advisors, and role models. Parents interact with their kids every day and, consciously or unconsciously, have a huge and powerful impact in shaping their lives. We lead by example and when kids see parents who are open to new ideas and embrace life-long learning it makes an impression. A child's life changes when his or her parents are teachers who will ask questions until they have a clear understanding of the answers, keep an open mind to other points of view, and encourage their children (and their spouses) to follow their dreams on the path to a rich and rewarding life.

I often see parents walk a fine line between sheltering and protecting their children from life's harsh realities and proactively preparing them for what, in today's world, is likely to be an uncertain future. The world of tomorrow belongs to those who can process information, see relationships and trends, and be agile and responsive to change as the world changes. And just as our world today is very different from the world in which our parents grew up, the world your child will face will be different, too. We can expect new and different challenges…as well as new opportunities.

Making the Case

Most Americans have heard references to "the 800-pound gorilla in the room." If you have not heard the phrase, it simply means that there is something—a topic or an idea that carries some weight or needs to be reckoned with—that everyone knows about, but no one wants to talk about.

There Are Four Gorillas in Your Child's Future

As I see it there are four gorillas—gorillas of the future—that your child will face. Few people are talking about them, but they're out there. Few people are talking to your child about these four gorillas—gorillas of the future—and your child needs to prepare for before he or she encounters them—later in life.

800-Pound Gorilla #1: The New Problem of Growing Old

The problem of growing old is a new phenomenon.

In 1935, the Social Security Act was signed into law by President Franklin D. Roosevelt. Back then, 65 was considered old age. Today, "65 is the new 45"—at least that's what many baby boomers would like to believe. In America, people fear growing old and the loss of there independence more than they fear dying. With advances in medicine and technology, the new *old* for your child may be 90 or even 120. In other words, growing old is a new and escalating opportunity… and problem.

> ***Is Age an Assets or Liability?***
>
> *During the Agrarian Age and Industrial Age, being older was an asset. Older meant wiser. In the Information Age, being older is a liability.*

In 2012, the U.S. government finally admitted that the Social Security fund will be bankrupt by 2033. How old will your child be in 2033? Most baby boomers will just be entering their 80s. The question is: How will governments afford to keep an aging population housed, fed, and given proper medical care?

In 2012, the Social Security Administration reported that 10.8 million Americans were now receiving disability benefits. That is a 53 percent increase over the past decade. More than 5 million people have applied for disability benefits since the economic crisis began in 2007. When unemployment rises, more people collect disability. What will happen if the economy remains flat for the next 20 years, as many predict?

Today, many governments are going bust, unable to fund the retirement pension plans of their public workers. The state of California's pension system is a disaster.

How will governments afford tomorrow's old people? This 800-pound gorilla will be your child's problem.

Aging Parents and Boomerang Kids

For years the American Dream was a house of your own. Housing today is become multi-generational. Two, three, and even four generations will be living under one roof. This is why many builders are designing homes with several separate dwell spaces, all under one roof.

Today, many American families have "boomerang kids"—kids who leave home and go to school, only to return unemployed and unable to survive in the real world.

On top of boomerang kids, many adults have aging parents who depend upon them for care. In the United States, long-term and assisted-living care can start as high at as $8,000 a month, which is more than many people earn per month.

Multi-generational survival will be your child's problem. Will your child move in with you, or will you move in with them and their kids? Will your child be able to afford your long-term healthcare if you are lucky enough to live a long life?

The Biggest Gorilla

The most expensive problem on the horizon is not Social Security or multi-generational housing. The biggest gorilla sitting quietly in the room is Medicare. Medicare was created in 1965 and today is an unfunded liability estimated at over $100 trillion, more money than all the money in the world. Your child will wrestle with this $100-trillion gorilla, one way or another.

President George W. Bush created the most expensive social problem in recent years, and the largest Medicare liability, when he signed into law Medicare Part D.

President Barack Obama's Obamacare sets the stage for another massive problem that your child will pay for, one way or another. I believe Obamacare is more problematic than Medicare.

Today, the first wave of approximately 80 million U.S. baby boomers has begun to collect on Social Security and Medicare. Keeping the math simple, if 80 million baby boomers collect $1,000 a month from the government, that is $80 billion each month in taxpayer money…yours and your child's taxes.

Baby boomers will live longer than their parents and demand expensive medical care to stay alive, as long as someone (your child and his or her peers…) is willing to fund their golden years. This leads to the next gorilla.

800-Pound Gorilla #2: Accelerating National Debt

Most of us have heard of the power of compounding interest. Albert Einstein is often credited with referring to it as the "most powerful force in the universe."

A parallel concept is the miracle of compounding debt. Your child will face the tyranny of compounding debt as well as the compounding interest on that debt.

In the year 2000, the national debt of the United States was over $5 trillion. By 2012, it had risen to over $16 trillion.

In 2011, riots erupted in Greece when the government of Greece declared bankruptcy. The United States, England, and Japan may not be far behind.

This leads to the next gorilla waiting for your child.

800-Pound Gorilla #3: The New Depression

Chairman Ben Bernanke is currently running the U.S. Federal Reserve Bank. He is arguably the most powerful banker in the world, simply because he has the power to tell the treasury to print U.S. dollars.

His first profession was as a college professor at Princeton, and he particularly studied the Great Depression. He believes the reason the last depression was so severe was because the Fed did not print money, which caused the economy to collapse. Hence, he believes the way to save the economy in this new depression is through "quantitative easing," aka printing money. That is why his nickname is "Helicopter Ben," for reportedly suggesting he would drop money from helicopters if the economy stalled.

History records two different types of financial depressions

1. The Great Depression of 1929 in the United States
2. The German hyperinflation in the 1920s

Summarized in simple terms, the American depression was caused by not printing enough money. The German hyperinflation type of depression was caused by printing too much money.

A few disturbing comments from the Fed Chairman Ben Bernanke, an "A" student, are:

- *"The U.S. government has a technology called a printing press [or its electronic equivalent today] that allows it to produce as many U.S. dollars as it wishes at no cost."* (2002)
- *"House prices have risen by nearly 25 percent over the past two years. Although speculative activity has increased in some areas, at a national level these price increases largely reflect strong economic fundamentals."* (2005)

In 2007, housing prices began crashing.

- *"The Federal Reserve is not currently forecasting a recession."* (2008)
- *"One myth that's out there is that what we're doing is printing money. We're not printing money."* (2010)

Chairman Bernanke is a distinguished academic. Unfortunately, he is not a businessman. From my viewpoint, his statements reflect being "out of touch" with the real world.

After 2007, it became apparent to me that Chairman Bernanke favored the German type of depression, a financial crisis that, if successful, will lead to hyperinflation. He believes printing money will solve the problem of printing money. It is like an alcoholic drinking more to cure his addiction.

Q&A

Question: How long did the last U.S. depression last?

Answer: It lasted 25 years. In 1929, the Dow was at a high of 381 before crashing. It took until 1954 before the Dow reached 381 again.

If the Great Depression lasted 25 years, the New Depression could last from 2007 to 2032.

Hyperinflation is a period of rapid inflation that leaves a country's currency virtually worthless. For people who work for money and savers who believe in saving money, hyperinflation could wipe them out. This is important to note because, during the last U.S. depression, the Americans who had jobs and had money saved were the winners.

During the German depression in the 1920s, those who produced products that were needed for survival—products such as shelter, debt, and fuel—did well. A few did very well because producers could raise their prices.

In the New Depression, savers, retirees, and fixed-income workers will be the biggest losers. Debtors and producers of food, fuel, and shelter (as well as those who hold gold, silver, and diamonds rather than cash) will be the biggest winners.

The point is, it is important to prepare your child for the possibilities of both types of depressions.

Sir Edmond Burke, who lived from 1729 to 1797, said:

"Those who do not know history's mistakes are doomed to repeat them."

This global financial crisis is a global condemnation because our schools fail to teach financial history, an essential element of financial education.

The Warnings of Economists

Today, many people claim that "printing money" to stimulate the economy is Keynesian Economics. That is rubbish. That is a lie told to a public that has no idea what Keynesian Economics are.

Rich Dad Lesson

Financial education must include lessons in financial history. He said, "If you want to prepare for the future you must know the past."

This is what British economist John Maynard Keynes had to say about devaluing the currency:

"Lenin is said to declared that the best way to destroy the capitalist system was to debauch the currency… There is no subtler, no surer means of overturning the existing basis of society than to debauch the currency… By a continuing process of inflation, governments can confiscate, secretly and unobserved, an important part of the wealth of their citizens… The process engages all the hidden forces of economic law on the side of destruction, and does it in a manner which not one man in a million is able to diagnose."

800-Pound Gorilla #4: Higher Taxes

Every time central banks print money, two things happen.

1. Higher taxes
2. Higher inflation (Inflation is another tax)

Taxes Are Not Patriotic

Many people believe paying taxes is their patriotic duty. Here again, they are victims of a lack of knowledge of financial history.

In 1943, the U.S. Congress passed the Current Tax Payment Act to fund another war, World War II. For the first time in history, the U.S. government began taking taxes out of workers' paychecks before the worker was paid. The workers allowed this to happen in the name of fighting for freedom and liberty. That is why many Americans believe it is patriotic to pay taxes. The problem is: World War II is over, but the United States never stopped collecting taxes.

As you know, bureaucrats running the government know how to spend money, but they do not know how to make money. They only know how to increase taxes.

Runaway spending and raising taxes is not a rich or poor problem. The rich have just as many welfare programs as the poor. The rich have corporate welfare programs, and the poor have social welfare programs. Regardless of what you call them, the taxpayer pays the price.

Welfare programs for the rich are often called "pork." Pork funds such programs as "bridges to nowhere" and "building weapons the military does not want." Pork is welfare for the rich because it funds projects that generate profits for rich business owners but that aren't needed.

Today, if government welfare to both the rich and the poor were cut off, there would be a crash bigger than the subprime crash of 2007. Granted, some government programs do a lot of good. The problem is that your child will pay the price for those programs with higher and higher taxes.

One discussion a parent should have with their child as early as possible is on the subject of taxes, and explaining who pays the most in taxes—and why.

To illustrate and explain the subject of taxes, rich dad drew the CASHFLOW® quadrant for me.

The letters in the four quadrants represent:

E for employee

S for small business or self-employed

B for big business (500 employees or more)

I for investor

Each of us resides in at least one of the four sections or quadrants of the CASHFLOW® quadrant. Which quadrant we are is determined by where our cash flows come from, hence the name CASHFLOW® quadrant. A person can have multiple streams of cash flow and reside in more than one of the quadrants.

Employees in the E quadrant are people with steady jobs who rely on paychecks.

Those in the S quadrant are the self-employed who work by the hour, on commission, or on a fee basis. Many "A" students, such as doctors and lawyers, reside in the S quadrant.

The B quadrant is filled with people such as Steve Jobs and Bill Gates, entrepreneurs who start large businesses.

People in the I Quadrant are professional, active investors like Warren Buffett.

Most people are passive investors who invest in pensions, IRAs, and 401(k)s. Since they are passive investors—not professional investors—their investments are taxed at higher levels.

Most CEOs are in the E quadrant. They are known as "managerial capitalists," employees who work for entrepreneurs. True capitalists are people like Steve Jobs, Bill Gates, or Mark Zuckerberg, entrepreneurs whose companies employ more than 500 employees and who transitioned from the S quadrant to the B and I quadrants.

Our school systems prepare people for the left side of the CASHFLOW quadrant, the E and S quadrants. That is why most parents advise their kids to "Go to school to get a job" (E quadrant) or "Become a doctor or lawyer" (S quadrant).

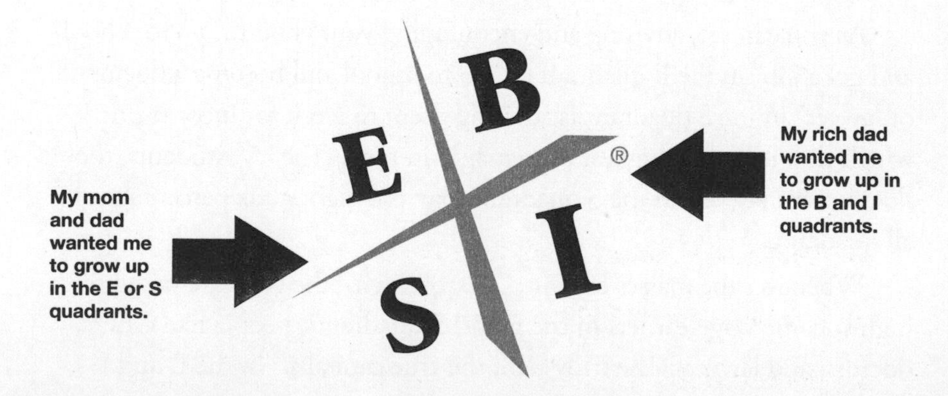
My mom and dad wanted me to grow up in the E or S quadrants.
E
B
S
I
®
My rich dad wanted me to grow up in the B and I quadrants.

The differences in taxes between the people and the quadrants are extreme.

Where a person resides in the CASHFLOW quadrant—meaning: where their income comes from—determines how that income is taxed. The diagram here depicts different types of income from different quadrants…and who pays the highest percentages in taxes today.

TAX PERCENTAGES PAID PER QUADRANT

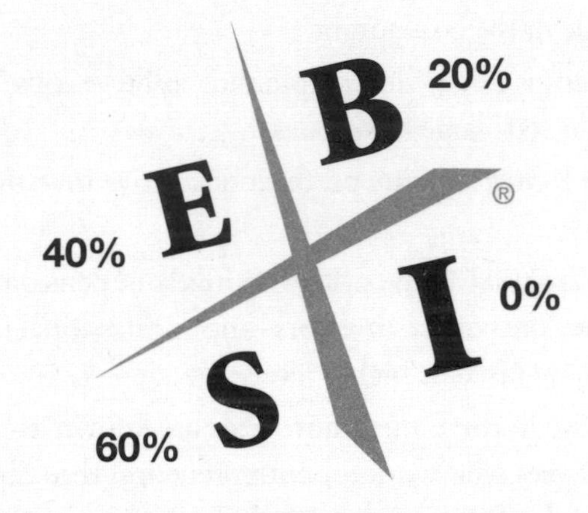

Now you know why President Obama paid 20.5% in taxes and Mitt Romney paid 14%. The difference is the blended differences in income earned in different quadrants. President Obama looks at the world from the E and S quadrants. Mitt Romney views the world from the B and I quadrants.

Most socialists live in the E and S quadrants. The true capitalists live in the B and I quadrants.

As you can see, advising and encouraging your child to "go to school and get a job" in the E quadrant or "go to school and become a doctor or lawyer" in the S quadrant is advising them to work for income on which they'll pay the highest percentages in taxes. The "A" students, the doctors and lawyers in the S quadrant, pay the highest tax percentage of all quadrants.

Whenever the masses cry out, "Tax the rich," the taxes are raised on high-income wage-earners in the E and S quadrants, people like CEOs, doctors, and lawyers. The truly rich, the true capitalists in the B and I quadrants, pay very little, if any, in taxes. To some people, people like President Obama, this may sound dishonest and unfair. Later in this book, we'll look at why tax breaks for those in the B and I quadrants are not only fair but also important to keep the wheels of the economy turning.

> ***Salary: $1 a Year***
>
> ***Question:*** Why was Steve Jobs' salary only $1 a year?
>
> ***Answer:*** He was a true capitalist. His income did not come from the E or S quadrants.

By understanding taxes early in life, your child has time to make better life decisions about what they want to study and which quadrants are best for them. A person should never choose a quadrant just to pay less in taxes, but understanding the fundamental differences is a part of financial education. Understanding the quadrants, different types of income, and the taxes on that income, will give your child a foundation for making informed choices about money, business, and investing.

Preparing your child for the B and I quadrants takes time. Steve Jobs, Bill Gates, and Mark Zuckerberg started their journey to the B and I quadrants as teenagers. These three men all dropped out of great schools, such as Harvard and Reed College, because school, primarily, prepares students for the E and S quadrants, not for the B and I quadrants.

In preparing your child for the gorilla-wrestling that lies ahead, it is important that your child knows that there are different options open to them, options other than "go to school, get a job, work hard, and pay higher and higher taxes."

Later in this book I will go into why the tax rates are different in the different quadrants. You will also find out why it is that when people shout, "Tax the rich!" the tax authorities tend to leave the B and I quadrants alone. No matter how hard President Obama tries, those in the B and I quadrants will find legal ways to pay less in taxes.

The lesson on Capitalism begins with the first chapter of *Rich Dad Poor Dad*, the lesson, "The Rich Don't Work For Money." Simply said, the people who work for money, those in the E and S quadrants, pay the highest percentages in taxes. Those in the B and I quadrants are capitalist. Capitalists do what the government wants done—like creating jobs and affordable housing. Hence they pay the least in taxes. This is true in all Western economy countries.

This difference in taxes will be further clarified in coming sections, because taxes are an important part of a person's financial education.

Is It Too Late to Change Quadrants?

Question: Does a person need to be young to make the transition from the E and S quadrants to the B and I quadrants?

Answer: No. Colonel Harlan Sanders did not start his journey until after he was retired. At the age of 65, a new freeway bypassed his little chicken shop and his business collapsed. That was when he left the S quadrant and began his Kentucky Fried Chicken franchise in the B and I quadrants. The Colonel's advantage was that he was pretty good at making chicken in the S quadrant when he started his journey to the B and I quadrants.

The B and I quadrants are demanding, which is why a strong financial education and an early start are important. Many start the journey, but few succeed. Yet for those who do make it, the rewards are immense. Success in the B and I quadrants is like climbing Mount Everest, ascending to the top of the world, the top of the financial food chain. If your child starts preparing early enough, they have a better chance of making it.

The good news is that you do not have to be the smartest person to succeed in the B and I quadrants. You do not have to be an "A" or "B" student, which is more important in the E quadrant and especially the S quadrant. Success in the B and I quadrants is best described as a team sport. All you have to do is surround yourself with smart, trustworthy, hardworking people. And while that may seem simple enough, it is often the toughest challenge of the B and I quadrants.

> ***Inspiration vs. Motivation***
>
> ***Inspire:*** *The word comes from Latin "ispiratio" meaning "in spirit" or "inspired by god."*
>
> ***Motivate:*** *The word comes from Latin "motere" meaning "to move."*

My Story

In 1969, I graduated from the U.S. Merchant Marine Academy in New York. Since the Vietnam War was on, I volunteered to serve my country rather than begin my career as a merchant ship's officer, a profession I had prepared for with four years of schooling. I had a great job lined up as an oil tanker officer with Standard Oil, but I knew I had to serve my country.

So in 1969, rather than sail for Standard Oil, I volunteered for military duty as a Marine and went to flight school.

Driving through the gates of the U.S. Navy Flight School at Pensacola, Florida, was the beginning of a great adventure in learning.

High school was a horrible experience for me. The academy was tough and competitive. But flight school was my love affair with learning. No matter how challenging the flight school was, the love of learning never left me. For the first time in my life, I loved being a student.

Learning to love learning is important because education is a process, like the diagram below.

EDUCATIONAL PROCESS

Navy Flight School was truly a process of turning a caterpillar into a butterfly.

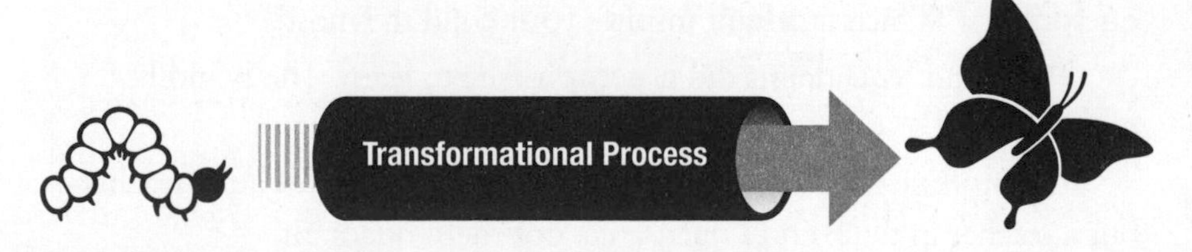

Flight school was more than educational. Flight school was transformational. Flight school challenged me mentally, emotionally, physically, and spiritually…and I loved the challenge. That is what education should do…inspire a student to learn more and become more.

I believe one important job of a parent is to find the educational process that brings out your child's gifts and inspires their love of learning. It might be in music, gardening, medicine, art, or law. For me, it was flight school. As I said, learning to fly renewed my love of learning, just as the game of *Monopoly®* inspired me to become rich.

Unfortunately, if you motivate externally rather than inspire internally, motivation becomes manipulation.

It is most important that the educational process inspires the child and brings out their genius, rather than punishing them for not doing well on tests and making them feel stupid.

If a child has a strong financial education from home, they can do what they love and still do well financially. Using myself as an example, today I am a teacher. For most teachers, their income comes from the E quadrant. And while most teachers complain about not making enough money, I don't have that complaint. Why? Because I am a teacher in the B quadrant. Since I am also in the I quadrant, I do not need a paycheck. Most of my money comes from the I quadrant, which is taxed at a much lower rate, often 0%, legally.

Use the Quadrants to Inspire

The lesson for parents is "The quadrant is more important than the profession."

Much of this book is about the differences in education, skills, and experience that are required to do well in the B and I quadrants. The real question is, "Which quadrant inspires your child the most?"

The E and S quadrants did not inspire me to learn. The B and I quadrants did.

The profession a child chooses makes little difference. I am a teacher—but a teacher in the B and I quadrants, not the E quadrant.

I never dreamed I would be a teacher, I just knew which quadrants I dreamed of.

The same was true for Steve Jobs. If you read his biography, you'll learn that he did not dream of becoming an employee or self-employed small business owner. His dreams were bigger than that.

Rich Dad Lesson

"It's not the profession that determines a person's earning ability. It's the quadrant."

My mom and dad were Es, in the employee quadrant. They often said, "The rich pay less in taxes because they're crooks." Although they were well educated, their education did not include the study of the quadrants, different types of income, and taxes.

Preparing for the Worst

One reason why people have trouble changing quadrants is because most people choose quadrants out of fear rather than inspiration. For example, most people choose the E quadrant because they fear not having money, a financial fear which causes them to seek job security, benefits, and a steady paycheck.

Many people gravitate to the S quadrant due to a lack of trust. It's my experience that most S-quadrant people do not trust many people. They want to do their own thing and be their own boss, which is why they often say, "If you want something done right, do it yourself."

The problem with the S quadrant is that you do not really own a business. You own a job. If you stop working, your income often stops. This means you own a "busy-ness," not a business.

A business in the B quadrant, on the other hand, continues to generate revenue, whether you work or not.

Training for Life

The reason Kim and I retired at 37 and 47 is because we had income coming in from the B and I quadrants. We had no income from the E or S quadrants.

One reason I loved flight school so much was that we were inspired to face our fears every day. I was not in flight school for a steady paycheck or early retirement benefits, although I knew many student pilots who were. Career Marines are employees of the U.S. Government.

I was in the Marine Corps and flight school for the inspiration, the preparation for war. Rather than seek security, our instructors forced us to practice "emergency maneuvers" on each and every flight. Rather than hope and pray things would go right, the instructors would intentionally cripple the aircraft in some way, sometimes even killing the engine. They forced us to face our fears, keep our cool, and still fly. It was perfect training for life in the B and I quadrants.

Many people will struggle financially simply because their emotions run their lives. Rather than face their financial fears, they hide from them. Many employees in the E quadrant hide under the blanket of a steady paycheck and job security. The self-employed in the S quadrant hide behind the veil of rugged individualism, the need to be the smartest and the best.

Tell Your Children About the Gorillas

Rather than shelter your children from the real world, advising them to get good grades and a good job that will protect them from the real world, tell them about the four gorillas that loom in their future. When it comes to money, all children are smart. Let them prepare for their futures, just as my flight school instructors helped me prepare me for Vietnam.

I know many experts will say that it is not good to scare kids, but this is not about scaring them. It is about preparing them for the future. By facing their fears and preparing for the worst, they have a better chance for a better life.

Then, if your *child* decides they would rather seek job security in the E quadrant or independence in the S quadrant, they will—at the very least—make a better-informed personal decision. If they believe their best chances for success are in the B and I quadrants, they have time to prepare. Just as Steve Jobs and Bill Gates started their process in their teens, it is best your child do the same, especially if they want to be entrepreneurs.

Your child will face a much different world than the world we live in today. The financial opportunities will be enormous, but so will the problems. The bankruptcies of entire countries have just begun. The near bankruptcy of Greece was only the beginning.

We hear people say, "The next generation of Americans will not do as well as previous generations." One reason that may be true is because our schools are not preparing them for the real world, the world of the future. Simply said, don't just protect your child from the future. Prepare them for it.

Final Words on Financial History

In 1971, President Richard Nixon took the U.S. dollar off the gold standard.

In 1971, the U.S. dollar ceased being real money. The U.S. dollar became currency, an instrument of debt, an IOU from the American taxpayers.

The good news is that after 1971, the world economy boomed, but it was an economy based on debt.

In 2007, the debt balloon exploded. Now we are in a financial crisis, a New Depression.

This may be the price we pay for not learning from the past.

History Repeats Itself

Mayer Amschel Rothschild, born in 1744 and founder of the Rothschild banking empire, explained the cause of this global financial crisis.

"Give me control over a nation's currency,
and I care not who makes its laws."

In 1971, when President Nixon took the U.S. dollar off the gold standard, it made no difference who made the laws. Republican or Democrat, it made little difference. The bankers of the world took control of the most powerful country in the world, the United States of America.

Yet President Nixon was not the first American to fall to the power of the bankers.

Thomas Jefferson, one of America's founding fathers, signer of the Declaration of Independence, and third President of the United States, stated:

"If the American people ever allow private banks to control the issue of their money, first by inflation and then by deflation, the banks and corporations that grow up around them, will deprive the people of their property, until their children will wake up homeless on the continent their forefather's conquered."

Jefferson also warned:

"I sincerely believe that banking institutions are more dangerous to our liberties than standing armies; and that the principle of spending money to be paid by posterity... is swindling futurity on a large scale."

In other words, the central banks, created in 1913 and of which the Federal Reserve Bank is the most powerful in history, have been stealing the future from our parents, our children, and their children's children. That theft has now spread throughout the world, and fueled the global crisis we face today.

The U.S. Federal Reserve Bank is not a U.S. enterprise. It is a cartel controlled by the richest banking families in the world. It is no longer Federal. You and I have no control over it. It has no reserves. It does not need money, it prints money. It is not a bank.

In 1913, the 16th Amendment led to the U.S. Constitution was passed. It gave the federal government the power to assess an income tax on its citizens. The 16th Amendment the creation of the IRS, the Internal Revenue Service, and gave it the power to collect those taxes.

In 1913, the citizens of the United States lost control over their money. The richest people in the world took control over the soon-to-be most powerful country in the world. A cash heist began with taxes, because taxes are how the rich and powerful put their hands into our pockets, via the government they control.

This theft of our future, via the banking families of the world, is the reason I believe we have no credible financial education in our schools. And why parents must fill that void and prepare their children for the financial realities of the future.

Thomas Jefferson, born in the 1743, warned of this…and this was a part of his warning:

> *"The banks and the corporations that will grow up around them, will deprive the people of their property, until their children will wake up homeless on the continent their forefather's conquered."*

This may explain why our government bailed out the mega-banks such as Goldman Sachs and Bank of America and bailed out corporations such as AIG and General Motors, bailouts paid for by the taxpayers. It was not to save jobs. It was to save the rich.

The End of the Fed?

During the Presidential election of 2012, Ron Paul, a Representative from Texas and candidate in the Republican primaries, talked about his book, *End the Fed*. In that book he writes about the power of a central bank that work against the personal interest of Americans. In other words, who pays Fed Chairman Bernake's salary?

He inspired an End the Fed grass roots movement.

Thomas Jefferson would agree. Back in the 1800s, Jefferson said, *"The issuing power [of money] should be taken from the banks and restored to the people to whom it properly belongs."*

Futile Effort

While it may be a noble effort, working to end the Fed is a waste of time. The entire corrupt system will probably collapse, just as the Roman Empire collapsed around the 5th Century. Will it collapse? When will it collapse? Who knows?

Rather than End the Fed, my rich dad taught his son and me to "Be the Fed." To "Be the Fed" requires a high level of financial education, which is why he started teaching us early in life.

By the end of this book, you will learn how you, too, can inspire your child to "Be the Fed" rather than work to "End the Fed."

By the end of this book, you will learn how I print my own money, as the Fed does, and pay less in taxes, like the country's largest corporations do…legally. And I make this point because with financial education, the type of education that can transform lives, you and your children can "print your own money," too.

I want to be clear here: I am not saying this is fair. There are lots of things in life that aren't fair. What I am saying is that "freedom" is a noble concept and one for which, I believed, I went to war. It includes the freedom to make choices. It is my opinion that our school system is dysfunctional if it does not give our students the freedom of choice over education in the four quadrants. Our world needs more men and women like Steve Jobs, people who needed to leave school to learn about the B and I quadrants. But why should they leave school to do so? Steve Jobs created jobs. Our schools produce enough CEOs, the managerial capitalists who are employees who need a job and often destroy jobs.

It is not fair when our schools teach history that is selective or distorted. Why not tell kids the truth? Much of history is about money. It is a distortion of the truth to say wars are fought for freedom. Wars are fought for money. War is very big business.

It is a distortion, a single-point-of-view opinion, to say that Christopher Columbus was an explorer. He was an entrepreneur, financed by Queen Isabella, who went in search of a trade route to Asia.

Columbus was the Steve Jobs of his era. His discovery of the riches of North and South America made Spain the richest country in the world at the time.

With all the gold stolen, by the great explorers (pirates) such as Francisco Pizzaro, Ferdinand Magellan, and Hernando Cortés Spain's economy boomed. Spain, once a great nation, is today one of Europe's economic basket cases along with Greece, Italy and France. This time, Spain's economy went boom and bust not on gold and silver but on debt, counterfeit money from Central Banks, just like the rest of the world.

The great pirates still roam the world. Today, they do not sail ships. Today they run international banks.

Mayer Amschel Rothschild's words, from 1838, are worth repeating:

"Give me control over a nation's currency, and I care not who makes its laws."

Today, he might say:

"Give me control over the world's currency and I care not who makes its laws."

Lessons from the Game of Monopoly®

The rules of *Monopoly* state:

"The Bank never goes broke. If the Bank runs out of money, the Banker may issue as much as needed by writing on any ordinary paper."

This is why rich dad used the game of *Monopoly* to teach his son and me about money. My rich dad often said, "*Monopoly* is the real game of life."

The World Today

Today, the world runs on counterfeit money, debt, and IOUs from taxpayers.

The bankers who built this global house of cards became very rich, many receiving handouts and bonuses from the government, as millions of taxpayers became very poor.

This is not only true in America. It is true all over the world.

International Gorillas

Here are a few modern-day examples of what happens when pirates take control of a nation's money.

Japan

Japan's economy has been stagnant for over 20 years, although Japan has one of the highest savings rates in the world.

So much for the idea that Americans need to save more money to save the economy.

Greece

Greece went bust in 2012 and then retirees began committing suicide, unwilling to face old age in poverty. Spain, Italy, and Portugal are next. In many countries, the best and the brightest leave home in search of opportunity in other countries. This crisis is known as a "brain drain."

Italy

In Italy in early 2012, in just one day, the price of a gallon of gas went from $10 to $16. This was because of an increase in taxes to help pay the interest on the national debt. The problem with most highly educated bureaucrats is that they think increasing taxes will save the economy. Taxes kill economies, as bankers and politicians get richer.

Three things happen when banks print money: Taxes and inflation go up and people become poorer.

France

France, the second largest economy in Europe, is deeply in debt as growth slows. Rather than work harder, the French want more to have time off, work less, and take earlier retirements. As their productivity declines, so will France.

To solve the problem, France is raising taxes on the rich…just as the United States wants to do. When you tax the rich, the rich (and their money) leave the country.

China

China's engine of growth is sputtering as unemployment and its military power rises.

Mexico

In Mexico, America's neighbor, drug lords have more money, guns, and influence than the government. Obviously, this is not an ideal environment in which to raise children.

Give Your Child a Financial Headstart

If you want your child to have an unfair advantage in life, teach them about money and money's impact on history. Teach them the real rules of money and taxes.

In an upcoming section of this book, you will learn the real life unfair advantages that a financial education can give your child—unfair advantages that even "A" students do not have.

Your Child's Future

Repeating Edmond Burke's warning:

"Those that cannot remember the past are condemned to repeat it."

Personally, I would rather than learn from the history of money…than be crushed by the future of money.

Since 1971, it's been reported that the U.S. dollar has lost over 90% of its purchasing power. It's not going to take another 40 years to lose the last 10%.

Consider this: If you teach your children to be capitalists, educate them about the unfair advantages that the B and I side of the quadrant offers for capitalists, and inform them of the real rules of money and taxes there is less of a chance the four gorillas sitting in the room, will stomp on your child's future.

Action Step for Parents

Use money problems as opportunities to learn.

My mom and dad did their best to protect the kids from their money problems.

The problem was all four of us kids knew we had problems. Rather than learn to face our money problems, we learned to hide from them.

When my rich dad had money problems or employee problems, he would use the real-life problem as opportunity to learn. He would take the time to explain the problem and possible solutions to the problems.

Rich dad often said, "Problems can make you smarter. Problems can also make you poorer. It's your choice."

When money problems occur in your home, I suggest parents use this book or other resources to seek possible solutions to your personal financial problems. Then discuss the problem and possible solutions growing smarter and bigger than the problem.

A family can use money problems—and working through solutions—as a way to grow smarter together. Later in life, when your child is faced with money problems, this habit will help them see the problem as opportunities to grow smarter about money.

If your child is too young or not yet ready to handle the sometimes disturbing real-world money problems, take them grocery shopping and discuss how you budget your money to feed the family. That will be a real world education.

We all have money problems…even rich people. What makes us richer or poorer is how we handle our money problems. I've learned not waste a good money problem because every time we solve one we get smarter in the process.

At What Age Should You Start Teaching Your Child About Money?

Part One | Chapter Four

LESSON #4: WINDOWS OF LEARNING

I'm sure most parents are well aware of their child's awareness related to money. As a baby, shiny coins catch their eye and as they get older, children they begin to get a sense of what things cost. Many of us probably recall our parents' admonitions when we wanted a new toy or bike: "Do you think money grows on trees?"

They see money changing hands—at the grocery store, the movies, the gas station—and soon have an understanding of paychecks and expenses. They come to like the idea of having money of their own, whether it's a few dollars from the tooth fairy, $5 dollar from Dad for some extra help with the yard work or a cash birthday gift from Grandma.

Question: At what age should you start teaching your child about money?

Answer: The moment they can tell the difference between a $1 bill and a $5 bill.

Making the Case

All children go through three important windows of learning. The three early windows of learning are:

First window:	Birth to age 12
Second window:	Age 12 to age 24
Third window:	Age 24 to age 36

The Three Windows of Learning

When teaching children, it is important to be aware of the three windows of learning and what a child is experiencing as he or she ages and moves through stages of development.

Window of Learning #1

Birth to Age 12: Quantum Learning

Most educational psychologists agree that learning window #1 is the period of quantum learning in a child. Anything they can see, taste, and feel is a new and exciting learning experience. They may not understand the word *hot*, but they soon know what hot feels like.

During this learning window, the child's brain is like clay. Their brain is also whole at first. It is not until the age of four, that the brain begins to divide into a right hemisphere and a left hemisphere.

If a person is described as "right-brain dominant," the person is more artistic, creative, and more free-flowing in their approach to life. If a person is described as "left-brain dominant," the person is more bookish, less creative, and more linear. The left brain is where speech, reading, writing, and math skills and aptitudes are said to come from. Traditional schools believe left-brain-dominant students are smart.

Art, music, and dance schools tend to attract right-brain-dominant students.

If a child is left-handed, the tendencies the right-brain or left-brain dominance may be reversed.

A number of researchers believe that great geniuses are dominant on both sides. One researcher studied individuals like Winston Churchill who, as a young boy, often reported flashes in the brain that stunned him. A few minutes later, he was able to articulate his flash of genius. In overly simple terms, the flash of genius took place in his right brain, the creative side. Since speech comes from the left brain, the flash of genius had to travel from the right hemisphere to the left hemisphere, which allowed him to talk about his new ideas. Today, we might say, "A light went on in our head." As you might expect, not all researchers agree with this school of thought.

One reason why games, such as *Monopoly*, are great teaching tools is because games engage both the left and right hemispheres of the brain. Games have the power to engage the whole person, not just the brain's left hemisphere. This is true for children as well as for adults. In other words, learning is as much a physical and emotional process as it is a mental one.

Regardless of which side of this debate you land one, it seems to hold true that during this first window of learning, from birth to age 12, a child is a learning machine. Parents do not need to encourage them to learn. They learn actively, progressing from crawling to walking, talking, eating, and learning to ride a bicycle. The little learning machine often wears parents out.

Then the child goes to school.

This first window of learning is when the child learns language and accents. For example, the speech of a child born in Alabama may develop with a Southern accent, while a child born in New York may develop a distinctive New York accent. Later in life a child may learn another language, but the accent developed early in life often transfers to the new language.

Children raised in Europe have a distinct advantage because they spend their early, first window of learning years in a multiple-language culture. Later in life, this experience allows them to learn new languages and change languages with ease. In contrast, a child raised in a single-language environment often struggles to learn a second language later in life.

During the first window of learning, the child acquires preferences for cultures, foods, and music. A delicacy for one child is disgusting to another. A child growing up in the city will see the world differently than a child growing up on a remote farm. A child growing up in the ghetto will see the world differently than a child growing up in suburbia. Similarly, a poor child will develop differently than a child born to wealth. And an abused child will often face challenges later in life that a child raised with love may never understand.

Between birth and age 12, the child's brain is relatively smooth. As learning takes place, neural pathways are formed in the brain. In simple terms, neural pathways are like roads inside the brain. Just as a person moving to a new town needs to find their way around town—and learn the path from their home to the supermarket, to work, and to church—a child's brain is forming neural pathways when it learns to crawl, walk, talk, and ride a bike.

The reason age 12 is an important age marker is because after 12, the brain begins to erase, or wash away, parts of the brain that have not yet formed neural pathways. In other words: "Use it or lose it."

Once neural pathways are formed and the unused parts of the brain are erased, it becomes more difficult to learn new things. Connecting the dots in learning new things is not as easy after age 12. Rather than simply connecting the dots, bridges now have to be built over the ridges and valleys in the evolving, aging brain.

So there *is* some truth to the saying, "You can't teach an old dog new tricks." The older you get, the more learning slows, and the harder it becomes harder to build new neural pathways.

These age periods are called "windows" because that is what they are—a window, an opening, brief period of time during which to learn something. For example, there is a window to learn how to walk. If the child is deprived of learning to walk during the first window, there is a possibility the child may be crippled for life because the skeletal, muscular, and motor skills never developed. The same is true for learning to talk and socialize with other people. If a child fails to learn to read and write during the first window of learning, they may be challenged, even handicapped, for life. They can learn these skills later in life, it's just harder. If the window is missed, the window closes.

I recall a story of a child who was locked in a closet by her parents. The child missed the first window of learning and most of the second window before she was found. Although she is free today, she remains severely handicapped mentally, physically, emotionally, and socially. She never developed the normal neural pathways that most children develop while growing up.

Window of Learning #2

Ages 12 to 24: Rebellious Learning

As a child enters their teens, they learn by rebelling. For example, if you tell a teenage boy, "Don't drink," chances are he will drink or at least be more inclined to experiment with alcohol. If they borrow your car and you say, "Don't speed," chances are they will speed. And if you say, "Don't have sex," the more curious they become about sex, especially with the peer pressure kids face today.

The second window of learning is called the window of *rebellious learning* because that is how a child learns during this period of life. They want to learn what *they* want to do or what to learn. They want to make up their own minds, rather than be told what to learn. They begin to exercise their power to think and choose for themselves.

Most intergenerational conflict come from this window of learning. For example, in music, teenage and growth rebellion generates new forms of music. In the '50s, it was Chuck Berry and Elvis. Rock and roll shocked adults who were listening to jazz. In the '60s, The Beatles and the Rolling Stones exploded rock and roll through the new medium known as television. In the 1970s, John Travolta was the king of disco. In the 1980s, Nirvana introduced "grunge" music led by Kurt Cobain. Today's rap and hip-hop really started to take off in the '90s. And of course, Michael Jackson blurred the lines between black and white, music, dance, theater, music videos, and elaborate choreography.

The Challenge of Window #2

The real challenge of rebellious learning is that the child is not yet aware of the word consequences. For example, if you say, "Don't speed," they do not yet understand the consequences of speeding, the possible results of their actions, consequences such as traffic tickets, car accidents, and, even worse, death. As a parent, you are well aware of the risks and consequences, but the child is not.

The lives of many teens veer off track during this rebellious period. They can develop drug habits, drop out of school, father or give birth to children, or begin their careers in crime, primarily because they do not understand the ramifications of their actions.

It goes without saying that this second window of learning is a very important window. The child's relationship to his or her parents during this time is crucial. During this period of development, much like the first window of learning, a parent is the child's most important teacher.

This is not to say that a parent is a bad parent (or the child is a bad child) if the child gets into trouble during this time. This second window of learning has an important function: It's a time when a child instinctively rebels and experiments, because this is how he or she learns during this period of life.

The relationship between parent and child is often tested in dealing with consequences when a child gets in trouble. This is a critical time in the developing relationship between parent and child. For example:

- How do parents respond when their daughter wrecks the car? How do a parents respond if their son is arrested for drunk driving? This is when the parent-child relationship is tested. This is when the parent finds out how good a teacher they are… or are not.

- How does a parent respond when they find out their clean-cut, college-bound son is earning a few thousand dollars a month selling drugs? Does the parent have their son arrested, or do they do their best to cover up his criminal behavior?

- What does a parent do when they find out their child is cutting classes and has disciplinary problems in school? Blame the school for their child's problems? Or resolve the problem responsibly with the school, the teacher, and the student?

- What does a parent do when their teenage daughter comes home, announces she is pregnant, and does not know who the father is?

Obviously, there is no one, easy answer to any of these situations. Every circumstance is different, just as every child is different. In a home with more than one child, the differences between them can be astounding. The lessons between parents and each child are unique and oftentimes challenging. This is a time when communication is critical as well as a willingness to see other points of view.

I believe the most precarious time in an individual's life is during the second window of learning, ages 12 to 24. If a child can get through those years, they have a better chance of doing well in life.

So the question is: How well prepared are you, as a parent, to handle the second learning window, the years during which your child is learning by rebellion? If you have done a good job during the first learning window, you may have a better chance of guiding your child through the second. You're in good company if you've used this sentiment in navigating those years: "Hopefully they'll grow out of it." Most kids do, but as we all know, some don't. That's when the role of a parent becomes even more critical.

Window of Learning #3

Ages 24 to 36: Professional Learning

This learning window is where the adult learns to "make their way in the world." Obviously, this is another very, very crucial window of learning. This is where the parent observes how well they and the school system did as parents and teachers. As most adults know, the real world is not always fair, equal, or kind. The real world can be a very tough teacher.

During the third learning window, the individual begins to grow roots, professionally. For example, if they have gone to medical school, they begin to find out how good a doctor they are or are not. They find out if they chose the right profession. If they lack professional education, they may wander from job to job before finding themselves—if they ever do. Many young adults struggle to find the courage to follow their dreams. And, so often, that's where a child's genius—his or her special gifts and talents—are found.

During this learning window is traditionally when young people marry, start a family, and buy their first home. This is when the financial realities of the real world sink in. Life becomes more and more about money, and often the lack of it. How a young person addresses increasing financial pressures will depend upon what the child learned about money during the first and second learning windows.

Since 2007, millions of young people have been unable to find meaningful employment or have been underemployed during their third window. Failing to develop during the third window of learning can adversely affect the rest of their lives. That is why global youth unemployment is a greater problem than just young people "not finding a job." A generation of unemployment among young adults is likely to present massive problems years into the future, problems your child may have to deal with.

A schoolteacher may teach your child for a semester or a year, but a parent is a teacher for life. The consistency and stability that a parent brings to a child's life as that life-long teacher—throughout all the windows of learning—reiterates why parents are a child's most important teachers.

My Story

Obviously, I did not know about the windows of learning when I was nine years old. I just knew something was missing in school. What was missing was the subject of money. That's why I went in search of my rich dad. I instinctively knew I needed another teacher, a different teacher.

My search for a new teacher really began when I was seven and saw my mom sitting at the kitchen table crying. She was crying because bills were piling up and our family was out of money. I can still remember her showing me the family bank statement, filled with lines of red numbers.

In the 1950s, banks sent typed bank statements to customers. The statement came on gold-colored paper. At the beginning of the month, after my dad deposited his paycheck, the numbers were in black. As my parents wrote checks, the black numbers turned red, indicating that there was not enough money in the bank account to cover the checks. Their checking account was overdrawn.

It deeply disturbed me to find my mom crying. At the age of seven, I could not understand why someone would cry about money. My first window for learning had opened.

I asked her what dad was doing about this problem. She defended him, saying, "He's doing the best he can. He is working hard and going to school to get his Masters and Doctorate degrees so he can get a higher-paying job."

At seven years old, I really had no idea what she was talking about. I just knew something was wrong, something very important.

Today as an adult, I cringe and bite my tongue when I hear someone say, "I'm going back to school for another degree," as a solution to their financial problems.

I can still hear my rich dad saying, "If going to school made you rich, then schoolteachers would be millionaires."

My First Window of Learning

As I've said, my rich dad would teach his son and me our lessons on money after playing games of *Monopoly*. Rather than tell us what to do and warning us not to make mistakes, he used the mistakes we made during the game as the basis for discussion and lessons to be learned.

According to the learning-windows theory, then my neural pathways relating to money began to connect while playing the game of *Monopoly*.

My grades in school were never good. No matter how hard I studied, I was just an average student. Both my dads were concerned about my grades. And rich dad's son, Mike, was not much better in school than I was.

One day rich dad took us aside and said, "Your grades are important. But I will let you in on a secret to real life."

"What is the secret?" we asked.

Leaning forward, rich dad whispered, "My banker has never asked me for my report card. My banker does not care if I was a good student or what school I went to."

Curious, we asked rich dad, "What *does* your banker want to see?"

"My financial statement," rich dad said, reaching into a file drawer of his desk. Showing us his financial statement, rich dad said, "Your financial statement is your report card when you leave school. The problem is, most kids leave school and never know what a financial statement is."

When Kim and I created our board game *CASHFLOW*®, we built the game around a financial statement, like the one pictured below.

PROFESSION

PLAYER

GOAL: Get out of the Rat Race and onto the Fast Track by building up your **Passive Income** to be **greater** than your **Total Expenses**

INCOME STATEMENT

INCOME

Description	Cash Flow
Salary:	
Interest/Dividends:	
Real Estate/Business:	

AUDITOR

(Person on your right)

Passive Income: $ ______
(Cash Flow from Interest/Dividends + Real Estate/Business)

Total Income: $ ______

EXPENSES

Taxes:	
Home Mortgage Payment:	
School Loan Payment:	
Car Loan Payment:	
Credit Card Payment:	
Retail Payment:	
Other Expenses:	
Child Expenses:	
Loan Payment:	

Number of Children: ______
(Begin game with 0 Children)

Per Child Expense: $ ______

Total Expenses: $ ______

Monthly Cash Flow (PAYDAY): $ ______
(Total Income - Total Expenses)

BALANCE SHEET

ASSETS

Savings:		
Stocks/Funds/CDs:	# of Shares:	Cost/Share:
Real Estate/Business:	Down Pay:	Cost:

LIABILITIES

Home Mortgage:	
School Loans:	
Car Loans:	
Credit Cards:	
Retail Debt:	
Real Estate/Business:	Mortgage/Liability:
Loan:	

G101CT®v12

A financial game built around a financial statement is the evolution of the game of *Monopoly*. It's a way to apply the money and investing lessons of the game to real life.

During my first window of learning rich dad burned the image of a simple financial statement into my brain. This simple diagram became part of the development of my neural pathways, pathways that would someday guide the direction of my life.

This is rich dad's diagram of a financial statement, your report card once you leave school, the 'report card' your banker asks to see.

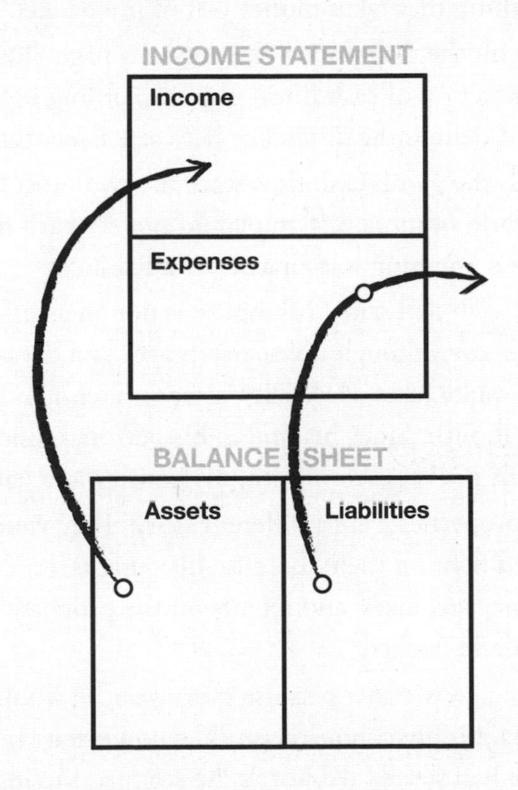

When it came to teaching us the language of money, rich dad used very simple definitions for the most common financial vocabulary words. For example, rather than the complex and confusing definitions for "asset" and "liability" found in the dictionary, he used simple definitions that anyone could understand.

For example, Webster's Dictionary defines an asset this way:

as•set noun \ˈa-ˌset also -sət\

a: the property of a deceased person subject by law to the payment of his or her debts and legacies

b: the entire property of a person, association, corporation, or estate applicable or subject to the payment of debts

Rich dad defined the word asset in simple terms: "Something that puts money in my pocket." His definition for liability was just as simple: "Something that takes money out of my pocket."

The arrows on the diagram on the previous page illustrate the cash flow. It is the direction of cash flow—money coming in and money going out—that defines the difference between assets and liabilities.

To rich dad, the words cash flow were the two most important words in the world of money. If you could not see cash flowing, you could not tell if something was an asset or a liability.

That is why rich dad said, "My house is not an asset." It was not an asset because, even though it was mortgage- and debt-free, he still had to pay real estate taxes, electricity, sewer, water, maintenance and insurance each month. Since his house, his personal residence, took money out of his pocket each month, his house was a liability.

His rental properties were a different story. They were assets—even though they had debt on them, because his tenants' rent payments covered the mortgage, taxes, and repairs on the property, and still put money in rich dad's pocket.

Every year he grew richer because every year he would buy more rental properties, his green houses, until he could start buying red hotels. Once he had several red hotels, he stopped buying little green houses.

Rich dad constantly repeated, "Assets put money in my pocket," and then drew a line on the financial statement from the asset column into the income column. The words, the explanation, and the diagram locked the definition into my mind and developed a neural pathway in my brain. Rather than using words alone for a definition (left brain),

I also had a picture (right brain) that I associated with the physical experience of playing the game.

Most important of all, I had a great teacher, a man who was patient and knew what he was talking about, a man who loved us and let us know we were important to him. A man who wanted us to do well in the real world. Although he was a very busy man, we played *Monopoly* together for hours. He was preparing us for the real world, a real world that ran on money.

Rich dad did not say something once and expect us to get the lesson. He believed in repetition as a key component to long-term learning. No matter how many times he told us something important, we could count on the fact that he would say it again and again. If I heard, "Assets put money in your pocket," followed by seeing his diagram with lines drawn from the asset column into the income column, once, I heard and saw it a thousand times. He also repeated, "Liabilities take money from your pocket," every time we played *Monopoly*.

Today, I know my home, my personal residence, is a liability because it takes money from my pocket. I also know my apartment buildings, commercial buildings, oil wells, businesses, and the intellectual property of my books, games, and patents are all assets putting money in my pocket every month. It's because of the cash flow from my assets that I don't need a paycheck or a retirement plan.

As Einstein once said, "Simplicity is genius." My rich dad was not an academic genius, but he was a financial genius. All he did was play *Monopoly* in real life.

Almost anyone, even high school dropouts, can play *Monopoly* in real life. It's important that each person find the game they love to play. Steve Jobs loved his game—the game of making people feel smart, hip, and like geniuses...which is why Apple stores have genius bars rather than service desks. Colonel Sanders loved the fried chicken business and the franchise game. Walt Disney loved making people happy and built the fantasy of a magical kingdom known as Disneyland. Not one of these three men finished college, but they all found the game they loved. Through their game, their genius came out.

The same thing happens for many athletes. Their genius may not come out in a classroom, yet once they hit the basketball court, football field, or golf course, they are in their element.

For someone with a love for music, it could be playing a musical instrument or singing that brings out their genius. Mick Jagger attended a prestigious school to become an accountant, but found his genius as a Rolling Stone.

Early signs of a child's special genius are often found in the dreams they have for their future. In the CASHFLOW game, before the first roll of the dice, each player chooses their dream.

During my first window of learning, I discovered the difference between capitalists and everyone else. I found the game I wanted to play. By the time I was 12, this picture was burned into my neural pathways.

Es and Ss focus on job security:

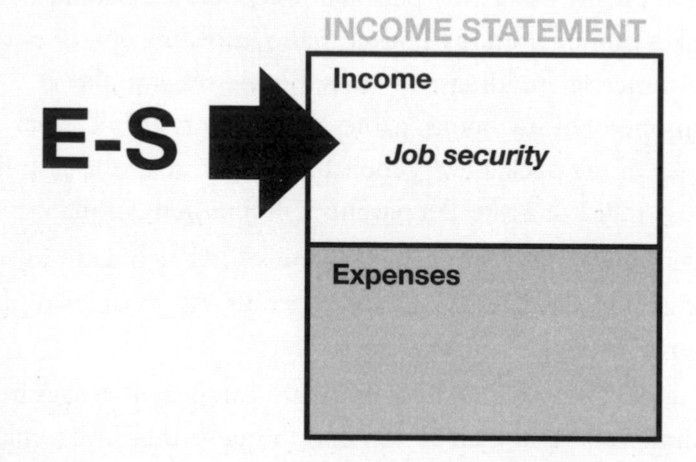

Bs and Is focus on property/production and asset acquisition:

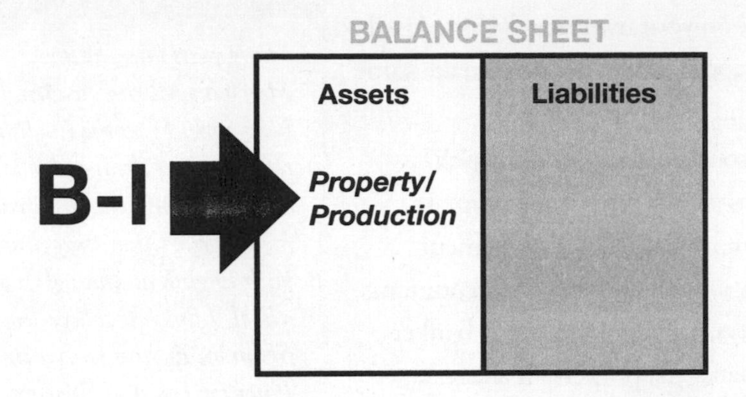

As a 12-year-old, I did not know how I was going to acquire assets such as businesses and property, but my neural pathways were forming and they were focused on the asset column. When I went with rich dad to collect rent or evict tenants, my neural pathways grew firm and I became more convinced of my path in life. Although I did not realize it at the time, I was making plans to become a capitalist.

My Second Window of Learning

The years between 12 and 24 were an interesting time for me. I was in academic trouble in high school and flunked out of English twice at ages 15 and 17. I'm thankful that my dad was the superintendent of education. If not for him, I might have dropped out of high school at age 15.

When I got into academic trouble the first time, my dad did not panic or scold me. He just said, "Often in life you will run into people you do not like and who do not like you. Learn from the experience, grow from it, and move on." My dad was talking about my English teacher, a horrible teacher who flunked nearly two thirds of his class.

My dad fired the teacher, explaining to the assembly of high school teachers, "A teacher's job is to teach, not fail, students. If a student fails, the teacher has failed."

When I failed English again at the age of 17, my dad smiled and said, "You're on your own now." This caused me to approach my teacher, retake some tests, and graduate with a D.

Also at the age of 15, my rich dad was allowing his son and me to sit in on his Saturday management meetings. Rich dad had his accountants, attorneys, architects, builders, bankers, sales managers, property managers, and human resource manager at these meetings to discuss the challenges facing his business.

Inspiring Genius

Many years later, at the Merchant Marine Academy in New York, I met the English teacher of my dreams. He was a great teacher who inspired me to write. After struggling with English all through high school, I finished college-level freshman English with a B. If not for Dr. A. A. Norton, I might not be known as a best-selling author today.

The Best Team Wins

Many of rich dad's advisors—like his attorneys, accountants, and bankers—were "A" students, individuals who were very smart academically. Others were great managers, "B" students, bureaucrats whose skill was the ability to deal with people, one of the toughest aspects of a business. Some of his managers had college degrees. Others came up through the ranks. Rich dad's team included his attorneys, accountants, bankers, managers, and other leaders. He often said, "Business is a team sport. The person with the best team wins."

Rich dad often said, "You have to be smart in the E and S quadrants. In the B and I quadrants, I don't have to be the smartest person. All I have to do is surround myself with "A" students."

My Own Advisors

Today, I have my own team of advisors. They are experts in very specific areas of business and investing. They have written books that share their expertise and experience and those books have become the Rich Dad Advisor series.

Thinking Is Hard Work

Henry Ford, another man who did not finish school, had a great team of advisors. There is a story about Henry Ford that goes something like this:

> A group of academics met in his office, in an attempt to prove him "stupid." Once the meeting got started, the academics began asking him questions. With each question, Henry Ford would simply pick up one of the many telephones on his desk and say, "Ask him," or "Ask her."
>
> Frustrated, the lead academic blurted out, "That is what we are talking about. You don't know anything. Every time we ask you a question, you just tell us to ask someone else."
>
> That was the moment Ford was waiting for. He paused for a moment, then said, "I hire the smart people your schools produce. They give me answers, like you train them to do. My job is to think."
>
> He then spoke words he is famous for today:
>
> *"Thinking is the hardest work there is...which is probably the reason why so few people engage in it."*
>
> The meeting was over.

The Power of Languages

I was not good at learning languages. Not only did I flunk English twice, but I also failed French, Spanish, and Japanese. Yet in my rich dad's meetings, I noticed that different professions spoke different languages. For example, attorneys spoke the language of law, accountants spoke the language of accounting, bankers spoke the language of banking, and gardeners spoke the language of landscaping. I realized that if I wanted to be a capitalist, I had to learn the different professional languages within the English language. I knew I could make more money than most "A" students if I studied the languages of money.

While still in high school, during my second window of learning, I made a mental note to pay close attention to the words different professionals used. In other words, I knew I would have an unfair advantage if I learned to speak and understand different words and languages of the different professions, even if we all spoke English.

During my second window of learning, between 12 and 24, I routinely observed rich dad—a man without much education who left school at the age of 13—leading very smart, talented, and experienced people.

When I asked him how a person without much formal education could lead such a diverse group of people, he replied, "Respect. We are all smart at something. We all have special skills and talents the others do not. They know I need them, and they need me. So mutual respect goes a long way." Respect is more important than money. If a person feels their genius is respected, they work ten times harder. If they do not feel respected, then they want more money and want to work less."

An important lesson I learned during my second window of learning was the importance of diversity. Having two dads allowed me to see that my poor dad operated in a mono-professional culture. Almost everyone around him was a teacher with at least one college degree. Those with PhDs tended to look down on those with Masters or Bachelors degrees.

Later in my life, this lesson would become more relevant as I recognized the truth in the saying, "Birds of a feather flock together." Today I notice that police officers hang out with police officers, attorneys hang out with attorneys, and real estate agents hang out with other real estate agents.

At the age of 18, as I entered the U.S. Merchant Marine Academy in New York, I was aware that if I wanted to be a "C" student—a student of capitalism—I had to learn to be a leader and a generalist, not a specialist such as a doctor, lawyer, technician, or teacher. I knew I had to learn to work with people from all walks of life, people with diverse educational, ethnic, and economic backgrounds.

Today, one of my personal role models for business leadership is Donald Trump. Although he is rich and successful, he treats most people, rich or poor, with respect. My experience in working with Donald is that his communication, even when it's tough, is always respectful.

One reason why both Donald and I acknowledge and support the network marketing industry is because success in this industry requires tremendous personal development and personal leadership skills. In other words, if you want to learn, there are people and organizations in that arena what are willing to guide you.

My key point is this: Too many students continue in school and become educated—and more specialized. Capitalists, "C" students, must be generalists, not specialists. Leadership skills and people skills are essential if you want to be a capitalist. If you are a genius who is an introvert, someone who enjoys texting over talking, your chances of becoming a capitalist are probably slim.

My Third Window of Learning

Returning from Vietnam in 1973 at the age of 25, I knew I had a few life decisions to make. I knew one thing for sure: I was definitely going to become a capitalist once my flying career was over.

Seeing my poor dad unemployed in the prime of his life at the age of 53—without any property or production options—my neural pathways to capitalism became highways. I knew I could go back to my old job with Standard Oil of California sailing as a tanker officer, or I could fly for the airlines as many of my fellow Marine pilots were doing. But that would be specialization—a narrow focus, where tanker officers spent time with tanker officers and pilots hung out with pilots.

The unfair advantage I had was my rich dad and his lessons on life's choices.

Different Classrooms

Pointing to the CASHFLOW Quadrant pictured on the next page, rich dad would often say, "Each quadrant is a different classroom. Each classroom teaches different subjects, develops different skills, and requires different teachers."

As I began my third window of learning as a young adult, I knew it was time for me to decide which quadrant, which classroom, was next for me. If I had chosen to return to sailing or flying, I would have chosen the E quadrant. At the age of 25, I was ready for my next educational experience into the B and I quadrants. I was going to become a student again. I did not know how long it would take me to graduate from the B and I quadrants, but at least I had my rich dad's education—beginning with the game of *Monopoly* at the age of nine—preparing me for the process.

In 1973, at age 25, I knew it was time to make a life decision, my first real decision as an adult. My poor dad suggested I go back to Standard Oil as a ship's officer or get a job flying for the airlines, as an employee in the E quadrant. When I told my dad my sailing and flying days were over, he suggested I go back to school, get my MBA, and possibly a PhD, as he had done.

I listened to my dad and enrolled in the MBA program at the University of Hawaii. It did not take long for the old memories of how much I hated school to come back to me. After learning to fly from real combat pilots, it was tough to learn from university professors who had little, if any, real-life business experience.

In my youth, during my first and second windows of learning, I had sat in on many of my rich dad's staff and management meetings. Now, back in college, I realized that I had more real-world experience than my college professors, most of whom had never started or run a business.

When I asked my college professors questions, I often received textbook theory rather than real-life answers and lessons. By my third month in the MBA program, I was once again flunking out. I really wanted to learn, but that environment—the MBA classroom—wasn't the right one for me.

A Business Is Not a Democracy

It was during one exceedingly boring class that I remembered a very intense meeting my rich dad once had with his advisory team. As tempers flared and his team disagreed, my rich dad finally laid down the law and said, "A business is not a democracy. I pay your salaries. Either you do what I ask, or look for a new job."

I believe I was about 16 years old at the time, and the exchange disturbed me. I had never seen grown men and women argue so intensely or emotionally. I also remember many of his staff backing down once rich dad threatened to fire them if they failed to do their jobs. He said, "All I ask of you is to do your jobs. I do not want your excuses. If you cannot do your job, look for a new job."

Once the meeting was over, rich dad took his son and me aside to make sure we were okay. It was then that I heard him say for the first time, "This is why "A" students work for "C" students. The "A" students may have been smart in school, but they do not have the guts to start, own, and run their own business. They went to school to become specialists, only knowing the law or accounting or sales and marketing. They know how to work for a paycheck, but they do not know how to build a business and make money. They have brains, but lack guts. They are terrified of risk. If you don't pay them, they don't work. If they do extra work, they want overtime or time off. They want me to do things their way, but they are not willing to pay for their mistakes if they fail." He added,"I have to pay for my mistakes as well as theirs. If the company fails, I am left with the mess, the debt, and the financial losses. They simply look for a new job. That is the primary difference between "A" students and "C" students."

He then told me, "People like your dad are "A" students, people who do well in school but never leave school. So they become "B" students, bureaucrats. They are people with responsibility who are terrified of risk. Most bureaucrats work for the government or other bureaucratic organizations, hiding in big corporations or organizations where office politics, laziness, and incompetence are tolerated. Most "A" and "B" students cannot survive in the B and I quadrants where managing risk and living or dying by the results of your decisions are everything."

Rich dad also criticized my poor dad for being the head of the teachers union. Although he did not say much to me on that subject, he did not hide his feelings toward union members. One day, a group of his employees got together to unionize his hotel and restaurant operations. He backed them down saying, "I'll shut down the business and all of you will lose your jobs if you unionize. I can start a new business and I don't need the money, but you need your jobs. I've been fair to you and your families. All I ask is for you to be fair to me and my family." When the vote was taken, the union lost.

As I sat in my MBA program classes, as an adult and a combat veteran entering my third window of learning and bored to tears, I better understood my rich dad's lessons. I realized my rich dad focused his life on his asset column by acquiring property and production. He was a true capitalist.

My poor dad and rich dad's employees, many of whom were "A" and "B" students, focused on job security and a steady paycheck. They had college degrees and jobs, but owned nothing. They had no property or production. It's not surprising that they needed security, benefits, and a pension plan.

Sitting in the MBA program, listening to my instructors drone on from textbooks and theory rather than real-life business experience, I realized I was learning from teachers I did not respect. That's not to say they weren't good people. Most teachers are like my poor dad—very good people dedicated to their profession. The problem with my MBA instructors was that they were "A" students who lived in the E and S quadrants. I wanted to learn from teachers who lived in the B and I quadrants.

I dropped out of the MBA program after three months, the only time I ever dropped out of school. Not surprisingly, poor dad was disappointed; my rich dad wasn't.

I didn't miss a beat in continuing my real-world education. I had signed up for a three-day real estate investment course on my rich dad's suggestion. I recall challenging his suggestion and saying, "But I'm not interested in real estate." I also reminded him that I didn't have much money. Rich dad just smiled and said, "That's why you need to take a course in real estate investing. Real estate is not about property. Real estate is about debt and using OPM, Other People's Money, to get rich."

It finally dawned on me that my rich dad was, once again, steering me to the education I was seeking, education for life in the B and I quadrants. The simple diagrams below illustrate this point.

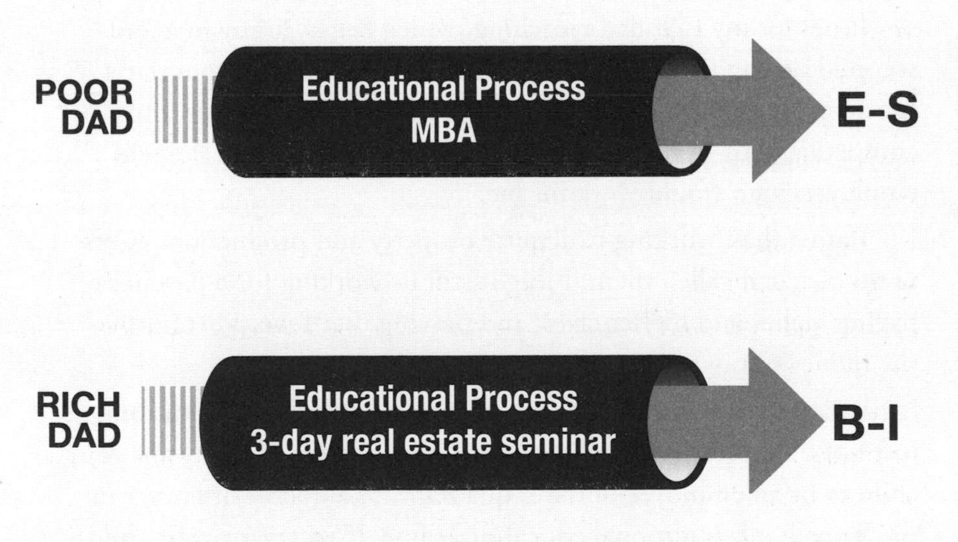

Education is a process. If you want to become a doctor, you go to medical school. If you want to become a lawyer, you go to law school. If you want to be come a capitalist in the B and I quadrants, you need to choose your teachers, your classrooms, and your educational process carefully.

In 1974, while still flying for the Marine Corps, I began applying to IBM and Xerox because they had the best sales and management training programs. Just before completing my contract with the Marine Corps, I was accepted into the Xerox Corporation's training program and was flown to their training headquarters in Leesburg, Virginia. Xerox was another step in connecting the dots, the educational process, to develop my neural pathways for the B and I quadrants.

At Xerox, I struggled to overcome my shyness, knocking on doors and learning to handle objections and rejection in order to sell Xerox copiers. Finally, after two years, selling started to come more naturally, an integral part of who I was becoming…a capitalist in the B and I quadrants.

Starting Early Is a Headstart

If not for my rich dad's teaching, which began in my first and second learning windows, I might have followed in my poor dad's footsteps—earning an MBA, climbing the corporate ladder, and competing with "A" and "B" students, rather than hiring them as employees who would work for me.

Rather than working to acquire property and production, assets as my rich dad called them, I might still be working for a paycheck, paying higher and higher taxes, and praying that I wouldn't outlive the money in my retirement account.

I want to repeat an important point: I am very pro-education—just not the education taught in traditional schools. If you want your child to be an employee in the E quadrant, or a doctor or lawyer in the S quadrant, traditional education is fine. If you want your child to have every opportunity for success open to them, then they must have every opportunity for education. And in many cases that means a departure from the traditional, into less conventional, real-world learning environments and classrooms.

The important lesson I've learned is: Each quadrant is a different classroom…requiring different teachers.

Question: What if I cannot get a job with a company like Xerox or IBM? How do I get my own sales training and experience?

Answer: Sales training and experience is vital for anyone wanting to be an entrepreneur, especially in the B and I quadrants. There are many ways to get sales training.

As I mentioned earlier in this chapter, Donald Trump and I both suggest that individuals look at network marketing companies for the training these companies offer. Many network marketing companies provide excellent personal development, fear management, rejection management, and sales training—especially for people who are afraid of selling or are new to sales.

Rich Dad Lesson

Remember, in 1971, once President Nixon took the U.S. dollar off the gold standard, the dollar became debt. This means those who learn to use debt—debt to acquire assets—will have an unfair advantage over those who never use debt, or use debt to acquire liabilities such as a house, car, or clothing.

The best thing about network marketing companies is that they will not fire you if you do not perform, as Xerox would have fired me if I had failed to sell its products and services. It did not matter how long I worked for Xerox. Every salesperson knew that they were only one or two months away from being fired, if they failed to sell.

Question: What if I don't have enough money?

Answer: That is why I recommend taking real estate investment courses. If you truly understand the skill sets in the B and I quadrants, you'll see that you're not supposed to use your own money. Your job is to learn to raise capital using OPM, Other People's Money (in this case: your bank's), not using your money.

Simply said, capitalists know how to use debt to make them rich. It is known as OPM, Other People's Money.

Becoming a capitalist is hard work and relatively few make it. That is why investing in your education—yours and your child's—

is crucial, especially today. People who are not actively studying and learning, regardless of which quadrant they live and work in, are falling behind rapidly.

When you read the stories of entrepreneurs—great capitalists such as Steve Jobs, Bill Gates, and Mark Zuckerberg—they began their path to capitalism and educational process in the first and second windows of their lives. So did The Beatles and many professional athletes.

This is not to say your child must know their professional calling in their first and second windows of learning. What I am saying is, regardless of their profession of choice, all children will be dealing with money. Why not begin their financial education early so they can better choose which quadrant is the best quadrant, the best classroom, for them?

My rich dad prepared his son and me for the real world of money. Most schools do not. This is why a parent's love, patience, and guidance are essential through all three learning windows, and why lessons about money need to be a part of what a child learns, from an early age, at home.

Old Dogs, Old Tricks

Today, as an older dog, I notice how slowly I learn and adapt to new technology. I often need to ask for help when using my computer or cell phone. My old neural pathways get in the way of creating new ones.

I have a friend, a doctor in his early seventies, who lost a lot of money in the 2007 market crash. He never managed his own money because he turned his life savings over to a personal money manager. The money manager made some bad decisions, and now my doctor friend will not be able to retire for years, if ever.

One concept he does not seem to grasp is the concept of cash flow. When I explain to him that cash flows into my bank account every month, he draws a blank. Even when I explain the concept of cash flow using the game of *Monopoly*—for example, one green house that pays $10 every month—his mind has difficulty with the concept of money always coming in, without the continual investment of his time.

All he knows is the concept of capital gains, the profit margin between what you pay for something—a share of stock, for example—and what you sell it for. That is how he was taught to invest when he was in college. He was doing well until the stock market fell from approximately 14,000 to 7,000. Now he is afraid to get back into the stock market, not sure if prices will go up and afraid that they'll go down. The same thing happened to his house. It fell in value from approximately $4 million in 2007 to $1.5 million today.

When I explain to him that I have thousands of rental apartment tenants sending me checks every month, a blank look crosses his face. He does not get it. He has neural pathways that only understand capital gains, but no neural pathways to comprehend cash flow, even though he played *Monopoly*® as a kid. He understands that one green house will pay him $10 a month, but in his mind *Monopoly* is just a game for kids.

> ***Windows of Wisdom***
>
> *As windows close, new windows open. After age 48, new windows to learning open. These windows are often called "Wisdom Windows." This means our new learning is filtered through what we've learned earlier in life.*
>
> *How well we use these "windows of wisdom" depends upon the quality of our wisdom. This means, if we have had a lot of experiences, good or bad in our earlier years—and learned from them—then our new lessons combined with wisdom can be very powerful. I'm sure you've heard people say things like, "I'm glad I went through that. It was a bad experience at the time, but it made me a better person today."*

Good News

Remember: Windows of learning open, and they close. And with age, in most cases, comes wisdom.

How well we use these "windows of wisdom" depends upon the quality of our wisdom. This means, if we have had a lot of experiences, good or bad in our earlier years—and have learned from them—then our new lessons combined with wisdom can be very powerful. I'm sure you've heard people say things like, "I'm glad I went through that. It was a bad experience at the time, but it made me a better person today."

Bad Experiences

The bad news is this: If all we have from your youth are bad experiences, and if we've failed to learn from them, we hold them as regret, anger, or resentment and any new learning will be tainted by the emotions surrounding those past experiences.

We all know people who live lives of regret. They often say, "I wish I had..." or, "I never got a break" or, "If only I had known" or, "It's too late for me." Knowledge of this can play a powerful role in taking action to move beyond regret and anger in our lives. Why harbor negativity that can keep you from moving forward and living the life you deserve?

I'm sure that holding on to the limiting and power-zapping energy of bad experiences is not the example parents want to set for their kids, and a parent's desire to give their child every advantage in life can be a powerful motivator. Parents lead and teach by example and the choices they make in life send messages to their children. When kids see their parents learning new things, being open to other points of view, and admitting (and learning from) their mistakes the message to their children is clear: Learning is a life long process.

These are the kinds of role models kids need…and if this role model is a parent who embodies the real-life lesson of learning from life's challenges and bad experiences then the child truly does have, in his or her parents, that special teacher who has 'walked the talk' related to the power of change and choices.

Action Step for Parents

Introduce new ideas, words, concepts, and experiences to your child on a regular basis and, ideally, in the course of everyday life.

This can take place at home, at the bank, at the movies, in the shopping mall, on vacation—even at church. Use the Windows of Learning as a guide for age-appropriate topics and exercises for experiential learning.

Parents can create a game or exercise around a new concept or idea and offer positive reinforcement throughout the process. Look for ways to integrate new vocabulary words and ideas into your everyday conversations so that the new concepts and words become second nature to your child.

Window of Learning #1: Birth to age 12—Quantum Learning

Investing time for games, fun, discussion, and family bonding will pay off when the child enters the second window of learning. This first window is when the brain is whole and neural pathways are being connected. After age 12, learning is a bit more difficult. In order to learn something new, a new neural pathway needs to be built from scratch.

It really is harder to "teach an old dog new tricks"—which is why this window is an important one and a time to work with your child to learn new words and definitions and begin to explain basic concepts like *debt*, *assets*, *liabilities*, *profit*, *inventing*, and *starting your own business*. The Study Guide, *Awaken Your Child's Financial Genius*, offers games, crossword puzzles and word-search games to reinforce these new words.

Window of Learning #2: Ages 12-24—Rebellious Learning

This is a stage at which to encourage exploration. So encourage your child to find answers to the questions that arise. Provide the tools to investigate the consequence of actions and be open to discussing the process with them.

This is a great time to introduce the concept of consequences. In this stage of rebellious learning, telling a child not to do something is likely to trigger the opposite response. Rather than say "Don't…" do something, ask: "What do you think the consequences might be if you did that?"

Encourage your child to make their own decisions and if they falter or fail don't rush in to rescue them. We learn from experiencing the real-life consequences of our actions and decisions and working though them. Look for ways to make the word "consequences" a part of your daily vocabulary.

One of the best ways to make a statement about the value of education and life-long learning is to learn and grow along side your child as they mature into adulthood.

Window of Learning #3: Ages 24-36—Professional Learning

As your adult child finds their path in life, it's likely that both your role as parent and your relationship has evolved. If you have established a good relationship with your child and time invested in family financial education nights chances are that will be paying dividends. You may even see your son or your daughter mirroring activities and discussion you had with them when they were in the first and second windows of learning.

A strong foundation of financial education in the home will prepare kids for the choices that will present themselves as they grow up and, ideally, your daughter or son began seeing how they could make money work for them as they moved through the second window of learning.

This is a time when parents see their adult child exploring and finding their passion in life and it's an opportunity for parents to support decisions and choices that will allow their son or daughter to create the life and lifestyle that celebrates their unique gifts and how they will share them with the world.

Many young adults leave school, even with a college degree, and still not know what they want to do when they grow up. Today a child has more choices, careers, and professions available to them. If they have a secure attitude towards learning, they may value learning over money.

Past Success
Does Not
Guarantee
Future Success.

Part One: Chapter Five

LESSON #5: WHY VALEDICTORIANS FAIL

Good grades and academic success can be a double-edged sword. In the short term, being lauded as an "A" student on the fast track to corporate success may open a few doors and help what colleges and universities anoint as the "best and brightest" graduates land jobs. And while academic success may prepare some students for life as an E, there's more to a rich and wonderful life than the job you leave school well-qualified to do. The real world is a whole new game—an exciting, fast-paced game where different rules apply.

Most people would agree that the majority of world-class entrepreneurs—Jobs, Branson, Gates, and Zuckerberg among them—*don't* fit this description:

> *"They obey the rules, work hard, and like learning, but they, are not the mold-breakers. They work best within the system and aren't likely to change it."*

The world of the future belongs to those who can embrace change, see the future and anticipate its needs, and respond to new opportunities and challenges with creativity and agility and passion.

Making the Case

Why Valedictorians Fail...Especially as Capitalists

In 1981, Karen Arnold, a professor at Boston University, began a study of valedictorians and salutatorians from graduating classes of Illinois high schools. Professor Arnold states:

> *While these students had the attributes to ensure school success, these characteristics did not necessarily translate into real-world success.*
>
> *I think we've discovered the "dutiful" people who know how to achieve in the system.*
>
> *To know that a person is a valedictorian is only to know that he or she is exceedingly good at achievement as measured by grades. It tells you nothing about how they react to the vicissitudes of life.*

What Happens to Valedictorians?

In her book, *Lives of Promise: What Becomes of High School Valedictorians*, Professor Arnold states that high school valedictorians go on to do well in college, averaging an overall 3.6 grade point average. Most went on to work in conventional careers such as accounting, medicine, law, engineering, and education.

Arnold says, "While valedictorians may not change the world, they run it and run it well...but just because they could get As doesn't mean they can translate academic achievement into career achievement." She also stated, "they've never been devoted to a single area in which they can put all their passions...The opportunities to become famous or change the world as an accountant, for example, are few and far between...They obey rules, work hard, and like learning, but they're not the mold-breakers. They work best within the system and aren't likely to change it."

Test Scores Equal Happiness

In another study, 95 Harvard students from the class of 1940 were followed into their middle age. The study found that the men with the highest test scores in college were not particularly successful in terms of salary, productivity, or status in their chosen fields when compared to their lower-scoring peers. The Harvard study also found that high test scores did not translate into greater happiness, better friendships, or superior family and romantic relationships.

The *Harvard Business Review* published an article about academic success stating:

"As it develops, academic-type success was not a good predictor of on-job productivity nor was IQ discovered to be a factor."

The Harvard article also states:

"Many people who get good grades have come to be quite smug about their intelligence even in the face of repeated failure outside the classroom."

Millionaire Mind

In his book, *The Millionaire Mind*, Thomas J. Stanley gives in-depth statistical research to identify which variables caused people to become successful in business and become super wealthy. Contrary to popular belief, there was no correlation between grades in school, class position, SAT scores, and success.

In fact, 33% of those on *Forbes 400* lists of wealthiest people did not start college or dropped out. And the dropouts' average net worth was much greater than that of their college-graduate peers. The dropouts had an average net worth of $4.8 billion. The college graduates' net worth averaged $1.5 billion. When the college dropouts' net worth was compared to their peers who graduated from Ivy League schools such as Harvard, Yale, and Princeton, the dropouts' net worth was 200 percent higher.

Lessons from the Cone of Learning

The Cone of Learning is again pictured, below. The cone explains why valedictorians do well in the E and S quadrants, but tend to fail in the B and I quadrants of capitalists.

Cone of Learning

After 2 weeks we tend to remember		Nature of Involvement
90% of what we say and do	Doing the Real Thing	Active
	Simulating the Real Experience	
	Doing a Dramatic Presentation	
70% of what we say	Giving a Talk	
	Participating in a Discussion	
50% of what we hear and see	Seeing it Done on Location	Passive
	Watching a Demonstration	
	Looking at an Exhibit Watching a Demonstration	
	Watching a Movie	
30% of what we see	Looking at Pictures	
20% of what we hear	**Hearing Words (Lecture)**	
10% of what we read	**Reading**	

Source: Cone of Learning adapted from Dale, (1969)

Reprinted with Permission. The original work has been modified.

Most valedictorians do well at the bottom of the Cone of Learning. Most valedictorians are excellent readers and learn well by listening to lecture.

Studies have found that only about 25 percent of students learn primarily via reading and lecture. Most students do not learn best that way. The educational system emphasizes reading and lecture as the primary ways to learn, even though long-term learning and retention through those methods is often minimal.

One reason why most valedictorians do not succeed at higher levels of the Cone of Learning is because "A" students are conditioned to think that making mistakes is bad and shows they are stupid. So they avoid the risk of making mistakes.

Hence, many do not succeed at the top of the Cone of Learning—"Doing the real thing." Again, Professor Arnold stated, "They obey the rules, work hard, and like learning, but they're not the mold-breakers. They work best within the system and aren't likely to change it."

My Story

My Dad Was a Valedictorian

My father came from a family of six children. Three of the six were valedictorians and my dad was one of them. All three valedictorians became PhDs. Two of the non-valedictorians received Master's degrees. The remaining sibling earned only a Bachelor's degree.

My dad was probably an academic genius. He read and just studied voraciously and graduated with his Bachelor's degree in two years from the University of Hawaii. Although he worked full time and raised a family, he also found time to attend advanced courses at Stanford University, the University of Chicago, and Northwestern. He ultimately earned his PhD from the University of Hawaii. At the same time, he was recognized as one of the two top educators in the history of Hawaii.

He lost his job at the age of 53 and was not prepared to do anything else. He was a teacher at heart, a former government employee, who had few marketable skills outside of teaching.

Cashing in his retirement fund and savings, he purchased a brand-name national ice cream franchise. His business venture soon went bust. I returned from Vietnam in 1973 to find my dad, a very good man, sitting at home looking through the newspaper's want ads for a job.

According to the Cone of Learning, my father attempted to "do the real thing" at the top of the cone and lost everything. Being a valedictorian did not help him in the real dog-eat-dog world of business. He went from the E quadrant straight to the B and I quadrants—and lost.

My dad did well in school as an "A" student. He did well as a bureaucrat in the government. Unfortunately, when it came to money, business, and investing, he missed learning in *all three* learning windows. He could not survive in the cut throat world of the B and I quadrants.

Success Does Not Guarantee Success

My message in this chapter is a simple one: Success in one quadrant does not ensure success in another. In my father's case, being a valedictorian helped him in the E quadrant as a government bureaucrat, but his good grades were of no help in the B and I quadrants.

This supports the findings of the Boston University and the Harvard University studies. That is why most valedictorians remain in the E and S quadrants, while college dropouts such as Jobs, Gates, and Zuckerberg and hundreds of others find and develop their genius in the B and I quadrants.

My rich dad often said, "Most "A" students are content to know that 2 + 2 = 4. But most "A" students do not know how to turn 2 + 2 into four *dollars* or millions more. Capitalists want to know how to make 2 + 2 = $4,000,000. To a capitalist, that kind of math is worth studying."

A Final Word

Most valedictorians succeed if they play it safe inside the E or S quadrants. But the moment they enter the highly competitive and fast-paced world of capitalism, the B and I quadrants, the college they went to and their grade point average may not do them much good. At the risk of repeating myself on this important point:

Success in one quadrant does not guarantee success in others.

The earlier a parent teaches their child about the different quadrants, the earlier their child can begin preparing for life.

Action Step for Parents

Discuss your child's dreams and the different ways success is defined outside of the school system.

I believe that a child's genius is found in their dreams. Creating an environment in which your child is free to discuss his or her dreams—even the most grandiose visions for the future—is a meaningful and important exercise, You may be surprised by the vivid and magical nature of what your child will share. And this is a time to encourage and support the thought that their future is theirs to create.

Use the Cone of Learning as a guide for discussion. Explain to your child why reading is not always the best way to learn. Explain the importance of simulations or practice and how it prepares us for real-world experiences.

You may want to take your child to a watch a sports team at practice. Explain to them that practice is where teams simulate doing the real thing—and where the mistakes they make are nothing more than opportunities to learn how to deal with challenges and setbacks that may arise in the future.

Transform Your Money.

Transform Your Life.

Part One | Chapter Six

LESSON #6: WHY RICH PEOPLE GO BROKE

The first step in making changes in our lives starts with a change, a shift in context, change in the way we look at things and the filters we use to process information and experiences. We often see the imagery of a caterpillar changing into a butterfly used to illustrate change. It's a good visual because change is a process, and what we become in the process is as important and powerful as how we emerge.

By learning to transform ordinary income into passive and portfolio income you will have the key to unlocking your future—and your child's future. In Chapter Seven, I will talk more about the different types of income and why understanding the differences is important. The world is an exciting and ever-changing place. This means new challenges, and opportunities, all the time. Preparing a child for the world of tomorrow is one of the most important roles a parent plays in a child's life. And it can be a daunting one. Taking on that challenge starts with understanding that our thoughts and actions—what we put into our brains and how we act on that information—needs to change...as our world changes.

Making the Case

Over 2,000 years ago, Greece was the most powerful empire on earth. Many words in our vocabularies today can be traced to the Greeks, including the words *democracy*, *theater*, *Olympics*, *marathon*, even the letters (A) alpha and (B) beta, which gave us the word *alphabet*. The Greeks also gave us the concept of "trial by jury" and, in theater, the tragedy. Today the spectacular country of Greece is on life support, the basket case of Europe, a modern day Greek tragedy.

A Greek Tragedy

On the world stage, Japan, England, France, and the United States also play roles in this Greek drama. If other powerful nations crash, it will be a global tragedy.

All over the world, millions of retirees—the global baby-boom generation, many of whom were once rich—now live in fear of outliving their retirement savings. Men and women of my generation feel as if they too have bit parts in this, their personal Greek tragedies. The children, grandchildren, and great grandchildren of the baby-boom generation are in the audience…wondering how the tragedy will end.

The Rise of Despots

If this global financial crisis is not solved, the final act will not be pretty. During times of financial crisis, a new type of leader often emerges, leaders known as *despots*. A few of these leaders are infamous. They are Franklin Delano Roosevelt, Adolf Hitler, Mao Tse-tung, Joseph Stalin, Robespierre, and Napoleon. It seems ironic that the word despot is a French word derived from the Greek word *despotes*.

I know it may seem like blasphemy to list FDR in this rouge's gallery. I am often severely criticized for doing this. He is one of our most beloved presidents. Before slamming this book shut, let me offer you my reasoning.

Reason #1

Both Hitler and FDR came to office in the same year: 1933

Reason #2

Both men were elected to solve the same problem: a depression

Reason #3

Both men failed to solve the problem. Hitler's solution was to go to war. FDR's solution was go to war, as well as initiate Social Welfare. The Social Security Act of 1935 is America's most beloved government program.

The problem is, FDR's solutions didn't work. Roosevelt simply "kicked the can down the road" pushing the problem to future leaders. Today Social Security and Medicare are huge elephants sitting in the room. The same is true in Greece, England, Japan, and other countries of the world. The problem is, the can cannot be kicked much farther. Does this mean the rise of a new despot?

My generation, the baby boomers, claim they deserve their Social Security and Medicare benefits. And they do. They contributed to the social programs. The problem is, all government social programs are Ponzi schemes. A Ponzi scheme is a swindle where the older investors are paid back from new investor money.

Most of us have heard of Bernie Madoff, the heavy weight champion in the arena of private Ponzi schemes. He went to jail. What he did is illegal, and, in my opinion, what the U.S. government is doing is immoral. Social welfare is destroying the soul of America. Social programs are cancers growing within the spirit of the people they were created to serve. Social programs do not make people stronger. They keep people weak, depending on the government to solve their problems.

I realize there are people who may deserve government programs. Some people are truly in need. The problem is, millions of able-bodied Americans are also on government welfare. This includes the leaders of our country—from the President on down. The President and Congress receive government "welfare" checks that would make even Bernie Madoff blush. The government bread line includes our military retirees, government employees, public servants such as the police and fire fighters, and teachers.

I do not criticize these people or their professions. I have tremendous respect for the work our military personnel, police, firefighters, teachers, and other government service workers perform. Their work is important.

What I am fearful of is the growing "entitlement mentality," the attitude that "the government should take care of me," which has become so pervasive in our culture. Today, when a worker loses his or her job, the first thing they do is apply for unemployment benefits. How can it be called a "benefit?"

How does the growing sense of entitlement related to this book and to parents as they work to prepare their children for the future? It's really pretty simple, when you think about it. I am critical of our school system and much of traditional education for failing to teach people to fish. Instead of teaching kids to fish—teaching kids the skills and attitudes that will make them strong and self-reliant and resourceful–our schools breed a culture of entitlement. It is this entitlement mentality that is eroding the foundations this country was built upon. The "entitlement mentality" is bringing down the American empire and the world.

The Fiscal Cliff

The dust had barely settled following the 2012 U.S. Presidential election when the Fiscal Cliff Battle engulfed Washington. The battle was between Democrats who wanted to "tax the rich" and Republicans who wanted to cut back on Social Security and Medicare—government welfare. The problems that underlie this crisis have not been solved and the crisis is morphing.

The reason that it has not been solved is because our *financial problems* are *social problems*. We have too many people who are not only *expecting* the government to take care of them...they *need* the government to take care of them. Because they can't, or choose not to, fish for themselves.

As you already know, this problem will soon be your *child's* problem, one of many that the next generation will inherit. So what is a parent to do?

The Entitlement Wagon

Insanity

Some people say that Albert Einstein gave us this definition of the word insanity:

Insanity is doing the same thing over and over again and expecting a different result.

It is insanity to say to your child, "Go to school and get a job," when jobs are being shipped overseas or replaced by advances in technology.

It is insanity to say, "Work hard," when the harder you work, to earn more money, the more taxes you pay.

It is insanity to say, "Save money," when money is no longer money…but debt, an IOU from the taxpayers.

It is insanity to say, "Your house is an asset," when it is really a liability.

It is insanity to say, "Invest for the long term in the stock market," when professional investment houses are using multi-million dollar computers to invest for the short-term, often in and out in milli-seconds for HFT, High-Frequency Trading, against amateur investors…in some cases their own clients. You may as well go to Las Vegas.

Albert Einstein is also credited with saying:

"We can't solve problems by using the same kind of thinking we used when we created them."

The following are some new thoughts on how to solve an old problem, the problem of how to prepare your child for the future and the role that money plays in it. Here is a different point of view on education.

We begin to solve the problem by changing our context of the problem.

Content vs. Context

Pictured below is a water glass, partially filled with water.

For purposes of this lesson, the water in the glass represents content. The water glass itself represents context.

Education Is About Content

Traditional education focuses on *content*: reading, writing, and arithmetic.

Traditional education does *not* focus on context: the *student*.

My problems in school began when I did not like the content (the water) my teachers were pouring into my head. Every time I objected, saying, "Why am I studying this?" their answers were uniformly the same, "If you don't get a good education you won't get a good job."

I've grown to understand that my teachers' responses demonstrated a lack of concern for my context. They assumed I wanted to be an employee.

What Is Context?

Context holds the content. Contexts can be visible, invisible, human, or non-human.

A person's context includes their:

- Philosophies
- Beliefs
- Thoughts
- Rules
- Values
- Fears
- Doubts
- Attitudes
- Choices

A poor person's context is seen in their words:

- "I'll never be rich."
- "The rich will not go to heaven."
- "I'd rather be happy."
- "Money is not important to me."
- "The government should take care of people."

The reason many poor people are poor is because they have a poor context. In most cases, more money will not make a poor person rich. In many cases, giving a poor person money keeps them poor longer… often forever.

This is also the reason why so many lottery winners are soon broke. The same often holds true for sports stars.

Notice the shift in priorities, values, and words that communicate a middle class person's context:

- "I must get a good education."
- "I need a high-paying job."
- "I want a nice house in a nice neighborhood."
- "Job security is very important."
- "How much vacation time do I have?"

People with a middle class context, typically don't get rich. Many go deeper in debt to, "keep up with the Joneses." Instead of investing, people with a middle class context just consume more. They buy a bigger house, take nice vacations, drive expensive cars, and spend money on higher education.

Since most people buy on credit, they often find themselves getting deeper in debt—bad debt, consumer debt—rather than getting richer.

When they hear "There is good debt and bad debt," their context closes. All they know is bad debt, debt that makes them poorer. Most cannot grasp the idea of good debt, the kind of debt that can make them richer.

For many of these people, it is best that they simply follow the advice of those who counsel "Cut up your credit cards and get completely out of debt." That is the content (the water) that their context can handle.

When it comes to investing, most middle class people have the context, the belief system, that supports the position that "investing is risky." That is because most invest in traditional education for college degrees, but fail to invest in financial education.

Examples of statements that reflect a rich person's context might include:

1. "I must be rich."
2. "I own my own business and my work is my life."
3. "Freedom is more important than security."
4. "I take on challenges so I can learn more."
5. "I want to find out how far I can go in life."

Most of these people are true capitalists. They know how to us OPT, Other People's Talents, and OPM, Other People's Money.

When a middle class person puts their savings or retirement fund into a bank, the banker lends that money to the capitalist.

This was rich dad's way of saying, "Context is more important than content."

One reason I had a tough time in school was because I had no plans to be an employee. I wanted to be an *employer*, an entrepreneur.

Every time a teacher attempted to motivate me with, "If you don't get good grades, you won't get a good job," I checked out…my mind just shut off. By the time I was 12, I had been working with rich dad for three years. I no longer had the context of an employee.

The statement, "You won't get a good job" worked on my classmates who wanted to be employees. It did not work on me.

If the teacher had said, "I'm going to teach you how to raise capital so you can start your own business," I would have been all ears. I would have been sitting at the front of the class. I would have said, "Pour that content in!"

My Story

Context Before Content

When rich dad talked about "teaching pigs to sing" he saw it as a lose-lose proposition: "It wastes your time. And it annoys the pig."

His message was:

"You cannot teach a poor person to be rich until they change their context. Teaching a person with poor or middle class person's context is a waste of time…and it does annoy them."

I have been teaching entrepreneurship and investing for over 30 years. Teaching the lessons my rich dad taught me. I can attest to the fact that rich dad was right. When *Rich Dad Poor Dad* was first released, it was more than rejected. It was trashed by the "A"-student society of the book-publishing world. That's why, in 1997, I had to self-publish that book. Most journalists are "A" students, academics, who do not share the same context as "C" students, or capitalists. In 2002, when the book *Why We Want You To Be Rich*, was published…it felt like déjà vu. That book, a book that Donald Trump and I wrote together, warned of the looming financial crisis and its potential impact on the middle class. It was not well received by the financial establishment. When I asked myself "Why would the financial community attack our work?" The possible answers weren't difficult to uncover, once I considered all the different contexts in play: media owners, their advertisers, the journalists, and their audiences.

Rich Dad Lesson

"Don't teach pigs to sing.

It wastes your time. And it annoys the pig."

Life Is Context

Our life is made up of contexts. Some contexts are invisible while others are physical and tangible. A few examples of other contexts are:

1. **The Constitution of the United States is a context.**
   The Constitution represents the values on which America was founded and which govern its operation.

2. **A religion is a context.**
   For example, Christians have a different context than Muslims. This means their content is also different. Christians believe Jesus is the Son of God and Muslims believe that Jesus is a prophet.

   In another example, if I said to a devout Christian, "Prophet Mohammed said…" the odds are their context would slam shut. But if I said, "Jesus said…" to a Christian, chances are their context would remain open.

   In other words, when someone says, "Keep an open mind," they are really saying "Keep an open context."

   During the U.S. Presidential race of 2012, opponents of President Obama called him a Muslim, although the President said he is a Christian. Opponents of Mitt Romney would whisper, "He's not a Christian, he's a Mormon." That is how powerful contexts can be.

3. **Economic philosophies are contexts.**
   For example, during that same election, many people called President Obama a socialist. Others called Mitt Romney a capitalist.

   Depending upon your personal economic context, you would accept or reject the candidate based upon their economic philosophies. For example, if you were a socialist, Mitt Romney being labeled a "capitalist" would be a turn off. If you were a capitalist, the idea of voting for a socialist would be unthinkable.

4. **A church building is a physical context.**
So is a gym. We go to church for one purpose and a gym for another. One is for spiritual revival and the other for physical revival.

5. **A school building is a physical context.**
So is an office building. Many schools now encourage parents to take their child to work. Unfortunately, when most kids go to work with their parents, they are confronted with the context of employees rather than the context of the entrepreneurs, the employers that created the business.

6. **A home is another physical context.**
As parents, ask yourself this question: What is the context of our home? Is it a context of a poor family, a middle class family, or a rich family?

Change Your Context…and Change Your Life

When I returned from Vietnam in 1973, my rich dad suggested I take a course in real estate. He said, "If you want to be rich, you have to learn to use debt to become rich."

Since my context already was "I want to be rich," I eventually acted on his suggestion. My context easily accepted the content "Debt will make me rich." So I was signed up for a three-day real estate investment course.

If I had had a poor or middle class context, I would have said, "I'll think about it. Before I take a class on real estate, I think I'll go back to school and get my MBA."

Today, when I say to people, "Real estate is about debt…debt that can make you rich. And the more debt you have, the less taxes you'll pay," it usually doesn't take long before their context slams shut. Fingers go in there ears and, like a child, they repeat the context of their parents instilled in them: Investing is risky. Debt is bad. The rich are greedy. Debt and taxes cannot make you rich.

Again, the lesson is, "Context determines content" or "Don't teach pigs to sing…unless they want to be pigs that can sing."

The three-day real estate course I took was great. Although I had learned a lot with rich dad and I owned the condo that I lived in, the course taught me a lot and made me realize that I still had a lot to learn.

The instructor was a great teacher. It was obvious that he taught because he loved teaching. He was a successful real estate investor who did not need a paycheck. He was for real. And he practiced what he preached. What made his class even better was he was not teaching pigs to sing. The whole class was there to learn.

When the class was over the instructor said, "Now your education begins." He smiled at us and said, "This is your assignment: In the next 90 days, your job is to look at, inspect, analyze, and write an evaluation on 100 or more potential rental properties."

Most of us were excited about the assignment. A few were not. They had allowed their "loser context" get in the way. Some of their excuses were:

1. "I don't have the time."
2. "I have to spend time with my family."
3. "I have a full time job."
4. "I was going on vacation."
5. "I don't have any money."

The instructor just smiled, saying, "I repeat what I said. 'The course is over. Now your education begins.'"

More than a Mindset

Many people think context is only your mindset. But context is more than your thoughts. Context is your core, your body, your mind, and your spirit. While mindset maybe easy to change, a complete change in context runs deeper.

Using money as an example, the reason so many people are poor is that they have a poor person's context related to money. Taking a three-day real estate course, without internalizing and applying what you learn, will not change your context.

When I told my rich dad of the instructor's assignment to look at and evaluate 100 properties in 90 days, he smiled and said, "Good teacher."

Rich dad did not use the word context. Instead he said, "If you do the assignment, you will change both yourself and your view on the world. You will begin to see the world through the eyes of a rich person. The assignment will not guarantee you success, or that you will become rich, but you will begin to do what rich people do."

You may recall the Cone of Learning from a previous chapter. At the top of the cone, and deemed to be the best way to learn something new and retain what you learn, is "doing the real thing." The assignment to look at 100 properties in 90 days was a simulation of the real thing.

Graduation

At the end of three-day real estate course, the instructor split the group into teams. There were six people on my team. We were to do the 90-day exercise together.

The first week after the course, two members of our team quit. They did not show up for our first meeting. We never heard from them again. Their context won.

That left four of us. We continued on our assignment for about four more weeks, then one more team member left, saying, "Real estate is not for me." Again, their context won.

By the start of the third month, 60 days into the process, a fourth person left after telling us, "I want to spend more time with my family."

Two of us finished the 90-day process. We evaluated 104 properties. John, the person who completed the process with me, went on to become a real estate developer and has made millions. I haven't done too badly either. We both paid $385 for that three-day course.

Education vs. Transformation

My choices of education changed my life. Within a few months of starting my MBA program, as a gesture to keep my poor dad happy, I lost interest and dropped out. The problem with that program was that I knew it would not transform my life. I already had two high-paying professions I could fall back on: One as a tanker officer for Standard Oil, the other as a pilot for the airlines. Even if I had completed the MBA program, I would still have to be an employee.

I signed up for the real estate class because I was looking for my next Navy Flight School experience. I wanted to be transformed. I wanted to evolve into a butterfly, not move through life as a caterpillar, a person clinging to a job, a steady paycheck, and benefits.

Contexts and the Quadrant

The four quadrants in the CASHFLOW quadrant are contexts. For a person to quit their job to start their own business, they first had to change their context. To evolve out of the E or S quadrant into the B or I quadrants is, again, a change of context.

Changing context takes time. It does not happen overnight. It is more than a change of mindset. It requires more than positive thinking. It is a process of mental, physical, and spiritual evolution. It requires tremendous faith, courage, self-esteem, and a hunger to learn quickly.

Donald Trump and I love speaking to young people at colleges. And we especially love talking to network marketing organizations. The reason is that the people in network marketing are voracious learners. They have high energy and are excited and anxious to learn. Why are they so energetic? Because they are in the process of transformation, a process that requires much more energy than just education. Most are evolving out of the E and S quadrants into the world of the B and I quadrants. They know they are not learning to look for a job. They

> **Rich Dad Lesson**
>
> *If you want to change your life…change your context.*

know the world they are entering is a world without a steady paycheck. That's why they are great audiences. Donald and I share their context, which is why they love our content.

> **_Rich Dad Lesson_**
>
> *If you want to transform your life...you need to learn to transform your income.*

The way a person transforms themself is by transforming their income. When a person transforms their income they transform their life.

Financial education must include knowledge of the three types of income.

Most people, even "A" students, learn about only one type of income. The rich work for the additional two types of income.

Three Types of Income

In the world of money, there are three types of income:

1. Ordinary
2. Portfolio
3. Passive

These three types of income exist all over the world. And, in most cases, the poor and middle class work for ordinary income. The rich work for portfolio and passive income.

Even the game of *Monopoly* teaches this vital lesson. In *Monopoly*, when you buy a green house—let's say you pay $200, and the green house pays you $10 a turn—the player converted their money. The player converted $200 of income from a paycheck into $10 of passive *recurring* income every month. You do not need to be an "A" student to understand that transformation of income.

Why Some Rich People Go Broke

The reason so many million-dollar lottery winners and well-paid professional athletes wake up one day to find they are broke is because they failed to transform their income.

Many doctors, lawyers, and high-income S-quadrant entrepreneurs are in trouble today, or not as rich as they could be, is because they failed to transform their income.

Financial experts say, "Work hard, save money, and invest in a 401(k)," but a person who follows that advice is not transforming their money.

When people work for money they are working for ordinary income, the most highly-taxed of all the three incomes. When people save money, they are working for ordinary income, in this case the interest on their savings. And when Americans withdraw their money from their 401(k)s and retirement plans, they withdraw their money as ordinary income.

This is true not only in America but also in most Western countries, although the names of the retirement plans or programs may be different.

It is crucial that parents understand the distinctions among the different kinds of income and teach their children how to transform their lives by learning to transform their money.

What are the key differences among the three types of income?

> **Ordinary income** is generally *paycheck* money. It is the most highly-taxed of all three incomes. Most people go to school to learn how to work for ordinary income. After graduation, most go on to become wage earners. If you work for money, you are working for ordinary income. Ironically, interest on savings is also taxed at ordinary-income rates. And when you retire, your 401(k) income will be taxed as ordinary income. In my opinion, there are better ways to save for retirement than a 401(k) plan.
>
> **Portfolio income** is also known as *capital gains*. Most investors invest for portfolio, income or capital gains. A capital gain occurs when you buy low and sell high. For example, if you buy a stock for $10 and sell it for $15, this is a capital-gains event with a profit of $5 and that profit is taxed as portfolio income.
>
> Taxes are one of the many reasons why I rarely invest in stocks. It makes no sense to me to take risks by investing in stocks only

to pay taxes if I win. Capital gains on real estate and stocks are currently taxed at 20 percent. Dividends from stocks are also taxed at 20 percent.

Passive income is also known as *cash flow*. In the game of *Monopoly*, the $10 a player receives for rent on one green house is an example of passive income or cash flow. Passive income is taxed at the lowest rates of all three incomes, sometimes zero.

Investing for tax-free cash flow requires the highest level of financial education and experience. This will be discussed more in later sections of this book.

Transform Your Life

The 90-day assignment following my three-day real estate class was a process of transformation. Just as the Cone of Learning illustrates, it was a process of simulation, before doing the real thing.

Simulation in the world of sports is known as *practice*. In the theater, simulation is known as *rehearsals*.

In school, there is no room for mistakes. A student takes the test, the teacher subtracts the number wrong from the number right, kicks out a grade and the class moves on.

One reason why many "A" students do not go as far as they could in life is because, from within their context, which in this case is their ingrained belief system, making mistakes means you are stupid.

In business, entrepreneurs know that mistakes are learning experiences, and—in many cases—are valuable feedback related to their business model, product, or service.

The reason I recommend that when people play the game *CASHFLOW* they play it at least 10 times is not to win the game but to make as many mistakes as possible and learn from those mistakes. Each game, especially the ones you lose, actually makes you smarter, and more prepared for the real world. As the Cone of Learning illustrates, simulations (games, practice, rehearsals) are what you do before you do the real thing.

Why Students Fail

One reason that being an "A" student does not guarantee success in life is because there is more than the one intelligence recognized by the school system.

In 1983, Howard Gardner, a professor at the Harvard Graduate School of Education, published his book, *Frames of Mind: The Theory of Multiple Intelligences.*

The following are brief descriptions of Gardner's Seven Intelligences.

1. **Verbal-linguistic**
   People gifted in verbal-linguistic intelligence tend to be good at reading, writing, and memorizing words and dates. They learn best by reading, taking notes, and listening to lectures. These people are left-brain dominant.

   School is relatively easy if you are strong in this intelligence. Most "A" students are strong in verbal-linguistic intelligence. Many go on to become journalists, lawyers, authors, and doctors.

2. **Logical-mathematical**
   Those gifted with this intelligence do well in math. They are comfortable with numbers, numerical problems, logic, and abstractions. These people are often left-brain dominant.

   Students with this intelligence also do very well in traditional education environments and often become "A" students. Many go on to be engineers, scientists, doctors, accountants, and financial analysts.

3. **Body-kinesthetic**
   These students are often gifted physically. They tend to learn better by moving around and by doing.

   This intelligence comes out through the gym, football field, dance studio, acting studio, woodshop, or auto shop.

   Professional athletes, dancers, actors, models, surgeons, fire fighters, soldiers, police, pilots, racecar drivers, and mechanics are often gifted with this intelligence.

4. **Spatial**
This intelligence is strong in art, visualization, design, and solving puzzles. These people are generally considered right-brain dominant.

Students gifted with this intelligence tend not to do well in traditional education environments. They do better in schools that focus on art, design, color, and architecture. These students go on to become artists, interior designers, fashion designers, and architects.

5. **Musical**
This intelligence is sensitive to music, rhythm, pitch, melody, and timbre. This person often sings and plays musical instruments well.

This intelligence does not do well in a traditional education setting. A person with this gift is better off in musical environments of learning, such as schools for the performing arts.

6. **Interpersonal**
These people are communicators. They are usually popular and extroverts, displaying sensitivity to other's moods, feelings, temperaments, and motivations.

A person gifted with this intelligence often does well in school, especially in popularity contests such as running for student government. These people tend to go into sales, politics, teaching, and social work.

7. **Intrapersonal**
This intelligence is often called emotional intelligence. This intelligence deals with self-reflection and being introspective. Emotional intelligence refers to having a deep understanding of yourself, knowing your own strengths and weakness, and what makes you unique, with the ability to handle reactions and emotions.

Intrapersonal intelligence is crucial for high-stress environments. In fact, intrapersonal intelligence is critical for success in almost any field or profession.

The Success Intelligence

Intrapersonal intelligence means communicating within yourself. It means being able to talk to yourself and control your emotions. For example, when someone who is angry says to himself, "Count to ten before you speak," that person is exercising intrapersonal intelligence. In other words, he speaks to himself before he opens his mouth and lets his emotions speak.

Intrapersonal intelligence is important for success, especially when times are tough and a person wants to quit or is fearful.

We all know people who are highly emotional. Rather than think logically, highly emotional people tend to let their emotions run their lives, often saying or doing something they may later regret.

Emotional intelligence does not mean being void of emotions. Emotional intelligence means you know it is okay to be angry, just not out of control with anger. You know it's okay to feel hurt, but it is not okay to do something stupid in the name of revenge.

Many of us know a person who is very intelligent, let's say in math, but allows their emotions to damage other parts of their lives.

Addictions are often caused by a lack of emotional intelligence. When frustrated, angry, or fearful, a person may eat, drink, have sex, or do drugs to numb the emotional pain. Some people go shopping when bored, spending money they do not have.

On the positive side, we all know people who have been subjected to extreme abuse and have risen above it. One example is Nelson Mandela. He was wrongfully imprisoned in South Africa, yet emerged a great man rather than an angry man. Eventually he rose to be the leader of the country that had imprisoned him. Greatness is often a reflection of a person with high emotional intelligence.

Again, emotional intelligence is often equated with "success intelligence" because successful people are successful at managing their emotions, especially in stressful situations.

These are all comments describing a person with high emotional intelligence.

- "She is cool under pressure."
- "She achieves her goals."

- "He controls his temper."
- "He can see both sides."
- "He quit smoking five years ago."
- "He'll be truthful, even if he looks bad."
- "She keeps her promises."
- "He's persistent and disciplined."
- "She doesn't make excuses."
- "He admits to his mistakes."

These are also comments often made about successful people.

Acting Like Children

Most of us have seen children…

- Cry when unhappy
- Complain when they do not get their way
- Quit when tired
- Become selfish with their toys
- Blame someone else for their mistakes
- Lie
- Run to mommy and daddy for security
- Become jealous when a friend gets a new toy
- Refuse to pick up their clothes
- Expect to be given everything

Most adults can tolerate these behaviors in children because, after all, they are just children. Most adults will say, "They'll grow out of it."

Unfortunately, many people do not outgrow these childish behaviors. Many adults become skilled at disguising or hiding their emotional immaturity behind their façade, their act.

We have all met adults who smile and are polite when you first meet them. Then, after you get to know them, you meet the rotten kid hiding behind an adult mask. Once we get past a person's act and get to know them a little better, we often see their lack of emotional maturity. You may hear this immaturity with statements such as:

- "You can't trust him."
- "She will tell you anything you want to hear."
- "He smiles, and then stabs you in the back.
- "He loses his temper easily."
- "He'll quit when the going gets tough."
- "She's a complainer."
- "He cheats on his wife."
- "She's greedy."
- "He can't take criticism."
- "She loves to gossip."

In other words, many people grow up physically, but fail to grow up emotionally. Many adults are still little kids on the inside. They go to school, get a job, and the little kid inside shows up at the workplace. They get their paycheck, and once again, the little kid shows up and spends the money. The years go by, and one day they wonder what happened to their lives. They've worked for years, but have nothing to show for it.

It is this lack of emotional development that often hinders adults in the real world. Many adults spend their lives doing what they *want* to do rather than doing what they *need* to do.

Emotional intelligence is essential for long-term success. In practice it may mean:

- Going to the gym rather than staying in bed
- Taking financial education classes even if you don't want to
- Being kind, when others aren't
- Going for a walk, rather than eating
- Not having a drink, even if you want one
- Telling the truth, even if it makes you look bad
- Making a phone call you don't want to make
- Volunteering even when you are busy
- Controlling your temper instead of losing it
- Turning the TV off and spending time with your family, especially if your favorite show is on

Simply said, growing into an adult often means growing up emotionally.

Caterpillar to Butterfly

When my three-day real estate course was completed, my transformation began. Evaluating 100 properties in 90 days was not really that hard. Almost anyone could do it. All I had to do was keep going for 90 days, and apply what I had learned. Like most people, I did not have much money. Marine lieutenants don't make much money. And I did not have much time, since I was still flying for the Marine Corps and taking night classes for my MBA.

The 90 days was a test of my emotional intelligence, the success intelligence.

At the end of the 90-day period I knew exactly which property was going to be my first investment. And, I knew why. I was excited. As rich dad often said, I was seeing a world few people ever see.

The property was a 1-bedroom condominium on the Island of Maui. It was across the road from one of the most beautiful beaches on the island. The entire development was in foreclosure and the price of the condo was $18,000.

I did not have the money. I didn't even have the down payment.

Following what I was taught, I used my credit card to pay $1,800 for the 10% down payment. The seller financed the remaining $16,200. After all expenses were paid, including the mortgage payment, I put $25 net in my pocket each month. This little deal changed my life.

Although the passive income was not big money, my personal transformation was huge. I now knew I could be rich. I now had my rich dad's context. I knew I would never need money again. I knew I could never say, "I can't afford it" again. More importantly, my life was transformed from that of a "C" student on the grading scale of academia to a "C" student in the world of capitalism. My desire to learn was exhilarating.

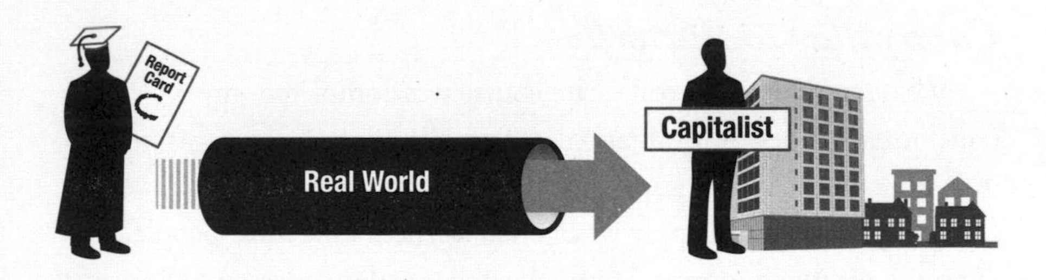

I no longer cared what my high school and college grades were. The only report card that counts for "C" students in the world of capitalism is their financial statement.

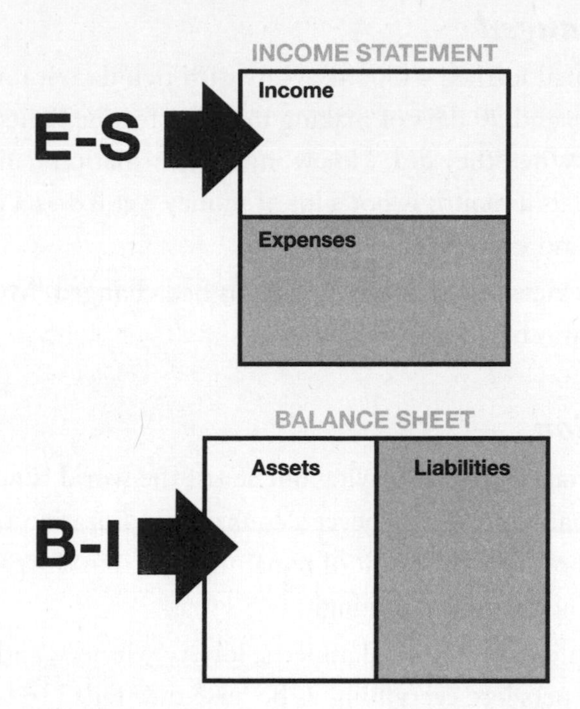

How Did You Do It?

When Kim and I retired, she was 37 and I was 47. Many people asked us how we did it. To say that it was tough to explain is an understatement. Imagine telling normal, often well-educated, people that we used debt and taxes to get rich and retire early.

Rather than talk, we spent the next few years creating our *CASHFLOW* game. It is the only game in the world that uses a financial statement as a scorecard.

The purpose of the game is to teach players how to transform their ordinary income into passive and portfolio income. Many players report the game changed their lives. It changed their lives because the game was designed to change a person's context.

My Life Changed

Although I had learned a lot after years with rich dad, it took a real estate course and 90 days of making mistakes for the lights to go on in my head. When they did, I knew my transformation had begun. Twenty-five dollars a month is not a lot of money, yet it was a giant step into the B and I quadrants.

My point of view had changed. My focus had changed. My transformation was beginning.

In Conclusion

The Greek tragedy that is playing out across the world is not a mistake. It is what happens whenever a country, organization or person rests on their laurels. It's the result of remaining stuck in the past—and forgetting that the world is changing.

The reason many professional athletes, lottery winners, and many high-income earners lose everything, is because they failed to learn how to transform their money…and, in transforming their money, they could transform their lives.

The problem with school is most kids come from homes (context) where parents work for ordinary income and went to school (context…reinforced) to learn to work for ordinary income. This is education, not transformation.

The reason transformation is difficult, even for "A" students, is because transformation requires emotional intelligence more than any other kind of intelligence.

When a person learns to transform their money from ordinary income to portfolio and passive income, they begin *their* transformation from the context of the E-S quadrants into the context of the B-I quadrants. It is the same transformation process a caterpillar goes through before becoming a butterfly.

If you want to change your life, change your context and learn to change the type of income you work for.

And remember, don't try to teach pigs to sing…unless the pig *wants* to learn to sing.

Action Step for Parents

Teach your child that money does not make people rich.

Many people believe that it's money that makes people rich. In real life, money can, and often does, makes people poor.

During your family Wealth Education Nights use the example of millionaire sports stars who go bankrupt. This paradox of thought will cause your child's mind to open and search for answers to understanding the relationship between *money* and *being rich.*

Then use the *Monopoly* game or the *CASHFLOW* game to explain why people with the most green houses and red hotels—the most assets on their financial statement—are the richest people in the world.

Talk about what makes people rich and use this book or the Study Guide to explain the reasons why rich people becoming poor. The discussions will lead your child to realize that their mind—not their money—is what makes them rich. And they may realize they do not need money to become rich.

Greed or Generosity... What Do Schools Teach?

Part One | Chapter Seven

LESSON #7: WHY GENIUSES ARE GENEROUS

What's the secret to raising a child who is generous? It's really pretty simple: Without financial education, many people leave school financially desperate, needy, and greedy. Financial education, the kind of financial education that transforms both the mind and spirit, opens our eyes to other points of view. It shows us how important it is to see both sides of a coin.

What are our schools teaching our children? Are they giving them fish to eat...keeping them needy and, often, greedy? Or do they teach kids to fish...to be self-reliant, innovative, and responsible enough to feed themselves?

As a parent you can show a child a path in life on which they can learn to use their gifts—their talents, their genius—to create a life in which they are free from the fear and worry of how they will survive. By finding and developing your child's genius you are also teaching them to be generous.

Making the Case

There are dozens of questions I ask myself when I think about what kids learn in school and how poorly most schools prepare our kids for the real world.

- Why do most student leave school needing job security?
- Why do so many employees expect their employers to take care of them for life?
- Why is Social Security one of the biggest government program in American history?
- Why will America go broke, unable to fund Medicare and other social welfare programs?
- Is our neediness caused by a school system's inability to prepare students for the real world?
- Do our schools foster the "entitlement" mentality?
- Are our schools killing the American Dream?

America: Land of the Needy

More than one hundred and fifty years ago, Alexis de Tocqueville, a French aristocrat, wrote about the power of the American Dream and how millions immigrated to America from all over the world in pursuit of that American Dream.

In Europe and Asia, at the time, there were basically two classes of people: the royals and everyone else. If you were born into the peasant class, you could never be a royal, no matter how hard you worked. The American Dream represented the opportunity for someone who was a peasant to become American "royalty," someone who could own property, control production (of goods or services of a business they could own), and work hard to create the life of their dreams. The American Dream, the spirit of entrepreneurship, is the driving force behind capitalism.

This dream was the spirit that caused people to leave their homelands and immigrate to America. While most were happy to join the American middle class, America did create its own nobility—entrepreneurs like Henry Ford, Thomas Edison, Walt Disney, Steve Jobs, and Mark Zuckerberg.

Alexis de Tocqueville believed that Americans could tolerate the gap between the rich and the poor as long as there was the hope that a person move from peasant to middle class—and maybe even become rich.

In 2007, when markets crashed, the American Dream began to die. As the economic crisis lingered and more people lost their jobs, homes, businesses, and retirement funds, the spirit that had been the driving force in this country began to die.

The bedrock of middle class status was to own a home. Today, millions of homes are worth less than the amount of the mortgage. Millions of people have lost their homes and are renting. Today, more people are moving out of the middle class and joining the ranks of the poor, rather than moving into the upper middle class or joining the rich.

In 2011, the number of Americans living in poverty grew to 46.2 million people. Approximately 1 in 6 Americans now lives in poverty, and the number is growing. When a person has no property, they join the ranks of the poor and become dependent upon the government to take care of them. Unfortunately, some turn to crime, crime in the streets and white-collar crime in business.

As more people lose their personal property, the more likely it is that the philosophies of communism, socialism, and fascism will fester within America. And capitalists will become the new enemy.

America became a great nation because people came here in search of opportunities for a better life. They wanted to succeed. They wanted to be capitalists. Then something changed. Today, rather than work hard in pursuit of the American Dream, many feel they are *entitled* to the American Dream.

All over the world, millions of people, not just Americans, seem to think the world owes them a living. Many people go to school, receive a great education, get a job, and then expect either the company they work for or the government to take care of them for life.

The growing entitlement mentality has played a role in the way individuals view personal financial responsibility.

These questions come to mind:

- To what extent are the financial problems, especially those faced by Greece, France, and the state of California, a result of an attitude of entitlement?
- Why do some of the best entitlement benefits go to our leaders—the President of the United States, our Congressional leaders, and other government workers? Once a President or congressman is elected, we the taxpayers take care of them for life. I ask myself: If they are qualified to be our leaders, why can't they take care of themselves?
- Why do our public servants feel entitled to financial security for life? When did the shift from public servants to *self-serving* servants occur? How many public servants work for the job security and benefits rather than to be of service?
- Why do CEOs and other corporate executives feel entitled to bigger and better financial packages than their employees? If they're smart enough to be high-paid employees, shouldn't they be smart enough to take care of themselves?
- Why do people the world over feel that they are entitled to have their government or their employer take care of them for life?

Where does this attitude of entitlement come from? Does it come from our schools and a school system run by teacher unions that fight for tenure and job security and benefits for life? Why do teachers grade students but refuse to be graded on their performance as professionals? Do they pass their entitlement mentality on to our kids? Could financial education have an impact on the entitlement mentality we see within the U.S. school system?

America's View of Capitalism

In the introduction to this book, I quoted from Dr. Frank Luntz's book *What Americans Really Want...Really*. Specifically, I quoted his comments on whom Americans respect today and whom they hate. I want to repeat what he wrote here, because it is so aligned with the key points in this chapter, the idea that our schools teach students to be needy and greedy.

"...it's hard to tell which has become the stronger emotion: respect for entrepreneurs or hatred towards CEOs."

Dr. Luntz also states:

"In fact, by better than a 3 to 1 ratio, Americans now trust entrepreneurs more than they trust successful CEOs."

"In today's world, 'Capitalists' frighten people, and 'capitalism' is short hand for CEOs taking tens of millions of dollars on the same day their pens wipe out 10,000 jobs."

Dr. Luntz found that Americans respect entrepreneurs still pursing the American Dream. He writes:

"The small business owner, even if she (female-owned small businesses are among the fastest-growing components of the shrinking economy) is successful, isn't making bonuses totaling tens of millions. She has no golden parachute, unless her business is providing skydiving lessons. She has to look her employees straight in the eye when it comes time to lay them off rather than just issuing a corporate edict. She has endured a lifetime of sleepless nights, tossing and turning about whether the business really was going to make it and whether she was going to let her employees down.

"Americans realize that there is far greater risk in investing your own time, your own money, and your own heart into starting a small business—and it's even harder to make it a successful one. And these risks made by the small-business owners are all in search of far less financial reward than their CEO counterparts."

Repeating Dr. Luntz's statement on MBAs:

"Forget about MBAs. Most business schools teach you how to be successful in a big corporation rather than start your own company."

Capitalists vs. Managerial Capitalists

John Bogle, an entrepreneur and *true capitalist*, is the founder of Vanguard Funds, one of the world's largest mutual fund companies. He is very critical of *managerial capitalists*.

In his book, *The Battle for the Soul of Capitalism*, Bogle addresses, "how the financial system undermined social ideals, damaged the trust in markets, robbed investors of trillions."

In an interview about his book he stated, "We have had what I describe in my book as a pathological mutation from traditional *owner's capitalism*, where the owners put up the lion's share of the capital and got the lion's share of the rewards, to a new form of *manager's capitalism*, where the managers are putting their interests ahead of the direct owners." By *direct owners*, Bogle is referring to the shareholders of pubic companies.

Bogle is saying that many of our largest corporations are led by *managerial capitalists*, not true capitalists. They are employees, not entrepreneurs. Many managerial capitalists are "A" students, graduates of the finest business schools. Managerial capitalists are not entrepreneurs. They did not start the business. They do not own the business. As managerial capitalists, they have responsibilities, but take no personal financial risks. They get paid whether they do a good job or bad job. They get paid…whether the business thrives or fails and even when employees lose their jobs or shareholders lose their investment.

John Bogle is especially critical of Jack Welch, former CEO of General Electric. Jack Welch was a managerial capitalist, an employee of GE. Thomas Edison is the entrepreneur who founded General Electric. Thomas Edison did not finish school and his teachers labeled him "addled."

Jack Welch, on the other hand, is a highly educated man, a chemical engineer with a doctorate degree from the University of Illinois. He is also one of the most respected CEOs in the world. Many believe him to be one of the best CEOs. Jack Welch is a frequent guest on financial talk shows as an authority on business.

Bogle disagrees, describing Welch as a managerial capitalist who did a great job for Jack Welch in lining his own pockets, but a poor job for General Electric's employees and shareholders.

Jack Welch's greed was exposed during his divorce proceedings. In his book, *The Battle for the Soul of Capitalism*, Bogle has this to say about Jack Welch:

"Jack Welch of General Electric gained an equally unwelcome spotlight for his extramarital peccadillos. His divorce proceeding illuminated the 'stealth' compensation typically awarded to retired chief executives but rarely disclosed. (If not for his divorce, even shareholders, the true owners of GE, would never have known how much Welch was being paid). While his total compensation as GE's CEO surely approached $1 billion, his lavish retirement benefits, valued by one commentator at $2 million per year, included a New York apartment with daily flower deliveries and wine, and unlimited use of a company jet. Nonetheless, he seems to have little to spare, given that his charitable giving came to just $614 per month."

Bogle notes Jack Welch's retirement compensation was awarded by GE's board of directors…also managerial capitalists.

"They made these awards despite the fact that the stock market did not think Welch did a very good job. In 2000, the market high for GE was $600 billion. When Jack Welch retired, GE's value had declined to $379 billion in early 2005."

If Thomas Edison was alive, I wonder if he would have rewarded Jack Welch so lavishly?

The Mutual Fund Industry

Expressing concerns about the 'retirement system' as a whole, Bogle takes aim at CEOs of investment firms. He believes retirement is going to be *the next big financial crisis* in this country.

Bogle, an insider in the mutual fund industry, is especially disturbed by the greed in the mutual fund industry. He says:

"When I came into this business there were relatively small, privately held companies, and these companies were run by investment professionals.

"Today, that has changed in every single respect. These are giant companies. They are not privately held anymore. They are owned by giant financial conglomerates, whether it's Deutsche Bank, Marsh & McLennan, or Sun Life of Canada. Basically, the largest portion of mutual fund assets are run by financial conglomerates, and they are in the business to earn a return on their *capital in the business—and not a return on* your *capital."*

Bogle points out that in mutual funds, you, as the investor, put up 100% of the money and take 100% of the risk. The mutual fund company puts up no money, takes no risk, and yet keeps 80% of the returns. The investor gets back 20% of the gains, if there are gains.

Warren Buffett Agrees

Warren Buffett is regarded as one of the greatest investors of our time. He is a capitalist. He is an entrepreneur. He is *not* a managerial capitalist.

This is what Warren Buffett has to say about these corporate money managers, managerial capitalists, most of whom are "A" students from great schools.

He says:

"Full-time professionals in other fields, let's say dentists, bring a lot to the layman. But in the aggregate, people get nothing for their money from professional money managers."

If this is true, it might be stated another way: Those who choose not to become financially educated or play an active role in their investments and, instead, turn their money over to professional money managers, are abdicating responsibility for their financial future—and, if Buffett is on target, getting little value for it. Positioned another way: How great is the risk of turning your money over to a 'professional' who brings little value to the undertaking of making your money work for you?

Bureaucrats: "B" Students

The vast majority of students who graduate from grade schools and high schools are "B" students. They're taught, by and large, by "A" students…some of the brightest students who continue their education to become teachers. What becomes of those "B" students as they choose their path in life? It's my opinion that they become bureaucrats.

What Is a Bureaucrat?

Decades ago, rich dad said, "The problem with the world is that it's now run by bureaucrats." He defined a bureaucrat as someone who is in a position of authority—such as a CEO, president, sales manager, or government official—but who takes no personal financial risks. Explaining further, he said, "A bureaucrat can lose a lot of money, but they do not lose any of their own money. They get paid, whether they do a good job or not."

When you look at the bureaucrats who run the country, especially our political leaders, I think you'll find that most are attorneys. Federal Reserve Bank Chairman Ben Bernanke is a former college professor. He is also an "A" student who became a "B" student (a bureaucrat) and the most powerful banker in the world. And we wonder why we are in a financial crisis.

Rich dad said, "A true capitalist, an entrepreneur, knows how to take a dollar and turn it into a hundred dollars. Give a bureaucrat a dollar, and they'll spend a hundred."

And we wonder why we have a global financial crisis.

What Do Schools Teach?

Without financial education, many people leave school financially desperate, needy, and greedy. Most of us have heard the saying, "Desperate people do desperate things." It could also be said that "*Needy* people do desperate things."

The diagram below is Maslow's Hierarchy of Needs. It depicts a theory first proposed by psychologist Abraham Maslow in his a 1943 paper titled "A Theory of Human Motivation." His theory is fully expressed in his 1954 book *Motivation and Personality*.

Maslow's hierarchy suggests that people are motivated to fulfill basic needs before moving on to other, more advanced needs. This hierarchy is most often depicted as a pyramid in which the lowest levels are made up of the most basic needs, while the more complex needs are located at the top of the pyramid.

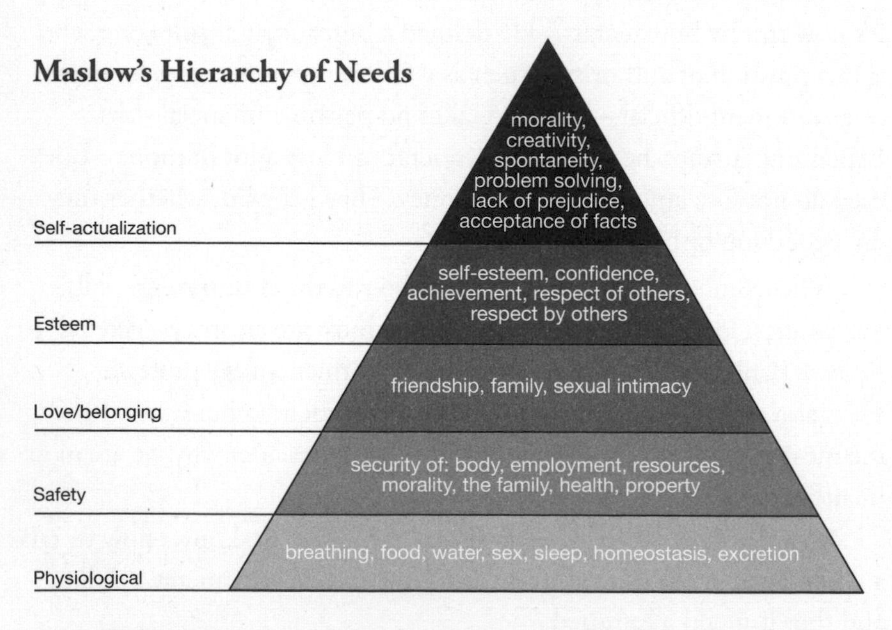

Source: Abraham Maslow
Reprinted with Permission. The original work has been modified.

Maslow's Second Level: Safety

In my opinion, our schools fail to fill a child's needs at Maslow's second level, Safety. This is why so many people leave school both needy and greedy.

Without a real financial education, people can never feel safe and secure, or in control of their resources, their family's security, their health, and their property.

Most people leave school in need of financial security, also called a steady paycheck. Many people will do anything to keep their job…and I do mean anything. Without financial security, people become desperate, clinging to a job and living in fear of losing their job, home, benefits, and pensions. Many end their working years in need of—dependent upon—Social Security and Medicare.

This is why some CEOs and money managers will violate their ethical and moral principles and values, in some cases actively cheating their employees, shareholders, or clients. I'm sure you can think of examples of corporate CEOs or money managers who used deception and cunning, or even criminal behavior, to create their own wealth.

Several of those who come to my mind made headlines and history, and may be in prison today.

This is why John Bogle's words, reiterated here, are so telling in terms of what goes on in the boardrooms of our biggest corporations:

> *"Jack Welch of General Electric gained an equally unwelcome spotlight for his extramarital peccadillos. His divorce proceeding illuminated the "stealth" compensation typically awarded to retired chief executives but rarely disclosed."*

In other words, if Jack Welch had not cheated on his wife, it may never have been discovered just how much he and his board had been cheating the true owners of GE. Again: Another morality issue. Note that the word "morality" is at Maslow's second level.

Is this what our schools teach the best and brightest students? I am afraid it is.

My Story

I believe that the American Dream is dying because many of us have lost our moral compasses. Our schools are not fulfilling the educational needs of our students, especially at Maslow's second level, safety, in the Hierarchy of Needs. We see so many kids, especially from poor neighborhoods, who turn to street crime and violence.

Rich dad often said, "Needy people become greedy people. Greedy people become desperate people. And desperate people do desperate things."

The greatest gift my rich dad gave me was showing me both sides of the Employee-Entrepreneur coin. He exposed Mike and me to the life of an entrepreneur and offered us an environment in which entrepreneurial thinking could thrive. Today, I do not need a job, a steady paycheck, money, bonuses, government support, or Social Security and Medicare. My wife and I have reached at Maslow's fourth level, the Esteem Level. This confidence allowed us to be entrepreneurs, starting The Rich Dad Company in 1996, two years after we "retired" in 1994.

The Rich Dad Company propelled us into Maslow's fifth level, the Self-Actualization Level. We do not need paychecks. We work because we love our work, sharing what we know so others can also grow and prosper. While we make a lot of money, most of that money does not go into our pockets. Most of the money is spent on growing the company, investing in new and better technology, more people, and new product development. That is what true capitalist do.

Unfortunately, a lot of money is also spent protecting the business from greedy people.

Greedy People

Like most business owners, we have run into some very greedy people in the course of doing business. We have been lied to, cheated, and ripped off by needy and greedy people, most of them

"A" students…a few of them white-collar criminals. Unfortunately, that is part of the entrepreneurial process and our so-called "justice system." Or, from a different point of view: our injustice system.

Rich or poor, we all have had our own challenges with dishonest or deceitful people. That is what happens when schools fail to fulfill students' needs at Maslow's second level. Many students, even "A" students, leave school needy, greedy, desperate, and—even worse—with a sense of "entitlement," the idea that the world owes them a living.

The Good News

The good news is that we have met some fantastic people along the way. We would never have met them had we not taken our leap of faith in starting The Rich Dad Company.

We would not have met them if we had retired in 1994, kept our money, and played golf every day.

I remember the first time Donald Trump said something that my rich dad often said:

"Out of every bad partnership, I have met good partners."

That is true for Kim and me as well. We met most of our Rich Dad Advisors through business dealings that were, initially, not pleasant or profitable. This lesson proves the saying that "Every cloud has a silver lining." My advisors were the silver lining, the positive outcome to some very dark and challenging times in my life.

Education's Failure

Question: What happens when the educational system fails at Maslow's second level?

Answer: A new American Dream emerges. Alexis de Tocqueville, told the world about the power of the American Dream, the dream that anyone could become rich.

More than one hundred and fifty years later, it seems like the new American Dream is that Social Security and Medicare will keep Americans alive.

The New America

According to the CBO, the U.S. Congressional Budget Office, the increase in incomes between 1979 and 2007 in the United States looked like this:

Poor:	**Income grew 18% over 30 years**
Middle Class:	**Income grew 40% over 30 years**
Rich:	**Income grew 275% over 30 years**

Then in 2007, the bottom fell out when the boom went bust. Today, incomes for the middle class and poor have stopped going up, yet the rich seem to be getting richer faster.

In 2011, the number of Americans living in poverty grew to 46.2 million people. That translates to approximately 1 in 6 Americans who now live in poverty, and that number is growing. When a person has no property, they join the ranks of the poor and become dependent upon the government to take care of them. Oftentimes this leads to increased violence, both on the streets and in our homes.

Students on Food Stamps

Nearly 47 million Americans rely on federal food assistance benefits (food stamps), a 12-year high attributed to the weak U.S. economy and high rates of unemployment over the last five years. A lesser-known fact is that college students are among the fastest-growing segment of our economy to rely on food stamps. As tuition fees go up and financial aid opportunities vanish—and parents who were once a source of financial support have lost jobs or homes and become ineligible for college loans for their children—students have had to fend for themselves.

The Next Poor

Are teachers headed for the ranks of the poor?

In 2011, the California State Teachers Retirement System, CalSTRS, realized it faced a long-term deficit of $56 billion. A deficit is the gap between assets and estimated liabilities. CalSTRS collects $6 billion a year, but needs $10 billion each year to meet its obligations. A shortfall of more than $4 billion a year is a lot of money, especially for government bureaucrats who do not know how to invest or how to make money. Most pension-fund managers are not from the I quadrant. Most are employees in the E quadrant, pretending to be professional investors. If they were true investors, they probably wouldn't be employees.

> **USDA Advertising**
>
> *Via Veronique de Rugy at NRO's Corner comes this amazing ad from the USDA about how food stamps will help you "look amazing!"*
>
> *In the radio spot, two retired ladies talk about their mutual friend "Margie," who "looks amazing." One asks the other: "What's her secret?" The answer, it turns out, is food stamps.*

If the California teacher's retirement plan goes bust, the taxpayers will be stuck with yet another massive bailout. Worst of all, millions of teachers will slide from the middle class and join the poor.

Again, repeating the words of John Bogle: "The whole retirement system…in the country is in, I think, very poor shape and it's going to be the next big financial crisis in the country…"

Generous Capitalists

Parents can teach their children to be *generous* capitalists. And it can start at home.

This is important because your child will not learn to be a capitalist, much less a generous person, in school. My rich dad taught his son and me to be generous capitalists using the B-I Triangle.

Our schools program students to look for work on the right side of the CASHFLOW quadrant, in the E and S quadrants.

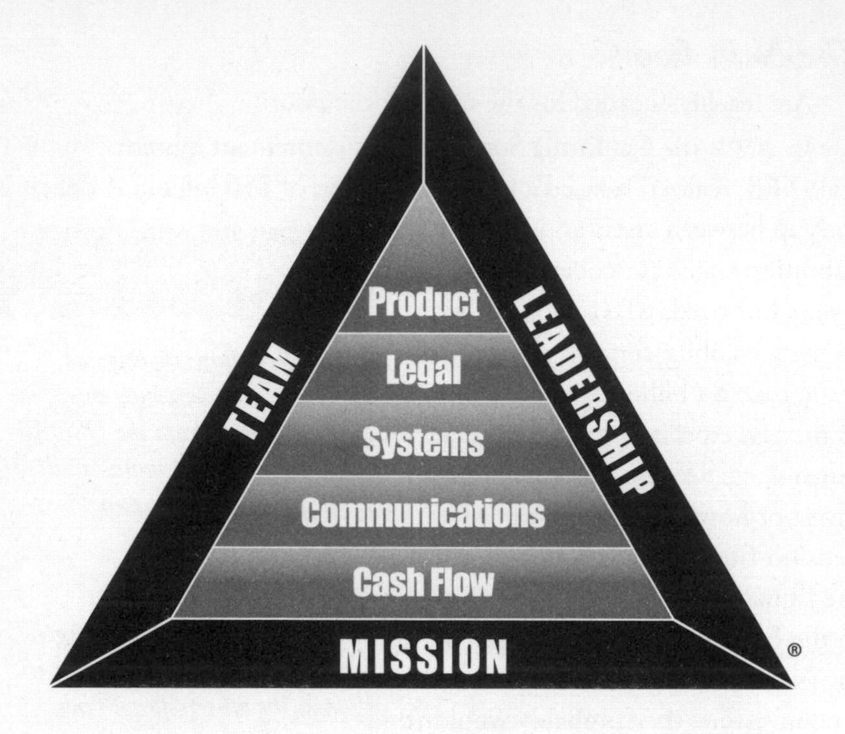

Notice that the B-I Triangle is made up of the 8 Integrities of a business. They are:

1. Mission
2. Leadership
3. Team
4. Product
5. Legal
6. Systems
7. Communications
8. Cash Flow

Specialist vs. Generalist

Most schools teach students to be specialists. Students who graduate with a degree in product design seek jobs at the *product* level of the B-I Triangle. Students who graduate from law school fill roles at the *legal* level of the triangle. Those with degrees in engineering or computer science tend to focus on jobs at the *systems* level of the triangle. Students who receive degrees in marketing focus on jobs in the *communication* section of the B-I Triangle. And students who receive a degree in accounting, typically find a job at the *cash flow* level of the triangle.

Entrepreneurs are generalists. One reason why entrepreneurs, like Steve Jobs and Bill Gates, leave school is because they did not want to be specialists. They hired *specialists*.

Generalists must be *mission* driven, have strong *leadership* skills, and surround themselves with a smart *team*, often "A" students with experience in the real world.

Why Most Entrepreneurs Fail

There are three primary reasons why most small businesses fail. They are:

1. **The entrepreneur does not have all 8 integrities in place.**
   For example, most new entrepreneurs focus on product. They may have a great product, but are likely deficient in some or all of the other 7 integrities.

2. **The entrepreneur is a mono-professional.**
   The saying "Birds of a feather flock together" applies here. For example, attorneys get together with other attorneys to form a business such as a law practice. Or techies get together with other techies to form a web company. Again, they may be smart professionals, but they will lack professional strength at the other 7 integrities.

3. **The entrepreneur lacks a sense of mission.**
   You will recall that, among the Seven Intelligences, emotional intelligence and a sense of mission is essential in carrying an entrepreneur through the ups and downs of starting a business.

Almost all notable entrepreneurs faced trials and tribulations that would destroy mere mortals.

Steve Jobs was kicked out of Apple, the company he founded. He was fired by the CEO he hired, John Scully, and his board of directors (All, by the way, managerial capitalists…) only to return years later to lead Apple to be the most profitable company in the world.

Bill Gates went to trial in a case known as *The United States vs. Microsoft*. The United States Department of Justice filed a lawsuit in 1998 for alleged violation of the Sherman Antitrust Act. Microsoft was accused of being a monopoly.

Mark Zuckerberg went to trial against the Winklevoss twins who claimed that they gave Mark the idea for Facebook. Mark settled the claim for $160 million. The twins are still asking for more.

As the saying goes, "Success has many parents, but failure is an orphan."

Without an entrepreneur's sense of mission and strong emotional intelligence, Apple, Microsoft, and Facebook might not be here today.

Generosity Is the Key to Success

Contrary to popular belief, many of the most successful entrepreneurs are generous. If you look at the B-I Triangle, you will see that to start a successful business, a B-quadrant entrepreneur must provide jobs.

Most students come out of school, *looking* for jobs. They need a job because schools don't teach students how to satisfy one of Maslow's basic needs, the need for Safety. That is why most "A" students work for "C" students.

If a parent will take the time to explain Maslow's Hierarchy of Needs and the B-I Triangle to their child, the child may, over time, realize their objective in life is to reach Maslow's fifth level, Self-Actualization, rather than get stuck at the second level, mired in the need for job security and a steady paycheck.

It is difficult to discover our genius, the geni-in-us and the magic we were born with, if we live in terror and fear at the second level of Maslow's Hierarchy.

I believe genius is found at Maslow's fifth level. At that level are found powerful and beautiful words, values, and abilities essential for today's world. The words are:

1. **Morality:** *you don't have to cheat people to be rich*
2. **Creativity:** *tap into your genius*
3. **Spontaneity:** *live without the fear of making mistakes*
4. **Problem solving:** *focus on solutions*
5. **Lack of prejudice:** *having a wider context on life*
6. **Acceptance of Fact:** *not afraid to face the truth*

A Final Word

Your child's ability to dream of the life they'd like to live and pursue it—is defined by the safety, confidence, and love they experience at home.

Action Step for Parents

Discuss the difference between greed and generosity.

My poor dad always thought my rich dad was greedy. My rich dad thought my poor dad was greedy. They had two different points of view based upon their contexts related to money, greed and generosity.

Entrepreneurs and capitalists are generous when they choose to invest in businesses, products, and services that create jobs and opportunities for others to thrive.

Also discuss why and how Steve Jobs became a billionaire, by sharing his genius and revolutionizing the way the world communicates. Then discuss Mark Zuckerberg or the founders of

Google… as well as gifted athletes or musicians who have generously shared their genius with the world.

On a regular basis encourage your child to find his or her genius—and share it.

Your challenge will be, the school system has it's own definition of what a genius is. It may not be the same definition of your child's genius.

Remember that different genius comes out in different environments. Thomas Edison's genius came out in a laboratory and Steve Jobs genius came out in his family's garage where he started Apple computers. Mark Zuckerberg created Facebook in his college dorm room as he created a way for his fellow students to connect and communicate.

One of your most important jobs as a parent is to encourage your child to find the environment where his or her genius shines.

Are You Climbing on The Entitlement Wagon?

Part One | Chapter Eight

LESSON #8: THE ENTITLEMENT MENTALITY

In January 2013, French actor Gerard Depardieu obtained a Russian passport and left France. The taxes on the rich were too high.

In 2013, the state of California raised state income taxes and the rich began moving to tax-free states such as Nevada.

In 2013, a friend of mine gave up his family's winery business in Italy and moved to a country that offered tax breaks for the rich.

In 2013, a friend of a friend who had a 400-employee construction business closed his doors after 24 years. He said, "Obamacare raised my employee's medical insurance by 24%. I lose money if I continue to stay in business."

In 2013, a pediatrician I know stopped practicing medicine. She said, "I cannot afford my malpractice insurance. It makes no sense to work for the insurance company."

Making the Case

In 1935, President Franklin Delano Roosevelt signed into law the Social Security Act. The act was an attempt to limit what were seen as dangers in modern American life: Old age, poverty, unemployment, and the burden of widows and fatherless children.

Today, Social Security is one of the largest government program in American history.

In 1964, President Lyndon Johnson launched his Great Society initiative, government programs designed to save the poor. That program led to the creation of Medicare, Medicaid, and the Older Americans Act. These programs were expanded under Republican Presidents Richard Nixon, Gerald Ford and George W. Bush.

Today, Medicare is the most expensive program in American history.

In 2010, President Barack Obama passed The Patient Protection and Affordable Care Act, more popularly known as Obamacare.

Unfortunately, this "Affordable Care Act" is costing American businesses approximately 29% more for medical insurance for their employees. When expenses go up for a business, it often means that jobs are lost. This means Obamacare will take a toll among the working poor and middle class, as well as the rich and the business owners.

Saving the Middle Class

In 2012, during the presidential race, both President Obama and Republican candidate Mitt Romney promised to "Save the Middle Class."

What happened to saving the poor? Why do we need to save the middle class?

Will today's middle class become the poor people of tomorrow?

My Story

For years my Sunday school teachers drummed this lesson into my head: "Give a man a fish and you feed him for a day. Teach a man to fish and you feed him for a lifetime."

Are our schools failing to teach people to fish? Or are our schools teaching students that they are entitled to their daily fish? Is this why there are more and more people dependent upon the government for life support?

In Chapter Seven, looking at Maslow's Hierarchy of Needs, it seemed obvious to me that our schools fail students at the second level of his pyramid, Safety.

Maslow describes the needs at this level to be:

Security of: Body, employment, resources, morality, the family, health, and property.

A dozen questions come to mind. Could the failure to teach children to fish be one of the reasons for the breakdown in American culture? Could it be that unemployment, dwindling financial resources, the loss of one's home, and inadequate healthcare are driving forces behind the rise in crime, immorality, obesity, and unstable families?

Do social programs such as Social Security, Medicare, and Obamacare make problems worse, or better? Does giving people fish increase their dependence on government programs? And is this why Social Security and Medicare—and now, Obamacare—are turning into financial disasters? Most importantly, will your children be expected to pay the bill?

As more and more of the 76 million baby-boomer Americans begin collecting Social Security and claiming Medicare benefits, will that cause more middle class Americans to slide into poverty?

Is this why, in 2012, both President Obama and Mitt Romney promised to save the middle class? As most of you know, it's the middle class that carries the heaviest tax burden. For many, taxes are their single largest expense. If you studied Obamacare, you'd find that it is really a tax—not an affordable healthcare plan. The question is: Who will pay the tax? Not the rich or the poor. This tax burden will fall on the middle class, possibly your child, due in large part to the fact that schools have failed to teach students to fish.

"I'm Entitled"

In 2012, I was listening to the radio while driving in my car. A U.S. Congressman was the guest and was answering questions from callers. One caller, a young man, said, "I joined the Navy in 1990. I retired in 2011. I am 39 years old. Where are the retirement benefits I am entitled to?"

The Congressman never answered his question. All he did was thank the young man for his service.

This sums up this troubling trend. And poses the inevitable question: How can so few people pull such a heavy wagon?

The Entitlement Wagon

As I listened to that radio show, I wondered where this "entitlement mentality" comes from. I fought in Vietnam. I served in the Marine Corps for six years. I don't think I'm entitled to anything.

As I drove, my thoughts drifted back to 1969, the year I joined the Marine Corps. I remembered that two of my relatives, both high-ranking Army officers when they retired, came up to me, shook my hand, and said, "Remember to stay in for 20." That meant stay in for 20 years, for the retirement benefits to which I'd be entitled, the paycheck and medical care for life.

At the time I thought that was strange. I had resigned from a high-paying job with Standard Oil of California, earning $4,000 a month (which in 1969 was a good starting salary and included five months off each year) and joined the Marine Corps, earning $200 a month. I joined the Marines to serve my country, not for the pay or a lifetime of entitlements. It was a teenager when President John

Kennedy took office, and I was responding to the words from his inaugural address, "Ask not what your country can do for you—Ask what you can do for your country."

In 1974, I resigned my commission and left the Marine Corps. I did not stay in for 20. The Vietnam War was almost over, I had served my country, and it was time to move on. For me, it was a privilege to serve my country. I was entitled to nothing. I was grateful for the experience. If anything, I felt I still owed more to my country.

Financial Crisis...or Education Crisis?

As the radio show continued, the young Naval retiree would not let the Congressman off the hook, demanding that he was entitled to more benefits.

Again, I asked myself: Where does this entitlement mentality come from? And why are so many people dependent upon the government for basic life support? Why is Social Security one of the largest program in U.S. history?

And what will Obamacare, this "Affordable Healthcare Act," do to my business? Will I be forced to let employees go as healthcare costs skyrocket? What will happen when 75 million American baby boomers, 38% of whom are classified as obese, begin collecting medical care they are "entitled to under the act."

And what will happen when baby boomers outlive their retirement savings? The average monthly Social Security benefit check in 2011 was $1,200. When inflation hits, there will not only be an increase in poverty, but increases in homelessness, crime, moral degeneration, and taxes as well as a government that prints more counterfeit money to solve the problem. We don't need hyperinflation—50% of Americans are *already* on the edge.

Why are 15% of all Americans—46 million people—on food stamps?

Today there seems to be many more questions than answers.

So again, I ask, "Why is there no financial education in schools?" And is the lack of financial education the reason why so many people feel the government should take care of them? Isn't it obvious that our financial crisis is a crisis in education?

In a February 2013 article, *The Week* reported that "Some 46.2 million Americans now live in families where someone is working but earning less than poverty line: $11,702 a year for an individual or $23,021 for a family of four." I realize that many people *do* need government support. I am also aware that many do not. Yet, not surprisingly, they must be asking themselves: Why work when the government is handing out cash, paying you not to work?

"Why Don't You Teach Me About Money?"

As a young boy, I often asked my teachers, "Why don't you teach me about money? Why don't you teach me how to be rich?"

I never received an answer to those questions. It took me years to realize that there were two reasons my teachers could not answer my questions. One, they themselves had no financial education so they could not teach me how to be rich. And two, they didn't think that learning about money was important because they expected the government to take care of them.

My teachers were much like my poor dad, also a teacher and head of the teachers' union. Today we have teachers (and teachers' unions) spreading the gospel of entitlement. Ask most teachers their ambition in life and their answer is, "tenure." Another word for *entitlement*.

146 Million Americans Classified as Working Poor

As reported by The Week in February 2013: "Many economists have a broader definition, saying that the working poor are those whose incomes do not cover basic needs: food, clothing, housing, transportation, child care, and health care.

"By that standard, there are more than 146 million Americans in the poor-but-working class. People in this category generally have no savings and survive from check to check, often filling in the gaps by going into debt."

Mass Entitlement Mentality

Millions of people want the security of a paycheck and benefits for life. The entitlement mentality is especially prevalent with "B" students, people who seek a lifetime of security working for government bureaucracies.

The legal system often fuels this entitlement feeding frenzy. Most trials are more about money than justice. And while judges perform an important role in society, the justice system has become a Roman circus of frivolous lawsuits, a battle between rich and poor.

Rich Dad Lesson

My rich dad often said, "You always get what you pay for. If you pay people not to work, you get more people not working."

The rising cost of medical malpractice insurance for doctors is only one reason for the rising cost of medical care. Many jurors rule against doctors simply because he is a "rich doctor" who has insurance. The high cost of malpractice insurance causes many doctors to leave the profession.

There is a lot of talk about "tort reform," which means limiting the outrageous sums of money that judges and juries can award a patient. One reason there may never be "tort reform" is because most of the lawmakers in Washington are lawyers. The rest are politicians who receive large campaign contributions from trial lawyers.

Television ads bombard us day and night as they troll for new clients. "Have you been injured in an accident?" they ask. "Call us. We're lawyers and we will get you the money you are entitled to."

Entitlement Mentality in the Gym

My wife Kim and I go to the same gym and work with the same coach. The gym is a no-nonsense gym. It is not fancy. The gym specializes in training professional athletes, such as NFL and NBA players, and Olympic hopefuls. You won't find a yoga studio, color-coordinated workout clothes, or smoothie counters for socializing. A large area of the gym is dedicated to physical therapy.

For over three years, a legal aid has come in three to four days a week for "physical therapy." He does not come in during his lunch hour or after hours. He comes in during work hours. He has his shoulder worked on by a therapist for about an hour and then goes back to "work." He does not lift weights, or do anything strenuous. He is about my age, in his 60s, and severely overweight. One day I asked him what he was doing at the gym. He smiled politely and said, "The government pays for my rehab so I take advantage of it. I only have two more years before I can retire and I want to make sure I get everything I am entitled to."

I know most public servants are good people. Yet I am disturbed every time I hear the word *entitlement*. It is difficult for me to be objective. Many public servants fail to realize that governments do not have money to support these programs and benefits. The money comes from taxpayers, fellow citizens, and, soon, your children.

But "I Am Entitled"

Many Americans say, "I am entitled to Social Security and Medicare. I've been paying into those programs for years." While that may be true, here are the facts: If you began paying into Social Security in 1950, you receive at least $30 back for every $1 you put in. This leads to the conclusion that Social Security is a Ponzi or pyramid scheme. Since the government has no money, the $30 comes from younger workers, robbing Peter junior to pay Paul senior.

Leaders with an Entitlement Mentality

The entitlement mentality starts with the President of the United States and prevails through the Senate and Congress. Over the years, these public servants have voted—for themselves—the most generous entitlement benefits package in history.

Is this what happens when our educational needs are not met at Maslow's second level. Safety?

The Real Campaign Issue

During the Presidential campaign of 2012, former governor Romney was secretly video taped speaking to an audience of wealthy donors at a private fundraiser. He was talking about the 47% of all Americans who do not pay income taxes.

The 30-minute speech, riddled with controversial statements, was posted on the Internet. Romney characterized the 47% of income-tax-exempt Americans as being "dependent on the government" and feeling "entitled to health care, to food, to housing, to you-name-it."

The video caused a firestorm of protest. The Democrats, sensing blood in the water, attacked. They gave reasons why the 47% were justified in not paying taxes. Many argued that Romney's facts were inaccurate.

Just the Facts

According to the bipartisan Tax Policy Center, here are the facts: In 2011 about 46% of Americans—76 million people—who filed taxes did not pay a penny in federal income taxes.

Whether his 47% figure was accurate or not, Romney took a punch to the chin and did not recover. The secret video proved to be one more nail in his campaign coffin. President Obama went on the offensive attacking the rich, saying the rich 1% did not pay their "fair share" in taxes.

Romney should have used facts to counter emotions. The facts are:

- To be in that richest 1% of Americans you must earn $370,000 a year. In 2011, the top 1% paid 37% of all income taxes collected in America.
- To rank in the lowest 50%, you earn $34,000 a year or less. The *entire* lower 50% pays 2.4% of all taxes paid.

In summary: If 1% of the wealthiest Americans pay 37% of all taxes collected, while the half of Americans earning $34,000 a year or less pay only 2.4%, it doesn't seem unreasonable to ask: Who isn't paying their fair share?

It's likely I'll get raked over the coals for even asking this question. If you are incensed by it, please ask yourself: How emotionally attached are you to entitlements? And instead of getting distracted by the political sideshow of "rich versus poor," wouldn't you be better off being financially educated?

Taxing the Rich

In 2013, President Obama kept his campaign promise to "tax the rich." But is he really taxing the rich? In 2013, taxes on individuals earning over $400,000 a year went up. Once again, the 1% is being asked to pay more than their fair share, more than the 37% of the tax load they already carry.

Millions of Americans think this is fair. They believe we should tax the rich.

My point of view is different. Obama is not taxing the rich. He is taxing high-income earners. It's the middle class that pays the lion's share of taxes collected.

This is why both President Obama and candidate Romney pledged to save the middle class. The middle class is slowly sliding into poverty. By the year 2020, millions of baby boomers who were middle class during their working years will retire and join the ranks of the poor, just as Social Security and Medicare move closer and closer to going bust.

Your child will pay for this.

This is what happens when we give people fish, rather than teach people to fish.

Question: Why do you say we are taxing high-income people, not rich people?

Answer: With a little financial education, the answer is clear.

A Simple Lesson in Financial Education

There is more than one type of income. There are three types of income. This is true in countries around the world.

1. **Ordinary Income**
2. **Portfolio Income**
3. **Passive Income**

Different types of income are taxed at different rates. When President Obama raised taxes in 2013, he raised taxes on people who earn *ordinary* and *portfolio* income. He did not raise taxes on the rich, because the truly rich earn *passive* income.

In overly simple terms, this is an overview of who works for what type of income:

1. **Ordinary Income:** *the Poor*

2. **Portfolio Income:** *the Middle Class*

3. **Passive Income:** *the Rich*...from investments in the B and I quadrants

What Do Schools Teach?

When schools advise students to land a high-paying job, their advice is to work for *ordinary income*, the highest taxed of all three incomes. When a teacher advises you to "save money," the interest income on savings is taxed at ordinary income tax rates. And when money mangers advise you to "invest in 401(k)," when that money is withdrawn at retirement it is taxed at *ordinary income* rates.

In January 2013, many working Americans found that President Obama had raised taxes on them, even if they were not rich. In January, workers found out their FICA (Federal Insurance Contributions Act), a payroll tax for Social Security went up when it returned to its pre-crisis level. Social Security is a tax on *ordinary income*.

Question: Why do schools teach students to work for ordinary income? Why not teach kids about the three types of income? Why not teach kids ways to keep more of the money they'll earn throughout their lifetimes?

Answer: Many teachers do not know there are three types of income. And most teachers work for ordinary income.

Words

It is important to know that different professions use different words to say the same thing.

For example:

Accountants say	Investors say
Ordinary Income	Earned Income
Portfolio Income	Capital Gains Income
Passive Income	Cash Flow Income

This is an example of why financial education can be confusing.

That's why I use simple language to explain concepts that are often complex and confusing. In my opinion, financial education is important enough to deserve a parent's time and focus so that you can teach your children.

Since I am a professional investor and not an accountant, I tend to use investor words—except when I am talking to my accountants. This is because most accountants are not professional investors. The same is true for attorneys and doctors. When I speak to my attorney, I do my best to speak his language, the language of lawyers. One reason why I make more money than most attorneys is because most attorneys do not speak the language of money. When an attorney speaks about money, they may say, "I charge $250 an hour," but that's ordinary income. Rather than speak about *money*, they speak about the cost of their labor.

1. **Poor people's income: *Ordinary Income***
   Ordinary income is poor people's income because the more you earn the less you keep. That is not financially intelligent. Many people go back to school, work harder or work overtime, hoping to earn more ordinary income. Earning more money pushes them into higher and higher tax brackets. Again, the more they earn the less they keep.

Most parents teach their children to work for ordinary income. That's what most people work for. They do so when they advise, "Go to school, get a job, work hard, save money, invest in a 401(k)." All generate ordinary income, the highest taxed of all incomes.

2. **Middle class income: *Portfolio Income***
   Middle class investors are counting on their stock market portfolio to keep them alive once their working days are over. The same is often true for many government employees. Many government-employee retirement funds have been counting on gains in the stock market (8% per year is the percent of increase we often hear talked about) to meet their obligations. If the returns aren't there, will the retirees get less money or will the government employee bureaucracy seek to raise taxes on the rest of us?

Stockbrokers and financial planners teach people to work for portfolio income. Portfolio income is also called *"capital gains,"* which means buying low and selling high.

Stockbrokers and financial planners advise investing for portfolio income, or capital gains, when they say, "The stock market goes up on average 8% per year" or "Invest for the long term" or "This stock pays a great dividend."

A real estate broker teaches people to invest for portfolio income, capital gains, when they say, "Your house will appreciate in value."

Here is a series of Q&As to further clarify portfolio income and capital gains.

Question: Did President Obama raise taxes on real estate investors?

Answer: He did in small ways. Yet, real estate in the United States still offers tax breaks that stock investors do not receive.

Question: What types of breaks?

Answer: If person buys a house for $100,000 and sells it for $150,000, the real estate investor does not have to pay the capital gains tax on the $50,000 gain, *if* the investor uses what is known as an 'exchange.' A stock investor would have paid capital gains taxes on the $50,000 capital gain.

Question: How much did President Obama raise taxes on portfolio income?

Answer: For high-income employees, those earning over $200,000 a year as individuals (or $250,000 a year for married couples), he increased taxes on long-term capital gains (portfolio income) by 60% in 2013.

Here's the math:

15% to 20% + 3.8% for Obamacare
OR
15% to 23.8% = 60% tax increase

As I have said, I am not a tax expert or specialist. And even at a basic level, taxes and numbers can be confusing. I encourage you to find a tax professional who is a good teacher as well as a good accountant. He or she can help you understand taxes and how they impact your life.

On the subject of taxes, there are two final points I want to make.

- Without financial education, most people actually believe politicians are raising taxes on the rich. The tax increases affect anyone who works for *ordinary income*. This is one reason why Lesson #1 in *Rich Dad Poor Dad* is "The rich don't work for money."
- Taxes were raised on those who invest in the stock market for portfolio income. This is one of many reasons why I do not invest in the stock market. Why pay taxes when I can invest for tax-free income with less risk and higher returns? On the other hand, if your investment plan cannot beat returns in the stock market, it may be best to stay invested in the stock market. It comes down to your willingness to become financially educated and move from being a passive investor (who turns their money over to a financial planner or money manager) to an active one.

How Do the Rich Avoid Paying Taxes?

It's simple: The rich work for passive income.

3. **Rich Income: *Passive Income***
   Passive income is also known as cash flow. The truly rich are rich because they have this type of income. President Obama did not raise taxes on most of this type of income.

Where do people learn about cash flow? The rich teach this to their kids at home. Rich dad began teaching his son and me by playing *Monopoly* with us after school. In the game of *Monopoly*, when a person lands on a property and pays $10 rent, that is cash flow.

Question: How do you know the rich work for cash flow?

Answer: It's common knowledge. For example, Steve Jobs worked for a salary of $1 a year. He did not need a paycheck. He did not want ordinary income.

Technically, with earnings of only $1 a year in ordinary income, he would be classified a poor man. Yet he was a multi-billionaire. It was his stock in Apple, the company he created, that made him rich. In effect, he printed his own money by creating a profitable company in which he was a significant stockholder. And while Es and Ss buy shares of stock, Bs and Is sell stock in the companies they create. That is what made Steve Jobs rich.

Question: How do the rich earn money?

Answer: By working in the B and I quadrants, not the E and S quadrants. You'll learn more about this later in this book.

Lessons from the CASHFLOW® *Game*

Pictured below is the board for the *CASHFLOW® 101* game.

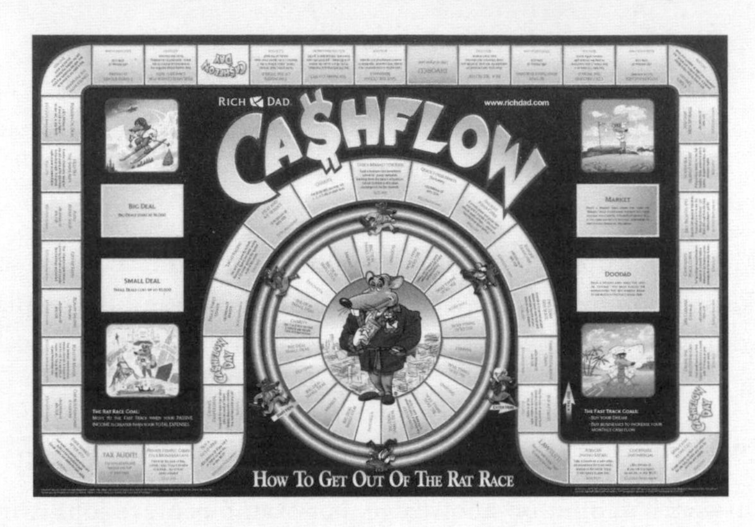

The *CASHFLOW* game offers another illustration of how the rich work and invest.

In the center of the game board is the Rat Race. When schools advise your child to get a good job and invest in the stock market, they direct your child to a life in the Rat Race.

The outside track is the Fast Track. This is where the rich work and invest.

The object of the *CASHFLOW* game is to transform ordinary income (your paycheck) into portfolio income and passive income. When you have enough passive income, you exit the Rat Race and begin to enjoy life on the Fast Track.

CASHFLOW is the only game that teaches players the differences between the three types of income.

As you know, in real life there really is a Rat Race and a Fast Track. Schools and most parents program their children for the Rat Race, a life of living paycheck to paycheck, reacting to the cards life deals them. Financial education gives your child choices. Which track are you advising your child to spend their life on…the Rat Race or the Fast Track?

Question: Is this fair?

Answer: No. But this book is about education. Education is not about being fair.

Most parents want their child to get a good education to get ahead in life. Education is about giving a child an unfair advantage in life. That is why many parents will spend small fortunes sending their child to private schools, hoping a private-school education will give their child a headstart in the world.

When it comes to grades, some students receive As and some receive Fs. Is that about being fair? Is it fair that our schools do not teach students about the three types of income? And while we're on the subject of 'fairness,' is it fair that 47% pay nothing in taxes and 1% pays 37% of the taxes?

Question: Are you saying to cheat on taxes?

Answer: No. I would never recommend cheating on taxes. Quite likely those most tempted to cheat on their taxes would be Es and Ss...because those quadrants have very few tax advantages. The bulk of tax advantages are found in the B and I quadrants.

This book is about education. Education is about having more choices in life. If your child knows there are three types of income, they have more choices. If you have more choices, you do not have to cheat on taxes. The rich avoid taxes legally by knowing what types of income to work for and controlling where their income comes from.

Question: What is the difference between the 47% who pay no taxes and the rich who pay little or nothing in taxes?

Answer: Financial education.

Most of the 47% who do not pay taxes can do very little to improve or change their financial status in life. Most lack the education and technical skills to change quadrants. A few simply lack the ambition or desire to change. Why work and pay taxes when you can just receive a check from the government?

The middle class only knows to work harder and longer for ordinary income. That is why so many go back to school or stay in school longer. Or they work overtime. Or they work at two or three jobs. Or they work hard to earn a raise in pay. All this does is push them into higher ordinary-income tax brackets. So while they may earn more money they keep less of it.

When the middle class invests, most invest for portfolio income, primarily in the stock market. Most buy, hold, and pray that their money will be there when they need it.

The rich have the financial education to acquire passive income. With financial education, the rich have the ability to increase income and reduce taxes by doing what the government wants done. Later in this book, you will find out that the tax code is not about levying taxes, but about tax incentives and how to, legally, reduce taxes.

Much of this book is about how to do what the government wants done. For example, if I provide jobs, I receive tax breaks. If I drill for oil, I receive substantial tax incentives. If I use debt to invest, I receive tax breaks. I also receive tax breaks for providing affordable housing for those that cannot afford to buy a home.

Unfortunately, most students leave school looking for a job rather than learning how to provide jobs. Most people use oil rather than drill for oil. Most people try to get out of debt rather than learn how to use debt. And most students leave school dreaming of buying their own home, rather than providing homes for other people.

> **Leading the Way**
>
> *Only one college in America has a financial education program. The college is Champlain College in Vermont.*

It all comes down to financial education.

The Entitlement Mentality

My primary concern is that the entitlement mentality is spreading. Without financial education, many people adopt an entitlement attitude toward life. I don't blame them. If I were out of money and did not have my rich dad's education, I probably would too.

As an entrepreneur, I have been out of money many times. The difference is that I knew I would become smarter and richer if I solved my own financial problems, rather than expect the government to take care of me.

If our educational system does not start addressing Maslow's second level of needs—Safety—I am afraid the growing entitlement mentality will cause a great country to dissolve into a poor country. It has happened before and, in my opinion, it is happening again.

Unfortunately, it will be decades before our schools offer much financial education. In the meantime, if you as a parent do not supplement your child's education with financial education, much of your child's future earnings will go toward funding entitlement programs—not just for the poor but for our President, judges, retired military, government bureaucrats, teachers, police and firemen, and Social Security and Medicare for America's retirees.

Lessons for Your Child

The good news is that you do not need to be a rocket scientist to understand the three types of incomes and taxes. If I can understand it, so can you. Even if you, as a parent, are learning this for the first time you can apply what you learn immediately. Millions of people around the world have done it. Here's an example. Do you know someone who has started a part-time business, owns a rental property, or represents a network marketing company? Generating income through any of these three avenues is a first step in moving toward passive income. The hardest part is getting started.

Draw these two lessons on a piece of paper and discuss them with your child:

1. **Three Types of Income:**
   - *Ordinary income:* Income of the poor
   - *Portfolio income:* Income of the middle class
   - *Passive income:* Income of the rich

2. **Who Pays the Most in Taxes?**

TAX PERCENTAGES PAID PER QUADRANT

Keep in mind that the intent here is not to discuss taxes but to discuss the importance of financial education, and how the educated choices and decisions a person makes throughout his or her life determines if they'll spend a lifetime working for money, or if they'll put their money to work for them.

The B and I quadrants require financial education and experience. The more you discuss these differences, the more open your child's mind will be to the real world he or she will someday enter. Remember, education is a lifetime process. It is more than an evening discussion.

These two simple examples hold true for most Western countries. When I am teaching, someone will always raise his or her hand and say,

"You can't do that here." I pause and then say, "You might not be able to do it here, but I can." I go through this banter in almost every country in which I teach…even in America. In other words, the rich are welcome everywhere. And the first step is a solid financial education.

The problem is, most will attempt to get rich, working for ordinary income, in the E and S quadrants. When they invest, most will invest for portfolio income from the stock market. Few will ever learn about passive income, or cash flow, unless that education starts at home.

College Student Survey

A CIRP (Cooperative Institutional Research Program) survey of college freshman reported that 81% of all college students want to be very well off financially.

The problem is, most will attempt to get rich, working for ordinary income, in the E and S quadrants. When they invest, most will invest for portfolio income from the stock market. Few will ever learn about passive income, or cash flow, unless that education starts at home.

Question: Why is it so important that my child understand the rules of the rich and how to become rich?

Answer: There are many causes for this financial crisis. An often-overlooked cause is the growing entitlement mentality, an attitude that is spreading across the world. Today, not only do we have poor people believing in entitlement, we have "A" students, the academics of the world, and "B" students, the bureaucrats, lobbying for and supporting more and more entitlement programs.

As Alexander Tyler, a Scottish history professor at the University of Edinborough, said:

"A democracy will continue to exist up until the time that voters discover they can vote themselves generous gifts from the public treasury."

The "A" and "B" students and the poor of the world want to tax the rich, not realizing they are raising taxes and expenses on themselves. They are also destroying the American democracy. They believe the rich are greedy, rather than entertaining the possibility that they are the greedy ones, living off the labors of others. Without financial education, how could they know anything different? All they can see is one side of the coin.

At the beginning of this chapter, I used an example of how the rich—in this case the French movie star Gerard Depardieu—may simply leave the country in search of a more friendly tax environment. True capitalists, like the builder with 400 employees who is unable to afford Obamacare, will just shut the business down. And medical doctors will stop practicing because the Robin Hood theory of finance, "Take from the rich and give to myself," is alive and well among judges, attorneys, and juries.

The United States has not had a new budget since 2009. This is because the battle between rich and poor, or class warfare, is alive and well. The reason the United States cannot balance a budget is simply because the cost of our entitlement programs, for the poor and the working class, runs into the trillions of dollars. Rather than cut entitlements, it is easier for the educated middle class to join the poor and chant, "Tax the rich." Yet it is the middle class that will, ultimately, foot the tax bill.

> ***Your Study Guide***
>
> *We've created an in-depth Study Guide to help structure and support you in driving your child's financial education. The title is* Awaken Your Child's Financial Genius*—because it was created to do just that: awaken your child's financial genius. Most children are interested in money and you can make learning about it fun for them.*

If your child leaves school and finds that high-paying job, the odds are they will join the high-income middle class in the rat race of life, working harder and harder for ordinary income, and paying more and more in taxes. And when they invest, it's likely they will invest in the stock market for portfolio income.

If that is what you want for your child, then a financial education is not necessary. But if you want your child to escape the middle class rat race, then becoming rich is one option. The other option is to be poor.

Living in a free country means you have the freedom to choose to be rich, poor, or middle class. That choice starts at home.

Rather than teach your child that he or she is entitled to free fish for life (the poor), or work for fish (the middle class), I believe it is smarter to teach your child to be a provider of fish (the rich).

The choice is yours.

Final Words

The Central Banks and investment banks of the world have looted billions of dollars from billions of people. It is also true that many greedy rich people have ripped off people in order to gain their wealth.

Yet, when you look at the balance sheet of many countries, it is entitlement programs that are the biggest threats to those countries and the world economy. In the United States, Social Security and Medicare alone are estimated to be $100 to $230 trillion in unfunded liabilities. When you add in all the military, state, and local, entitlement programs, the numbers are beyond imagination.

This is what happens when our schools fail to meet our needs at Maslow's second level. Rather than teach people to fish, we teach people that they are entitled to free fish. From my point of view, that needs to change.

The Creature from Jekyll Island

For anyone who wants to be a professional investor or entrepreneur, I recommend the book *The Creature from Jekyll Island*, written by G. Edward Griffin.

It is a big book, yet it's an easy read, reading more like a murder mystery—because that's what it really is. It's a book about financial murder…about banks and money, especially the U.S. Federal Reserve Bank.

Griffin believed that communism could not take hold in America simply because the American spirit of free enterprise and capitalism, was too strong. An intermediate step was required, and that intermediate step was socialism.

Today we have Social Security, Medicare, and Obamacare.

In other words, Americans have to first become dependent upon their government for life support, which would erode the American spirit. With a weakened and needy spirit, Americans become dependent, addicted to government handouts and entitlement programs. The result is a country ripe for communism. I am not saying that this is true. I leave that decision up to you.

As a person who joined the Marine Corps to fight for capitalism and against communism, then returned home to see the American spirit dying and entitlement mentality growing, Ed Griffin's views have a ring of truth to them. His concerns are my concerns.

This may be why there is no financial education in our schools. G. Edward Griffin states:

> *"Financial dependence on the state is the foundation of modern serfdom."*

It's been said that Abraham Lincoln stated:

> *"You cannot bring about prosperity by discouraging thrift. You cannot strengthen the weak by weakening the strong. You cannot help the wage earner by pulling down the wage payer. You cannot further the brotherhood of man by encouraging class hatred. You cannot help the poor by destroying the rich. You cannot keep out of trouble by spending more than you earn. You cannot build character and courage by taking away man's initiative and independence. You cannot help men permanently by doing for them what they could and should do for themselves."*

Action Step for Parents

Do your part to fight the entitlement mentality:
Don't give your kids money.

Today the Western world is on the verge of economic collapse because millions have the entitlement mentality. This entitlement mentality starts at home. Sometimes it starts by trading money for time or love...in rich and poor neighborhoods alike. Sometimes parents buy their kids clothes, high-end athletic shoes, toys—even cars—so the child can keep up with his or her classmates.

If your child's classmate is given a new bicycle it's easy to feel entitled to an new bicycle, too. That is where the entitlement mentality begins.

Many sports programs teach kids that everyone gets a trophy, even if they lose. What is that teaching a child? That everyone is *entitled* to be a winner?

Rather than teach your child that he or she is entitled to money and success, teach them that money is simply a medium of exchange. Exchange means I give you something and you give me something in return. And, I believe, the more you give the more you will receive. When a child is given something for nothing, the seeds of entitlement are planted.

Also discuss the concept of "give and you shall receive." That's another way of being generous.

I was fortunate. I had two dads and neither one of them gave me money. When I was 16, my real dad told me he would not pay for my college education. That gave me two years to prepare and find a way to fund my college education. That is why I applied for and received congressional nominations to the U.S. Naval Academy and U.S. Merchant Marine Academy. In service academies and in the Maine Corps we were taught to be of service to both god and country.

My rich dad insisted that I work for free. He did not want me to develop the mindset of an employee who would my time for a paycheck. In exchange for my work, rich dad gave me the best financial education in the world. With that financial education I have been able to create wealth out of nothing, which is what entrepreneurs do.

I have written two books with Donald Trump. An added benefit of that has been getting to know his three children. They are bright, attractive, respectful, and do not have an entitlement mentality. They have worked for what they have. Both of his sons, Don Jr. and Eric, have said to me, "Our dad would not hesitate to fire us if we did not do our jobs."

One day, Don Jr., Eric and a few of my friends were together on the island of Kauai in Hawaii. Don and Eric were texting their sister Ivanka. When they were through, I asked them what the three of them were talking about. Both boys said, "We were sharing recipes."

"Recipes?" I replied. "You know how to cook? I thought you had servants?"

Both boys laughed and Eric said, "My parents had servants. We didn't. We had to learn to cook and clean. Our parents made it very clear that their wealth was *their* wealth. We knew from an early age that we were expected to create our own wealth. We know we have had many privileges, but we got very little for free."

Part Two

ANOTHER POINT OF VIEW

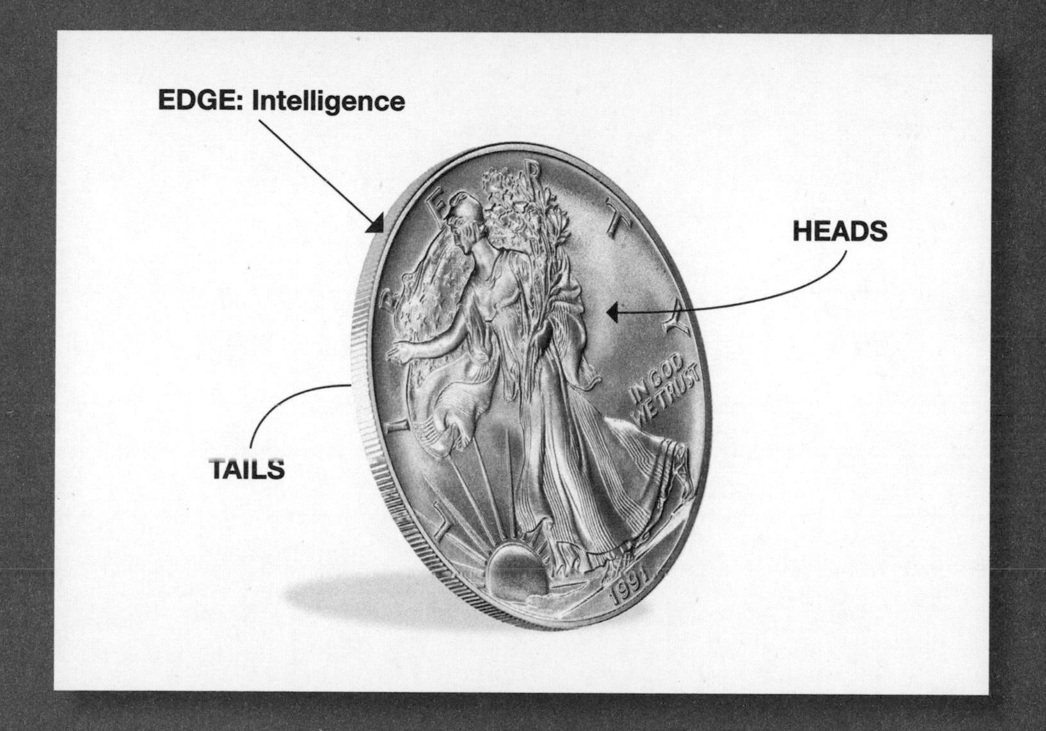

"The test of a first-rate intelligence is the ability to hold two opposed ideas in the mind at the same time, and still retain the ability to function."

– F. Scott Fitzgerald

Part Two
INTRODUCTION

Rich dad said that one of the problems with school is that kids are taught to live in a world of "right" or "wrong." That isn't realistic and it isn't intelligent. In real life there are often more than one answer or solution to questions or problems.

In school there is only one right answer. As teachers grade tests they are looking for right answers.

In school, you are intelligent if your right answers agree with your teacher's right answers. If your answers agree with the teacher's answers, you are an "A" student.

The idea of only *one right answer* is the foundation of academic education.

Right Answers in Real Life

In real life there is more than one right answer.

Here's an example. When I asked my poor dad what 1+1 equaled his answer was "2." Rich dad's answer to that same question was different. His answer was "11."

This is why one man was poor and the other rich.

Definition of First-Rate Intelligence

This statement from F. Scott Fitzgerald supports the core lessons of Part Two of this book:

> *"The test of a first-rate intelligence is the ability to hold two opposed ideas in the mind at the same time, and still retain the ability to function."*

Discussing the two sides of a coin is nothing new. I propose a spin on this and believe that all coins have *three* sides: heads, tails, and the edge. According to F. Scott Fitzgerald, the most intelligent people live on the edge, able to see both sides.

Many students leave school believing that only one answer can be right. Rather than open a student's mind, traditional education closes minds. Kids leave school believing in a world of right or wrong, black or white, smart or stupid. This is the primary reason why so many people do not like school, including many "A" students. If a student never gets to the edge, that vantage point from which they can see both sides, they see only one side of the coin. One answer, one point of view, one perspective.

Rich vs. Poor

Literature that's studied in school is filled with stories of rich vs. poor. Books such as *A Christmas Carol* by Charles Dickens, the story of an unhappy rich man named Scrooge, or stories of Robin Hood, who took from the rich to give to the poor, tend to vilify the rich and honor the poor.

Very few schools recommend their students read *Atlas Shrugged* by Ayn Rand, who takes the other side of the coin, vilifying the socialists and honoring the capitalists.

The Bible, a book of books in which money is the single most discussed subject, is a bit more balanced. It has stories for believers on both side of the coin.

Both Sides

Part One of this book is about financial education.

Part Two of this book is about financial intelligence, the ability to look at the subject of money from the edge of the coin and see more than one point of view.

Fitzgerald refers to "the ability to hold two opposed ideas in the mind at the same time" as the test of a "first-rate intelligence." In other words, the idea of right vs. wrong, which is taught in school, is unintelligent. In fact it is ignorant, since 'right vs. wrong' ignores, rather than explores, the other side.

In my opinion, the idea of right versus wrong is the basis of all disagreements, arguments, divorce, unhappiness, aggression, violence, and war.

Lines and Waves

In school, all teaching is linear, as in the following diagram:

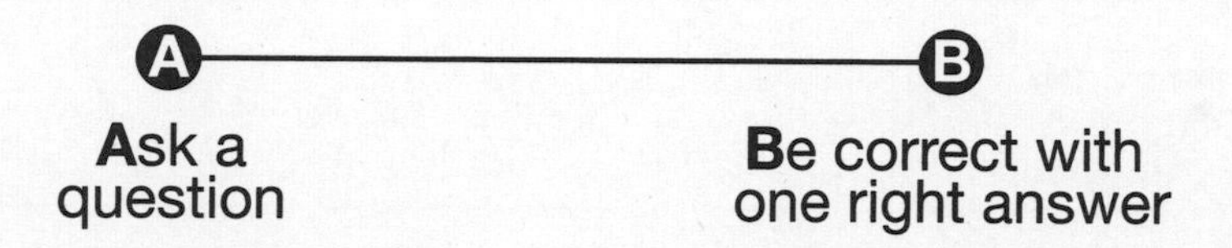

In this method, there is no room for anything but the right answer. For schools, there is only a direct, linear connection between the question and the correct answer.

The problem is that in all other facets of life nothing linear. Nothing is so simple. As R. Buckminster Fuller has noted: "Physics has found no straight lines." Instead, the physical universe consists of only waves undulating back and forth allowing for corrections and balance.

An example of this universal theory is found in NASA's Apollo 11 space mission that landed two Americans, Neil Armstrong and Buzz Aldrin, on the moon. The capsule was on a straight-line trajectory for only 5% of its time in space. There was no one, linear, 'correct answer' for getting there from Point A to Point B. Instead, 95% of the trip was correcting course, left to right, starboard to port, to reach the intended destination.

Think of driving your car. If you followed the school model—direct line from Point A to Point B—you'd be a menace to society. There is definitely an accepted way to drive, and that is to use the steering wheel.

As you leave school you quickly learn that nothing is linear. As you navigate your life's course you'll have ups and downs, course corrections, that create waves of experience and education. This is how we learn—and it is anything but linear.

The following is diagram is an example of the ups and downs of my path:

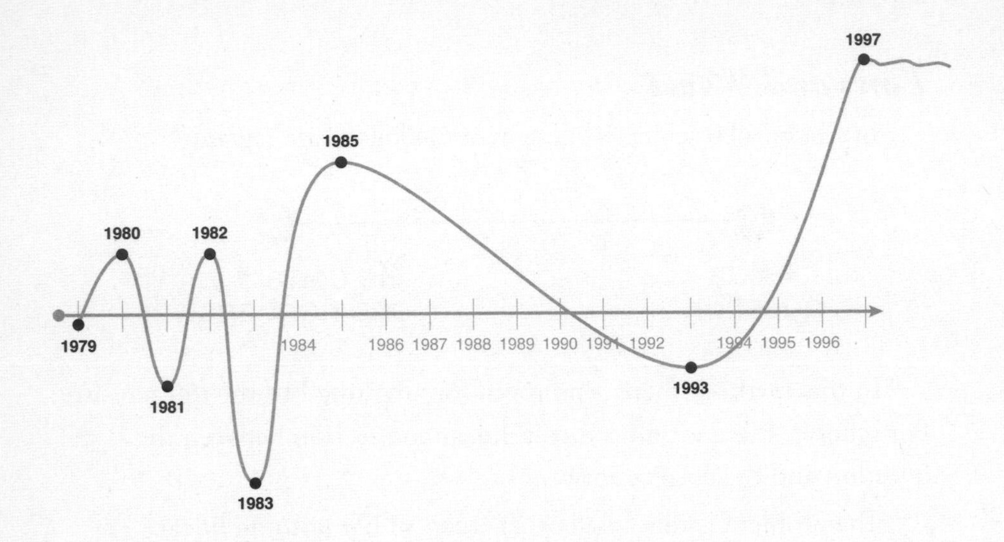

In 1979, two friends and I started the Rippers wallet business. By 1980, life was good. We were millionaires on paper, which led to fast cars and faster women. As you might expect, we took our eye off of the business and by 1981 we hit bottom. But we were resilient and got right back into it. We set up some joint ventures with radio stations in Hawaii and high-profile rock bands (including one of my favorites, Pink Floyd) and by 1982 we were back. But the problems from our first failure were, in hindsight, never fully addressed. A few of the partners had marital problems and that, among other things, led to dissolving the partnership in 1983.

Fortunately, I had started studying entrepreneurship in 1981. And better yet, in 1984 I met Kim and we moved to California later that year to teach entrepreneurship for a seminar company. The business thrived and we expanded internationally to five offices in Australia. One day a reporter from the Australian Broadcasting Company (ABC) showed up. The TV network was interested in our seminars and wanted to report "all the good work we were doing."

That's what they told us. But it wasn't the truth.

Their intention was to expose what they saw as a 'cult.' David Koresh and his Branch Davidian followers (some of them Australian) had died in a government siege outside Waco, Texas in April of 1993. The ABC wanted to expose Americans who were, in their opinion, conducting cult-like activities in Australia. The negative and devastating ABC broadcast sunk our business. (Interestingly, an unsolicited letter-writing campaign by all the people our seminars had helped began immediately. The higher-ups at the ABC soon realized they had a problem: Their report was a monumental falsehood. They recanted the story, out of fear they'd be sued.)

While we certainly had the grounds for a lawsuit (starting with their initial misrepresentation) we chose to view the experience as a sign that we should step back and refocus.

Kim and I realized it was time for a change. In 1994, we started to create the *CASHFLOW 101* board game. It was launched in 1996. And in 1997, the "marketing brochure" I wrote for the *CASHFLOW* game was published as a book: *Rich Dad Poor Dad*. Most of you know the rest of that story, and while we've had a few bumps along the way we have enjoyed a high level of success and personal satisfaction in supporting the important work for financial education advocacy.

The point here is that in the grandness of the physical universe—and the unique journey of your own life—*nothing* is linear. Instead, there are only waves and peaks and valleys.

I encourage you to chart your own life, as I have done and celebrate the high points of your life. On the flip side of the coin, take time to recognize the lessons that the low points have delivered. And explain to your children that there is not one right answer to most of life's questions...but rather a wave of choices, from different perspectives and different points of view.

Opposing Points of View

Part two of this book will explore the opposing points of view found in the CASHFLOW quadrant.

For example,

On the E-S side…	**On the B-I side…**
taxes are bad	*taxes are good*
debt is bad	*debt is good*
the rich are greedy	*the rich are generous*

Communist vs. Socialist vs. Fascist vs. Capitalist

Part Two will tread lightly on the minefields of economic philosophies, philosophies of communism, socialism, fascism, and capitalism. Many people have heard these words and know that they can be very emotionally charged.

Part Two of this book will attempt to diffuse the emotional booby-traps in these words so that people can better decide if they, or their children's schools, are teaching kids to be communists, socialists, fascists, or capitalists.

What Is Intelligence?

Intelligence has many definitions and many meanings. Intelligence, for the purposes of this section, is to simply the ability get out of the trap of a right-or-wrong world that our schools promote and look at the world of money from as many sides, as many perspectives, as possible.

As Abraham Maslow described in his Hierarchy of Needs, the fifth level, the highest level of human existence, is the level of Self-Actualization. Self-Actualization is the level at which a person is able to face the world with a "lack of prejudice" and "acceptance of facts." One such fact might be: There is more than one right answer.

Attaining Self-Actualization also means that a person is generous, giving back rather than being a taker. As I've stated in an earlier chapter, I believe that the reason so many people are greedy is because schools do not prepare people for Maslow's level two, Safety. When people live in fear, when they do not feel safe, it is human nature to become a taker instead of a giver.

The lesson is: "If your mind is open to opposing ideas, your intelligence will go up. If your mind is closed to opposing ideas, your ignorance is in control." Intelligence or ignorance? Your ability to keep an open mind and appreciate multiple points of view is a conscious choice. And one that can open your world, and shape your child's future.

Who Must Be Smarter: Employees or Employers?

Part Two | Chapter Nine

ANOTHER POINT OF VIEW ON INTELLIGENCE

If you read *Rich Dad Poor Dad*, you know my poor dad was very upset that rich dad did not pay me with money for the work I did for him.

Rich dad was a very generous man. He believed in "fair exchange." He also believed that financial education was much more valuable than money.

He paid his employees money. In most cases, he paid them quite well. Many worked for him for most of their lives. He often said, "My employees value money more than financial education. That's why they are employees."

Making the Case

Rich dad did not believe in the concept of *free*. He believed a free education was not valued, which may be the problem with the government's public education program. They're free.

Rich dad had a lot of compassion for my poor dad and the teachers who worked for the government. He often said, "How can teachers teach when kids and parents *expect*, rather than *respect* their free education?" He also felt the concept of a free education, while a noble idea, is one of the reasons the entitlement mentality is so pervasive today. From a young age, children are trained to believe "The government will take care of me."

Rich dad believed the financial education and coaching he was giving me were much more valuable than money. That is why he did not pay me in money. In exchange, I worked for him for "free," doing things that would have cost him money.

Question: How did you survive without money?

Answer: By working for money during my free time.

My Story

My mom and dad started giving me an allowance of $1 a week in high school. Even in the 1960s, a dollar a week did not go far.

Rich dad did not pay me because he did not want me to think like an employee. He felt the rest of the world would teach me to think that way. In other words, he was training me to think differently about money, which was priceless. He did not tell his son and me what to do. He gave us choices.

Rather than telling me to "Look for a job," rich dad encouraged me to think like an entrepreneur and instead "Look for opportunities."

With that advice, I did many things to make money. For example, on Saturdays, I would be up at five o'clock in the morning to surf with my friends, since the surf is usually better in the morning. I would then go to rich dad's office and work for him for a few hours. To earn money, I would then go to the golf course in the afternoon and work as a caddy, carrying a golf bag for 9 holes for $1. It was only a nine-hole course, so I could make $2 by carrying two bags. I could make more on a Saturday afternoon than the *weekly* allowance my parents gave me. On top of that, I got in shape for football season.

The advantage to this was that instead of looking for a job, I was always looking for *opportunities*. By looking for opportunities, rather than a job, rich dad was training me to look at the world as an entrepreneur from the S quadrant of the CASHFLOW quadrant, rather than an employee in the E quadrant.

If I saw a pile of rubbish in someone's yard, I would knock on the door, and negotiate a fee for clearing away the rubbish. It was great education in business, as well as self-esteem.

I got to be pretty good as an entrepreneur in the S quadrant. I was making a nice sum of money, while still working for rich dad for free.

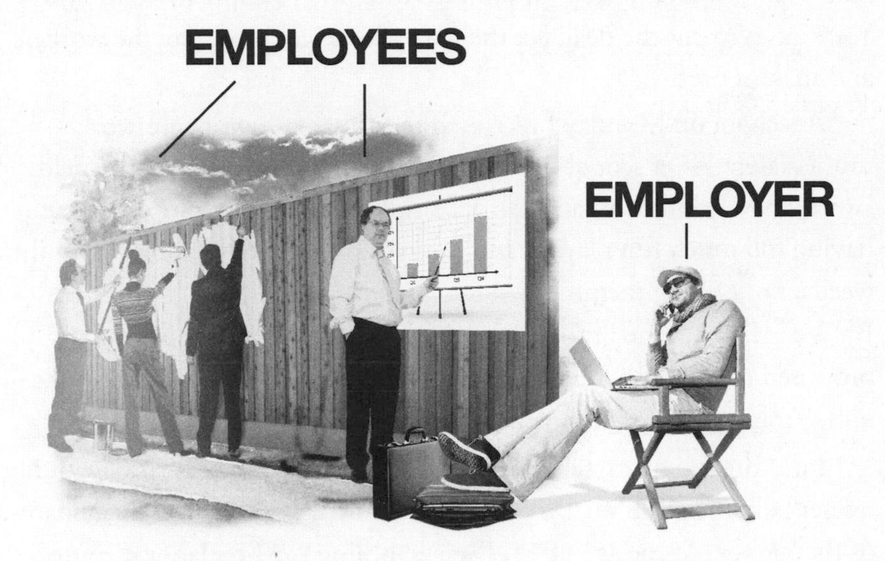

Bigger Opportunities

Once rich dad realized that I was pretty good in the S quadrant, his new lesson was for me to move on to the B quadrant. To begin the lesson, he had me read the story of *The Adventures of Tom Sawyer*. In that story, Tom takes on the task of painting a fence. Rather than paint the fence himself, he gets his friends to paint the fence for him.

Rich dad's assignment was for me to find a job so big that I could not do it myself. He said, "People in the S quadrant take on tasks they can do themselves. For example, a lawyer can do most of the legal work himself. But an entrepreneur in the B quadrant takes on the impossible. That is why they are the richest people in the world."

For about a week, I looked around for a really big opportunity. Finally, I saw a man staring at a rather large field filled with very tall weeds. I went up to him and asked if there was anything he needed done. The elderly man said he needed the weeds in the field cleared. He used to do it himself, he told me, but now he was getting too old. The field was about two acres in size. He told me he would pay me $50 if I would pull, not cut, the tall weeds. Once I heard "$50" I heard nothing else. I took the job, of course. He then told me it had to be done by the next weekend.

Calling rich dad with the news, he added to my assignment. He said, "Like Tom Sawyer, your job is to hire other people to do the work. Your job is to cut the deal, get the work done, get paid, pay the workers, and make a profit."

At school on Monday I recruited ten classmates to begin work immediately. After school on Monday, only six showed up at the field. By Tuesday, not much had been accomplished. My "employees" were having too much fun playing and not working. They were rolling in the weeds, not pulling them.

By Wednesday, none of them showed up to work, even though they promised they would. On Wednesday night, I talked to rich dad, who said, "You had better keep your word and get the job done."

I did the job by myself on Thursday and Friday. On Saturday, the owner paid me the $50. On Monday, my "workers" wanted their share of the money. At the age of 15, I was handling my first labor dispute, which I lost. I paid them because the pain of seeing them every day at school, being harassed, and possibly beaten up, was not worth $50. In the long run, it was an experience I couldn't put a price on.

When I told rich dad the story of doing all the work but not making any money, all he did was smile and say, "Welcome to my world."

In collecting rents for rich dad, sitting around the table at rich dad's office with his advisors, his "A" students, and now dealing with my employees, *my* view of the world of business was taking shape. At 15, and entering my second window of learning, I knew that if I wanted to be an entrepreneur, I had to learn a lot more than people who wanted to be employees. My intelligence was increasing. My mind was opening. I was beginning to see both sides of the coin.

It used to be that instead of going to college you worked as an apprentice. Unlike college, an apprenticeship allowed you to be wrong, to make mistakes, and to take the time to really learn how to do something well. It is no wonder that Donald Trump's television show,

The Apprentice, is so popular. The idea of an apprenticeship, of gaining real mastery over your area of interest, appeals to all of us.

Looking back, I know why rich dad never paid me in dollars. He paid me with an apprenticeship of real-life lessons, lessons that in hindsight have proven to be priceless.

Action Step for Parents

Explain the concept of three sides to every coin.

Select any coin and use it as a teaching tool. Explain to your child that schools and the traditional classroom environment are often focused on right answers. Think of a few examples in which there could be several answers to a question or problem as an example of how to look at things from several different vantage points.

Use the coin to illustrate heads on one side, as one point of view, and tails on the other.

Also discuss the edge of coin, and how intelligence is the ability to use the edge as a vantage point to see and appreciate multiple points of view.

Real-life challenges and questions are seldom as black-or-white or right-or-wrong as schools would have us believe. Intelligence is the ability to see both sides of the coin, from the edge.

Why Your Banker Does Not Ask You for Your Report Card

Part Two: Chapter Ten

ANOTHER POINT OF VIEW ON REPORT CARDS

I was a poor student in school. My report cards were never very impressive.

So when I realized that a banker was more interested in the cash flow of a property than the grades on my report card, I knew I had a shot in life. Thanks to my rich dad, I understood cash flow. And I learned that our report card, in real life, is our financial statement. A banker can tell a lot about a person from their financial statement and in the real world financial intelligence is more prized than As and Bs in school.

Making the Case

Schools have students believe that good grades are important. In this chapter, you will find out why good grades are important in school, but are less important after a student leaves school.

The reason a banker does not ask you for your report card is because your banker is not interested in your academic intelligence. Your banker is interested in your financial intelligence.

Your financial statement is your report card after you leave school. It's your report card as an adult.

The problem is, most students leave school living in the past. A few bask in the glory of having been "A" students in school. Many fail to focus on the report card for their future, their personal financial statements. This is why many "A" students who may have had good grades in school have failing financial report cards as adults. And, on the flip side, why many students who struggle in school become financial geniuses once they leave that academic environment and enter the real world.

Your choices and your actions are determined by which report card is important to you.

What Is a Financial Statement?

A financial statement is made up of two parts: an Income Statement and a Balance Sheet.

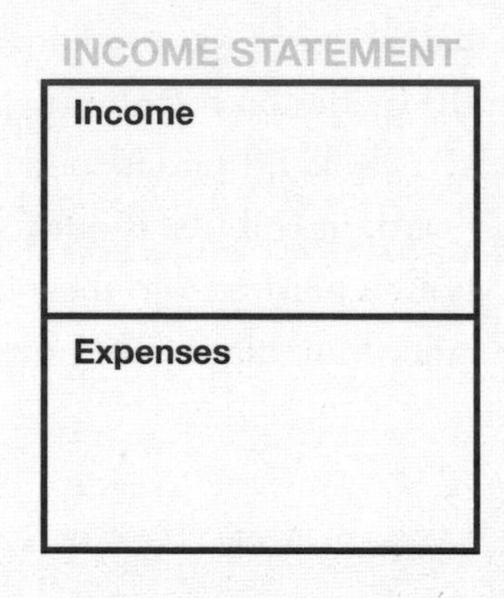

BALANCE SHEET

Assets	Liabilities

Both the income statement and balance sheet work hand in hand. Financial intelligence involves the ability to know and understand the relationship between them.

When most students leave school, their primary focus is on the income statement. They are looking for a job and a paycheck.

They need income to pay for living expenses. The graphic shows the cycle.

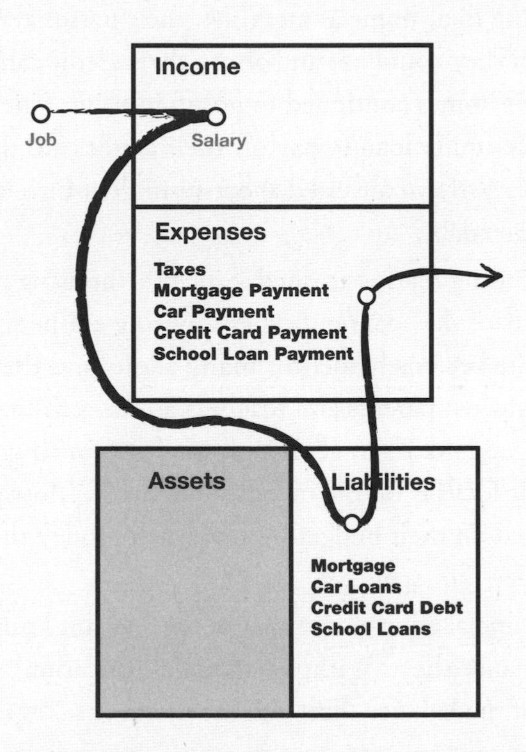

For many young people in America, their first expenses are rent, food, transportation, and entertainment. If they do not have the money, some moms and dads give them the money they need. This does little to increase their financial intelligence.

As they enter the third window of learning, from ages 24 to 36, many get married and start a family. When the first child arrives, so do more expenses. And as most parents know, children become more expensive with age. When children arrive, many parents are forced to grow up.

In the third window of learning, people begin to think about earning more money. Many take their work more seriously. Some go back to school. By the time they are 36, the end of their third window of learning, most young couples are trapped in the Rat Race of life. Life becomes a scramble to earn enough money to cover increasing expenses, with most people living paycheck to paycheck.

Between the years 1971 and 2007, many people survived the Rat Race by using their home as an ATM, their personal Automatic Teller Machine. They could use and abuse their credit cards, because the value of their homes continued to go up in value. They would then apply for a home equity loan to pay off their credit card debt. In the language of money, they converted short-term debt into long-term debt, even lifetime debt.

Then the housing market crashed. Since the housing market is one of the key drivers of the economy, when housing crashed, jobs began disappearing. Life became harder for many adults and their kids. This is what happens when parents and teachers advise a child to "go to school and get good grades to get a high-paying job." If you follow that advice, your focus is on the income statement. Most people spend their lives focused on their budget—how much money they make and how much money they spend.

Without financial education, most people do not know about the power of the balance sheet. Without financial education, most people use the power of the balance sheet against them. It takes financial education to use your balance sheet to make it work in your favor.

Without financial education, many people abuse the balance sheet. The result: They become poorer. The financially educated know how to use the power of their balance sheet to make themselves richer.

My Story

At nine years old, I knew I was going to be rich. Playing *Monopoly*® with my rich dad, I knew I would someday use the power of the balance sheet to become a rich man.

At the same time, my poor dad, then in his thirties, was focused on his income statement. He was constantly in school, taking courses for his Master's degree and his PhD. He was in school to make more money, a bigger paycheck.

When I was 14, my dad finally worked hard enough, saved enough money, and bought his first house. Although I was just a kid, I would cringe every time my poor dad proudly said, "Our house is an asset and our biggest investment." Even at 14, I knew our house was not an asset. I also knew there were better investments than a personal residence. I already knew that four green houses or a red hotel, producing income, were much better investments.

Assets and Liabilities

My poor dad wanted me to do what he was doing, which was to go to school and focus on the income statement:

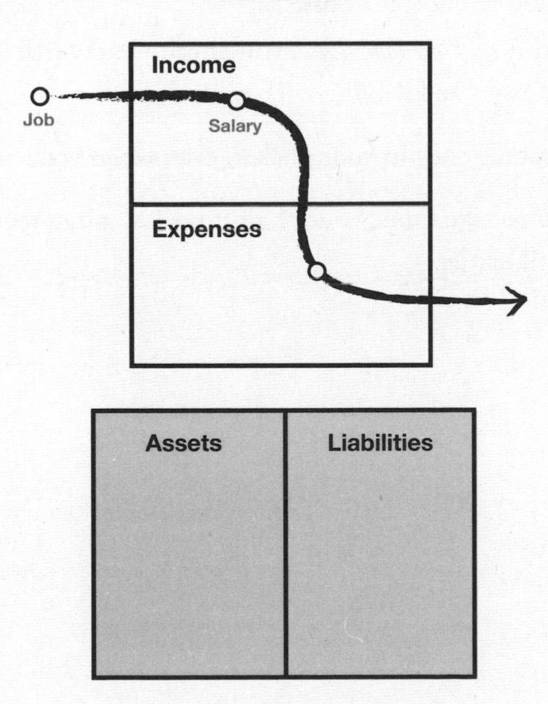

My rich dad was teaching me to focus on the balance sheet.

BALANCE SHEET

Assets	Liabilities

From playing *Monopoly* with rich dad, I knew the power of little green houses and red hotels. You do not have to be a college graduate to know the difference between assets and liabilities. You don't have to be a college graduate to know that a personal residence is a liability, or that green houses and red hotels are assets.

If you read *Rich Dad Poor Dad*, you already know rich dad's simple definitions for assets and liabilities. They are:

- *Assets* put money in your pocket, even when you're not working.
- *Liabilities* take money out of your pocket, often requiring you to work harder.

The following simple line drawings explain the differences between assets and liabilities.

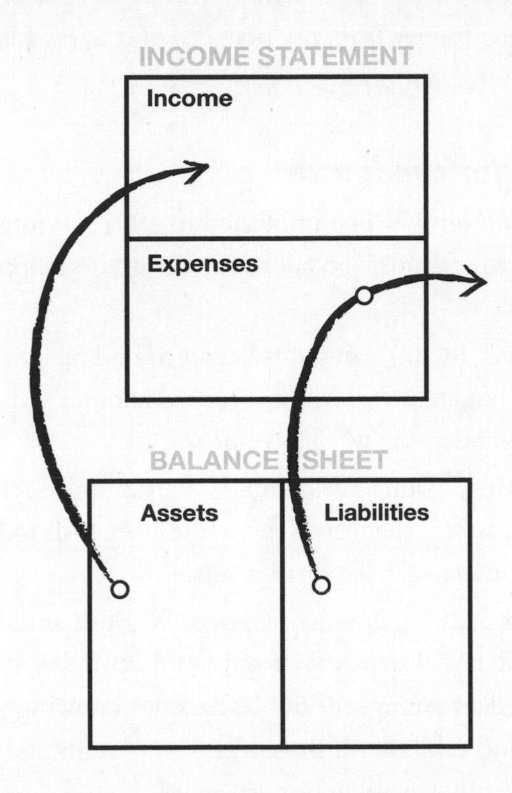

In this simple diagram, you can see the relationship between the income statement and the balance sheet. This relationship is very important. It is the other side of the coin. It takes both documents to determine which are assets and which are liabilities.

If you do not understand the relationship between the income statement and balance sheet, please review it again or ask someone to assist you in understanding it. You may recall that, in the Cone of Learning, discussion is a higher level of learning.

If you do not understand the relationship between the income statement and balance sheet, don't feel that you're alone. Many people—even accountants, attorneys, and CEOs—do not know the importance of that relationship or, in some cases, even how the two are related.

Simply stated, "You cannot tell assets from liabilities without first checking the income and expenses on the income statement."

A financial statement is not rocket science. All a person has to do is ask, "Is this taking money from my pocket?" If it is, it's a liability. If it's putting money into your pocket, it's an asset.

A Warning for the Future

In *Rich Dad Poor Dad*, first published in 1997, I wrote, "Your house is not an asset." My friends who are real estate agents stopped sending me Christmas cards.

Ten years later, in 2007, millions began to find out the hard way that their house was not an asset. Millions learned another important word in the language of money, the word *foreclosure*.

I am not saying, "Don't buy a house." I am simply saying, "Do not call a liability an asset." The reason the world is in crisis today is because our leaders continue to call liabilities assets.

On October 3, 2008, President George W. Bush authorized $700 billion for TARP. TARP stands for Troubled Asset Relief Program. And TARP is an excellent example of our leaders not knowing the difference between assets and liabilities. If those assets were really assets, they would not be in trouble. They would not need relief.

The real problem was that those assets were actually liabilities. If our leaders were financially smart, they would have named the program LRP, for "Liability Relief Program," or RPL, for "Relief Program for Losers."

Even "A" students do not always know the difference between assets and liabilities on a balance sheet. Like my poor dad, most people focus on a paycheck in the income statement. On top of that, they call their personal residence an asset.

No wonder we have a global financial crisis. What do you expect when our leaders—our best, brightest, and most educated—call liabilities the assets!

What Are Assets?

Rich dad's definition of assets applies to anything, not just real estate. Businesses, stocks, bonds, gold, and even human beings can be classified as assets or liabilities. Anything that takes money from your pocket is a liability. Anything that puts money in your pocket is an asset.

Assets cannot exist without liabilities. Remember that there are always two sides to every coin. For example, if you take the time to write down your monthly expenses, you will see where your cash is flowing into someone else's asset column.

If your home has a mortgage, your mortgage payment is your liability. But you and your loan are your banker's asset…as long as you keep paying on that mortgage.

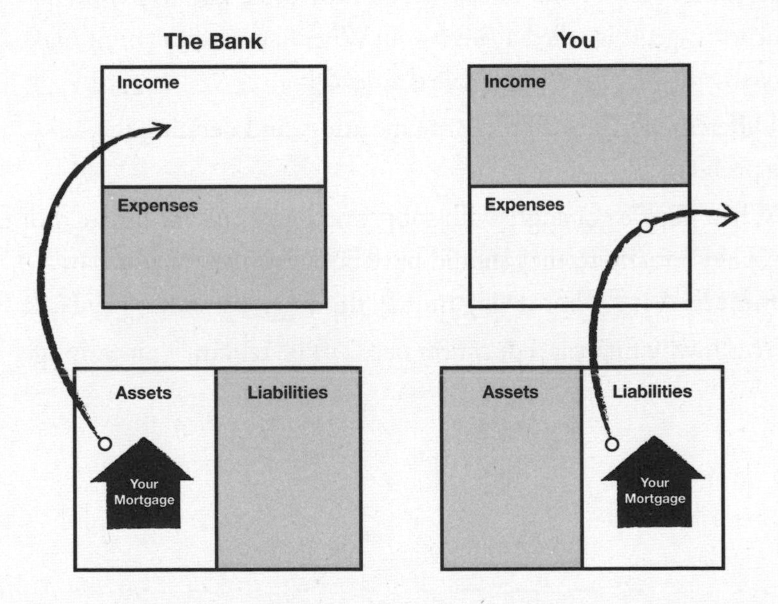

If you stop paying on your mortgage, your banker's asset turns into his liability. Knowing this is key. Assets becoming liabilities is a major factor of the global financial crisis.

The reason banks needed bailout money was simply because people had stopped paying the banks. The result: The bank's assets have become the bank's liabilities.

That is why knowing the power of the balance sheet is essential to your financial well-being. Since many of our leaders do not know the difference between assets and liabilities, it is important that you do.

Consequences

In an earlier chapter, I wrote about the second window of learning,—from ages 12 to 24. During this window a child learns by taking risks without fully understanding the consequences. Young people often learn the hard way about the consequences of their actions.

It seems our banking and political leaders are learning the hard way, too. The problem is that we, the taxpayers, foot the bill for the consequences of their financial ignorance.

In the language of money, when an individual fails to pay on their mortgage, it is called a *foreclosure*. When a country cannot make the payments on its debt, it is called a *default*.

Different words, with the same meaning, and defining the same problem.

When people got angry with subprime borrowers for buying homes they could not afford, they should have been even angrier with our subprime leaders for borrowing money they, too, can never pay back.

This is why financial education needs to be taught at an early age.

Three Financial Classes

When a banker looks at a person's financial statement, it is easy to see which of the three financial classes the person fits in. For example:

THE POOR

Income
$5,000 to $35,000

Expenses
Low expenses

Assets	Liabilities
0	0

The working poor tend to have low-paying jobs and, as a result of that, limited expenses. Generally, they have no assets and no liabilities. Most of the poor rent and use public transportation. This class tends to live at the survival level. They live paycheck to paycheck, if they have a paycheck. If they require banking services, they prefer to use pawn shops or payday-loan companies for emergency financing.

THE MIDDLE CLASS

Income
$50,000 to $500,000

Expenses
Taxes Mortgage payment Car payment Credit card debt Lifestyle expenses

Assets	Liabilities
Savings	Home mortgage Car loans Student loans Credit card debt 401(k) retirement plan

The middle class earns more money but, generally, has more expenses and liabilities. New cars, bigger houses, exotic vacations—as well as *keeping up with the Joneses*—impact the Expense column and the Liabilities.

I am often asked why I place a 401(k) plan as a liability. The answer is simple. Your retirement plan is an unfunded or underfunded liability, that actually takes money out of your pocket.

After a person retires and the retirement plan begins to put money back in your pocket, it then becomes an asset—an asset that, hopefully, provides enough cash flow to cover your living expenses for the rest of your life.

There are three problems with most retirement plans.

1. Due to market fluctuations and inflation, your may never know how much money you really have.

2. You never really know how long you will live.

3. You never really know how much money you will need.

THE RICH

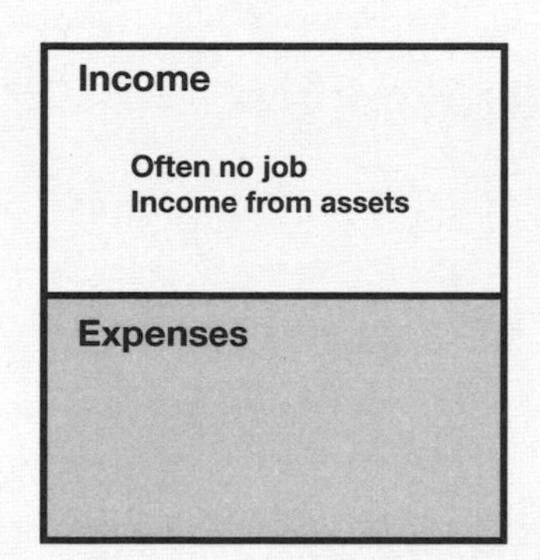

Assets

Businesses
Real estate
Paper assets
Commodities

Liabilities

Obviously, many of the rich have jobs, expenses, and liabilities. But I intentionally left salary from a job and the expenses and liabilities columns blank in order to emphasize the difference between the rich, the poor, and the middle class.

The point I want to make is that the rich focus on the power of their asset column. The middle class, by and large, have few assets and many liabilities. The truly poor have no idea what assets and liabilities are.

This is a copy of the financial statement from Rich Dad's *CASHFLOW 101* game. Notice the highlighted lines in the income column. Those lines represent the income from assets in the asset column.

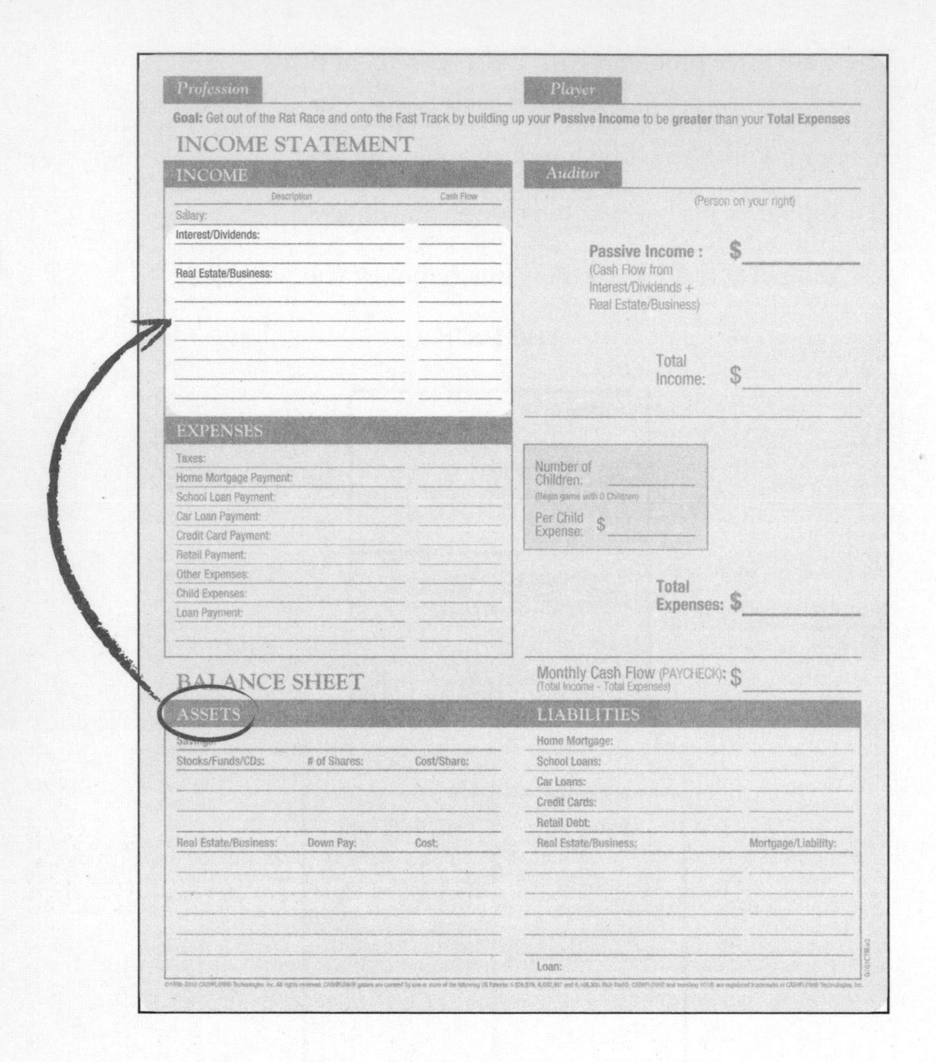

Profession

Player

Goal: Get out of the Rat Race and onto the Fast Track by building up your **Passive Income** to be **greater** than your **Total Expenses**

INCOME STATEMENT

INCOME

Description	Cash Flow
Salary:	
Interest/Dividends:	
Real Estate/Business:	

Auditor

(Person on your right)

Passive Income : $
(Cash Flow from Interest/Dividends + Real Estate/Business)

Total Income: $

EXPENSES

Taxes:
Home Mortgage Payment:
School Loan Payment:
Car Loan Payment:
Credit Card Payment:
Retail Payment:
Other Expenses:
Child Expenses:
Loan Payment:

Number of Children:
(Begin game with 0 Children)

Per Child Expense: $

Total Expenses: $

Monthly Cash Flow (PAYCHECK): $
(Total Income - Total Expenses)

BALANCE SHEET

ASSETS

Savings:

Stocks/Funds/CDs:	# of Shares:	Cost/Share:

Real Estate/Business:	Down Pay:	Cost:

LIABILITIES

Home Mortgage:
School Loans:
Car Loans:
Credit Cards:
Retail Debt:

Real Estate/Business:	Mortgage/Liability:

Loan:

The *CASHFLOW* game was designed to teach players, young and old, to harness the power of the balance sheet. A player's financial intelligence increases the more the player's mind recognizes the power of the balance sheet. There are thousands of subtle financial lessons embedded in all of the *CASHFLOW* games. Since every game is different—different professions (and incomes), different Deal cards, different Doodad expenses, different market conditions—a player's financial IQ increases every time they play.

The more a person plays the *CASHFLOW* game—whether it's *CASHFLOW for Kids, CASHFLOW 101, CASHFLOW 202,* or one of the new Rich Dad social mobile games—the more obvious it becomes why bankers do not ask you for your school report card. The more you play the game, the more you realize why your banker does not care if you were an "A" student, "B" student, or a college dropout like Steve Jobs, Bill Gates, or Mark Zuckerberg.

A banker wants to know:

- If you know how to harness the power of the balance sheet
- If you know the difference between assets and liabilities
- How many assets you really own
- How much money your assets are putting in your pocket

If you can teach your child what your banker wants to know, then you have given your child a massive financial headstart in life.

Action Step for Parents

Discuss why bankers do not ask for your report card.

Talk about school report cards and what they measure and represent. Then discuss the types of reporting related to money and finance. The goal of credit ratings (like a FICO score) or credit reports are much the same as a report card. They communicate how a person is doing in terms of managing their financial life. As a person begins to make purchases and invest, the lender—a creditor, bank, mortgage company, or auto dealership—will make determinations related to a person's credit worthiness based upon credit scores or a person's financial statement.

If a person is seeking a business loan or financing for an investment property, a banker will ask for a financial statement.

A financial statement is your real-world report card. It shows a banker your financial strength and the level of your financial education and that is important information to a banker.

If you have a financial statement, share it with you child…to the extent that parts of it are age-appropriate. It's a great tool to reinforce new vocabulary words and the concepts of income and expenses and assets and liabilities.

The real game board of the *CASHFLOW* game is the financial statement that players fill out and update as the game unfolds. The *CASHFLOW* games teach players, young and old, the power of the financial statement…and how to see the world through a banker's eyes.

Give
and You
Shall
Receive.

Part Two | Chapter Eleven

ANOTHER POINT OF VIEW ON GREED

Many people believe the rich are greedy. That's one point of view. Certainly there is another side to this coin.

A capitalist is often driven by this principle: The more people I serve, the more effective I become. Capitalists serve people in many ways, the least of which is stepping up to the challenge of free markets in producing more with less...including better products and services at better prices. From my point of view, that's not greed. It's ambition and drive.

Should they become wildly successful and insanely wealthy... I first think of all they jobs they create and the innovations they bring to our lives. They've enriched other lives on the road to becoming rich...and I have a hard time labeling that as "greed."

Making the Case

A California government retiree is claiming that the reduction in his government pension is "elder abuse." Bruce Malkenhorst, 78, is fighting CalPERS, California Public Employee's Retirement System, for reducing his retirement pension. His pension was reduced from $45,073 per month, or $540,000 year, to just $9,644 a month or approximately $115,000 per year.

Elder Abuse

Bruce Malkenhorst also claims that denying him an additional $60,000 a year for golf fees and massages is another example of elder abuse. His justification for his high retirement pay and fringe benefits, such as regular massages and free golf is, "I'm from an era where you made as much as you could for as long as you could."

This sounds like greed to me.

Malkenhorst is not an isolated example. The city where he was *making as much as he could for as long as he could* is the tiny industrial town of Vernon, near Los Angeles, with a population of just 100 people. How can 100 people (112, actually, as reported in the last census) afford such dedicated public servants? Six other government officials of Vernon are also under investigation.

In the end, Bruce Malkenhorst was fined $10,000 and ordered to pay back $60,000 in green fees. It seems that government workers protect their own.

Throughout the world, there seems to be a popular sentiment that capitalists are greedy—hence the term, capitalist pigs. A person does not have to be rich or a capitalist to be greedy. One definition of greed is, "wanting more than you are willing to give."

When a mutual fund takes 80% of their clients' gains, that is greedy. When a politician does "favors" for special interest groups that can benefit the politician, that is greedy. When a worker expects to be paid for more than they produce, that is greed. When an employer cheats an employee, the employer is greedy. There are as many greedy poor people as greedy rich people. It seems to me that greed knows no boundaries, class or otherwise.

America's New Civil War

In the 1860s, America was embroiled in a Civil War, a war between the North and the South, a war fought over the economic and moral issue of slavery.

Today, America is engaged in a new civil war. This time it's a civil war between civil servants and the people they serve.

In 2012, a battle broke out in the state of Wisconsin. The fight was an election to unseat (recall) their newly elected governor. Many workers were angry with Governor Scott Walker for cutting their pay and retirement benefits, benefits the state could no longer afford to pay. All across America, people and the press began taking sides.

Although the recall failed, the battle in Wisconsin brought to light the generous pay and benefits that government employees enjoy. No longer are civil servants the low-paid servants of the people. Once taxpayers realized that public servants were being paid more than many private-sector workers, the civil war spread to other states.

In California, arguably one of the most socialist states in America, total pension costs for government employees rose by *2,000 percent* between 1999 to 2009. In 2011 alone, California spent $32 billion on public-employee pay and benefits, which is up 65 percent over the past 10 years. At the same time, spending on higher education is down 5 percent.

In bankrupt San Bernardino, California, one third of the city's population of 210,000 live below the poverty line, making it the poorest city of its size in California. But a senior police officer can retire in his 50s, and take home $230,000 in one-time payouts on his last day on the job, as well as a guaranteed, $128,000-a-year pension.

When police officers or other civil servants retire with that much in pension benefits, many cities cannot afford to hire replacement police officers. The size of police forces across the country is decreasing—and this may be one of the major reasons. Is this public service or personal *self-service*?

The police unions put money behind city council elections and the city council poured money into pay and pensions for unionized employees. And three months before the city of San Bernardino declared bankruptcy, the city council paid out an additional $2 million to retiring city employees. Other words, in addition to greed, come to mind.

California's civil war spread to the cities of San Diego and San Jose when voters in those cities cut benefits and pensions to government workers. Once again, the voters' anger flared. They were tired of government workers ripping off the people they were hired to serve. And example of what fueled the anger: It's projected that pension and retiree healthcare costs would equal 75% of San Jose's public safety payroll and 45% of its non-safety payroll by 2014. In order to afford these high-paid public servants, the city was forced to close libraries, cut back on park services, lay off government workers in other departments, and ask the remaining civil servants to take a cut in pay.

Twenty-five years ago, San Jose, the tenth-largest city in the United States, had approximately 5,000 public servants. Although the city sits in the heart of Silicon Valley, San Jose can afford only 1,600 public servants today. For years, it seems, public servants were serving themselves, resulting in fewer public servants and less and less service.

And this isn't just a problem in California or the United States. In many ways, the problems with public servants in California are the same problems Greece and France are facing—more and more money paid for less and less service.

Ohio's government pension liability is now 35 percent of the state's entire GDP. Residents will have government services cut while their public servants, many of whom are paid more than most of the people they serve, enjoy a guaranteed retirement with generous cost-of-living increases year after year. Is this public service…or greed?

How Did This Happen?

All over America, powerful public-sector unions are asking for regular pay increases. Politicians give in to the unions because they need union support at election time. Due to balanced-budget requirements, most governors and mayors are limited in terms of how much they can grant in salary hikes. Instead, they hand out generous pension benefits that will impact the state's budget years after the politicians themselves are out of office and enjoying a comfortable retirement. In other words, politicians, bureaucrats, and unions have been stealing from our kids' future.

That is why America is fighting a new civil war. The elections in Wisconsin, San Jose, and San Diego mark the beginning of America's war against greedy *government* pigs, rather than greedy capitalist pigs.

Foolish Government Bureaucrats

At the heart of this civil war are corrupt government pension plans. In theory, government employees and the city and state governments must finance their retirement plans with monthly employee and employer contributions. The size of their contributions is determined by assumptions made in the investment plan. The better the assumptions on rate of return, the less the workers and the government need to contribute.

The big problem is with the assumptions that the state governments have been using. The assumption was that the stock market would grow 40 percent faster in the 21st century than it did in the 20th century. The stock market grew 175 times in the 20th century. To make their assumptions, the stock market will have to grow 1,750 times in the 21st century. Can government bureaucrats truly be that naïve? Who can actually believe the stock market will grow at that rate? While 1,750 times growth might be possible, anyone who bets their future on such projections must also believe that pigs will fly in the 21st century.

Words of Warning

Long before the financial crisis took down giant banks like Lehman Brothers in 2008, Warren Buffett warned the world about derivatives. He called them "weapons of mass financial destruction." A derivative is like the juice of an orange. The juice is the derivative of the orange itself. Just like a mortgage is a derivative of a piece of real estate. A more technical definition of derivative is: A security whose price is dependent upon or derived from one or more underlying assets and its value is determined by fluctuations in the underlying asset.

Today Buffett, often called "the Oracle of Omaha," is sounding a new alarm. He is calling the costs of public-sector retirees a "time bomb, the biggest single threat to America's fiscal health."

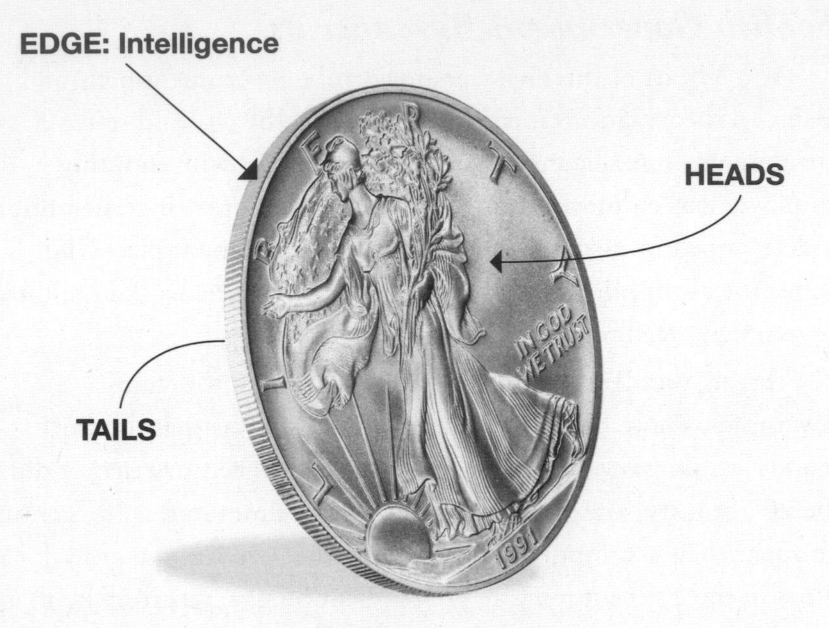

The Other Side of the Coin

A friend of mine in Phoenix, Arizona, Councilman Sal DeCicio, has been fighting government greed and corruption for years. His fight has come at a price. He and his family have been threatened many times, yet he continues to fight. I asked him to write about the battle he fights in Phoenix.

These are his words:

As a Phoenix City Councilman, I've learned that the Number One rule of government is to not to serve the public, but to serve and protect yourself. This applies across our country in every city, county and state.

What if you found out some government employees were handed a check for $500,000 or more when they retired? Retired in their 50s, with generous pension and health care benefits for life?

Would you be upset to learn this...and would you look at government differently if you found out this were true? Well, that is exactly what is happening. And it is happening, to some degree, in every city in the nation.

If you think government is out to protect you and your family, you are wrong. They will protect themselves at your expense. And they make you believe that they are protecting you as they protect themselves.

Let's take the most cherished positions in government: firefighters. They save cats from trees and rush into buildings when we run out. It also doesn't hurt that most are good looking and buff. Who doesn't love a firefighter? Let's see if that image fits reality.

In Phoenix, and in most U.S. cities, a firefighter can typically walk away with about $500,000 in pension after working for 25 years—in addition to a generous retirement with health and many other benefits.

Here are some stats:

- *$340,000 is handed to them at full retirement. In a firefighter's last five years of work the employee officially "retires," but keeps working and drawing a salary. While still working and drawing their salary, they collect a pension for the next five years, put into an account with a taxpayer-guaranteed 8% return.*
- *5% of gross pay goes into a tax-deferred 401(a) account—regardless of employee contribution. That's about $94,000 over a 25-year career, not including gains. This is in addition to the firefighter's pension.*
- *$33,880 by selling back accrued sick pay. This is the big scam. These employees are allowed to accrue sick leave year after year—and it never disappears. The accrued sick days act as casino chips at retirement.*

  They get to cash them in, and it bumps their pension benefits too. Ready for the double whammy? Pensions are based on a firefighter's last few years of pay and those sell-backs and other devices spike their pension…a pension they receive for the rest of their lives (with 80% going to a surviving spouse). The union contract also guarantees the most senior (and therefore highest paid) employees get first shot at overtime, another means by which to spike pension.

- *$76,000 in post-employment health benefits, paid out as they are used. That's firefighters. What about an entry-level clerk? Here are few benefits they receive…in their first year on the job:*
    - *40.5 days off a year (holiday, vacation and sick days)*
    - *$8,000 in annual education benefits*
    - *$150 contributed weekly to a post-employment health plan*
    - *Pension funding by the city at 20% of pay; employee contributes 5%*
    - *Cadillac health care funding at $150 per month for postemployment health benefits.*

So how did public workers here fare during the Great Recession? While millions of Americans lost their jobs and homes, Phoenix government employees received pay raises, called "step increases," averaging 4.5% a year. Then they announced they were taking cuts in pay, to make it seem as though they were making sacrifices like millions of other Americans. For most, the "cut" was a cut in the pay raise that they got, not their base pay. What about layoffs? Phoenix has 17,000 employees and only 15 got a pink slip. Small companies were hit much harder.

During the Great Recession, average compensation per public servant went up more than $20,000 from $80,347 (in 2005-06) to $100,980 (in 2011-12). That's about 26%. How did you do during those years?

So while millions have been scraping by to make ends meet and keep their home during the recession, taxpayers have been paying more to ensure government workers get healthy pensions. Many employees "pension hop," which means they retire in their 50's and move to another government entity—sometimes to a position similar to the one from which they just retired. They get another pension and start the cycle all over again.

These are just the high points of public employees' benefits that taxpayers pay for. There are many smaller perks, like free bus and light rail passes. It's also worth noting that it's nearly impossible to have anyone fired. Phoenix once had an employee being paid while on Death Row.

If government workers were compensated on a par with private sector employees—and if they had competition for their jobs, like in the private sector—you would have a different relationship with government. You would either have more money in your pocket or more services, or some combination of the two. And the people who served you in government would be responsible to a standard of good service, not to their union representative.

Respectfully submitted,
City Councilman Sal DeCicio • 2012

Please note that it is not my intention to criticize public servants as professionals. Government workers, including teachers and especially police and firefighters, perform essential and sometimes dangerous functions of civilized society. I realize and appreciate that their professionalism protects and serves my family, business, property, and community on a 24-hour, 365-days-a-year basis. This purpose of this book is raise questions and challenges on issues that are tied, in my opinion, to a lack of financial education, which leads to an entitlement mentality, a mentality that causes all of us, public and private, to suffer.

My Story

My poor dad, a schoolteacher, was truly a public servant. He dedicated his life to education. He even took two years off from work and a cut in pay to serve in the Peace Corps. He signed up the moment President Kennedy announced the creation of that service organization. The years my mom and dad spent in the Peace Corps were some of the happiest years in my family's life, although the sacrifices were high.

But as the years went on, my dad's bitterness grew. He grew angrier and angrier with his classmates who chose to go into business while he chose government service. My dad resented the fact that he was successful professionally, but not financially, while some of his classmates enjoyed both professional and financial success.
As his classmates grew richer, my dad began calling them "fat cats" rather than "friends."

At first, he was not an active member of the teachers union. But as his resentment toward his fat-cat classmates grew, his involvement in union activities increased. He eventually became the leader of the HSTA, the Hawaii State Teachers Association. It was from this position, as the head of one of the most powerful unions in Hawaii, that he vented his frustrations at his fat-cat friends.

If not for my rich dad's lessons on money, I might have grown up siding with my poor dad. I, too, might have grown up thinking that the rich are greedy.

Why Bankers Want to See Your Financial Statement

By the age of 12, I understood financial statements. Because I understood financial statements, I could tell who was greedy and who was not. It hurt to realize that it was my poor dad who was greedy, not my rich dad.

Comparing my poor dad's financial statement against my rich dad's financial statement was an eye-opening experience. The following is a comparison of their balance sheets.

	Poor dad	**Rich dad**
Jobs created	0	Hundreds of jobs
Housing provided	0	Hundreds of units

My poor dad was a highly-paid government employee. My dad did not own a house until he was in his 40s. Our family rented the home we lived in. Although he hired people, he never created any jobs. Taxpayers paid the salaries and benefits of the workers he hired. If my poor dad hired a bad employee, the taxpayers paid for his hiring mistakes. He didn't. And in many instances, my dad could hire, but he could not fire. That is one reason why many of our government institutions are so inefficient.

In contrast, my rich dad created hundreds of jobs and paid tens of thousands of dollars in salaries every month. His investment in real estate provided homes for hundreds of low-income renters.

My poor dad could not see my rich dad's actions as generous. From his point of view, my rich dad was a greedy person who exploited workers and took advantage of people like him, people who could not afford to purchase their own home.

My two dads were on opposite sides of the same coin. Each one thought he was right and the other one was wrong.

This is the same battle as America's new civil war, a battle between government workers and taxpayers, between the rich and everyone else. Which side a person is on depends upon the person's definitions of the words *greed* and *generosity*.

Having two dads, I could see both sides…from the edge of the coin.

Beyond Emotions

Having two dads got me past the emotions and down to the facts. The real battle between capitalists and everyone else is the asset column. Capitalists make the asset column a personal priority. Socialists don't. They tend to see the asset column of capitalists as public property.

As is often the case, a picture is worth a thousand words.

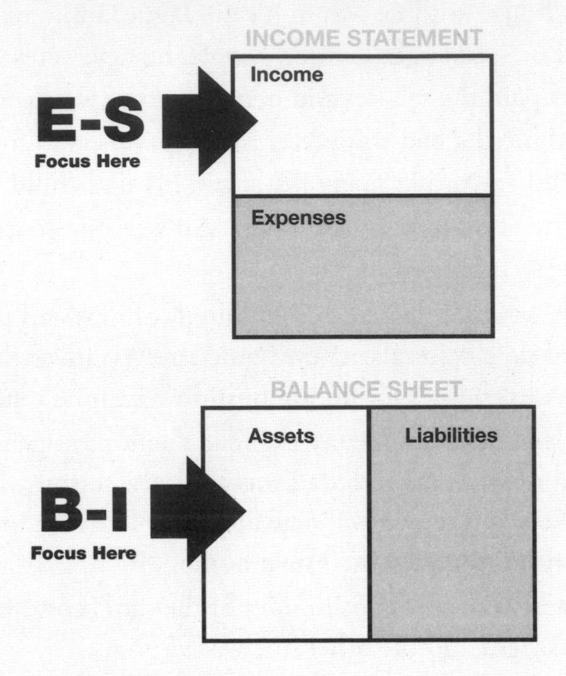

The Most Important Concept

The lack of financial education in school is one of the causes of the battle between the rich and everyone else. I believe that if children knew the difference between assets and liabilities, the gap between the rich and poor would be narrower—or at least the poor and middle class might realize why the rich are growing richer and decide to put what the rich know to work in their lives.

Many people have the "Tax the rich" or the Robin Hood "Take from the rich and give to the poor" philosophy of government. Many people believe the rich are greedy. Period. I see another side of the coin. I know of many rich people who are generous, with both their time and their resources.

If this economic crisis is not solved soon, this centuries-old sentiment against the rich will soon dominate the economic, social, and political agendas. It may be disguised as "taking from the rich and giving to the poor," but the core issue will be financial ignorance caused in part by the lack of financial education in schools.

The Four Economic Groups

Today, there are four economic groups.

1. The poor
2. The middle class
3. The rich a million dollars a year in income
4. The mega-rich a million dollars a month or more

Here are some examples of rich versus mega-rich:

- **A medical doctor may be rich.**
  The owner of a pharmaceutical company may be mega-rich.
- **A professional athlete may be rich.**
  The owner of the sports team who signs the athlete's check may be mega-rich.
- **A lawyer who lives in a mansion may be rich.**
  A person who invests in apartment houses has a better chance of becoming mega-rich.

Young people should know those differences. It will help them see both sides of the coin and give them more choices in life.

What Is a Millionaire?

Many people dream of becoming a millionaire. The question is, what kind of millionaire?

The following are examples of different types of millionaires.

Net Worth Millionaires

This is the largest group of millionaires. Many people in the middle class are in this category. An example would be a baby boomer who bought their home in 1975, for $100,000, just as inflation took off. That $100,000 home today may be valued at $2.5 million—and the homeowner may own it free and clear. They may have a portfolio of stocks worth $500,000. This person is a net-worth millionaire. The problem is, many in this category still worry about day-to-day living expenses, since they may have little cash flow from their net worth.

Rich dad's accounting does not follow traditional accounting methods. Rich dad based his accounting on "cash flow." If something "put money in his pocket" it was an asset. If it "took money from his pocket," it was a liability. In this example, the $2.5 million home is not an asset, since it is taking money from his pocket for expenses such as repairs, upkeep, insurance, utilities, and taxes. If the homeowner sells his house, the house would *then* be an asset, putting money in his pocket, as capital gains rather than *cash flow.* The $500,000 in stocks may or may not produce cash flow from dividends.

Millions of Americans are "net-worth millionaires," which means they are millionaires on paper only. Very little cash is flowing into their pockets.

High-Income Millionaires

These are millionaires who receive million dollar paychecks from the E and S quadrants, people like CEOs, high-income employees, lawyers, professional athletes, doctors, film stars, and lottery winners.

Although they are millionaires *in income*, many of these millionaires still worry about losing their job or running out of money if they stop working for any reason.

Cash-Flow Millionaires

These people receive income from assets. They are the truly rich. They do not need a job. This is why Steve Jobs did not need a paycheck and took a salary of only $1 each year.

When people refer to "the 1%," the truly rich in America, most of this group of rich people are in this category of cash-flow millionaires.

What Are Your Teaching Your Children?

Kids learn by example and mirror what they see and hear. Exposing your child to seeing multiple points of view—both sides of coin on a variety of thoughts—opens their mind to new ideas and new ways of thinking. Many parents encourage their child to "Go to school to find a high-paying job" in the E quadrant, rather than learn to create high-paying jobs for as many people as possible in the B quadrant. Which path will your child travel?

Many people focus on buying their dream home rather than investing to provide homes for others. Many people invest for the long-term in a pension plan for themselves rather than investing in assets for cash flow...assets that can be passed on to their children or charities for years and generations to come. Challenge yourself, and your children, to see another side of the coin on greed.

> **Rich Dad Lesson**
>
> *Rich dad encouraged his son and me to become generous rich people by becoming "cash-flow millionaires." It was a little easier for Mike because he inherited his father's assets. I started with nothing.*
>
> *Today Kim and I provide over a 1,000 jobs, have over 4,000 rental units, as well as books, games, and oil wells...assets producing millions in cash flow. If we stop working, the money continues to come in. When we pass on, these assets will continue to provide cash flow for the charities that are the beneficiaries of our estate.*
>
> *In our minds, we had to be generous if we were to produce cash flow that would be sustainable, to continue for generations to come. Yet, in the minds some people, we are greedy capitalist pigs.*

In Conclusion

The real issue between the rich and the poor and the middle class is one of focus. The rich focus on acquiring assets in the asset column. The poor and middle class focus on their income, how much money they earn, in the income column. The poor and middle classes then tend to save money, even as their own government bureaucrats devalue the purchasing power of their savings. Rather than understand—and address—their financial problems, many of those in the poor and middle classes get angry with the rich, accusing them of being greedy.

The gap between capitalists and everyone else begins when a parent says to their child, "Go to school to get a job," rather than, "Go to school and learn to acquire assets."

The poor own few real assets. This is also true for the majority of the middle class. Notice that I'm referring to real assets—investments that put money in your pocket every month. Most only have jobs or professions.

- Most people have only one job, their own.
- Most people have only one house, their own.
- Most people have one retirement plan, their own.

The true principle of capitalism is, "The more people I serve, the more effective I become." That is why those in the B and I quadrants must be generous. You must be generous if you want to serve as many people as possible.

Many of us are familiar with this Bible verse:

"Give, and you will receive. Your gift will return to you in full—pressed down, shaken together to make room for more, running over, and poured into your lap. The amount you give will determine the amount you get back."

– Luke 6:38 (NLT)

Unfortunately, many people want to be paid more, do less, and retire early. Doesn't this violate the principle of generosity?

So who has to be the most generous?

When offering your child another point of view, please discuss the power of generosity, the principles of being generous—regardless of the quadrant they choose—and results of being generous and sharing, rather than greedy.

Action Step for Parents

Discuss what generosity means and ways everyone can be generous.

Ask your child to think about ways in which he or she is generous. They may be surprised to see how may small but meaningful ways generosity is a part of their everyday life. Generosity is sharing their toys, being patient when Mom or Dad is busy, being kind and helpful to a younger brother or sister, volunteering at a homeless shelter, and tithing.

It is important for your child to know that greatest entrepreneurs such as Henry Ford, Walt Disney, and Thomas Edison have been very generous people, creating millions of jobs and tremendous wealth for the country and the world. This may inspire your child to learn to be more generous rather than believe *capitalists*, or the rich, are greedy people and that *capitalism* is a four-letter word.

Debt Can Make You Rich

Part Two | Chapter Twelve

ANOTHER POINT OF VIEW ON DEBT

Often the only financial education that students or young people get is to "save money" and "get out of debt." Many say that's the smart thing to do. In this chapter you will learn why these are outdated ideas that may, in fact, put speed limits (and speed bumps) on your child's road to financial freedom.

Making the Case

In 2012, a 5-star hotel near our home in Phoenix was sold to the government of Singapore, purchased via the Singapore Sovereign Wealth Fund. Where did that money come from? The money came from Americans who used their dollars to buy TVs, computers, iPhones and other products made in Asia—products that lose value over time. Those dollars then return to the United States to buy our wealth, assets that increase in value over time.

Today, the employees who work for the hotel are now employees of the country of Singapore, assisted by financing from international banks.

Losing our Wealth and our Jobs

This is an example of globalization. The American people, always in search of a bargain in the name of "saving money," send the money they earn to countries that produce these low-cost bargains. That money costs them their jobs and as well as our country's wealth. It is an expensive lesson in global economics.

Globalization also means the U.S. government has already surrendered massive amounts of political and economic power to global organizations such as the United Nations, the WTO (World Trade Organization), the IMF (International Monetary Fund) and the World Bank. In particular, the U.S. economy, in large part, has been merged into the emerging one world economy. For the average person, globalization means your leaders are *not* your leaders, nor can they protect you.

Lessons from History

President Richard Nixon did two things to contribute to our modern economic crisis.

1. In 1971, President Nixon took the U.S. dollar, the world's reserve currency, off the gold standard.
   The *gold standard* was converted into the *debt standard*, and for over 40 years, the world economy boomed. Inflation took off, debtors became winners, and savers were losers.

   Immediately, housing prices began to go up. Homeowners, many who never expected to be rich, suddenly discovered they were because their house had "appreciated" in value. In reality, it wasn't that the value of their home had appreciated, it was the value of the dollar *depreciating*.

2. In 1972, President Nixon opened the door to trade with China, and suddenly low-priced Chinese goods began flooding the U.S. market. American production and manufacturing shifted gears and Americans became consumers first and producers second. And as Americans bought more and more low-priced Chinese products, more American jobs were exported to China. As American factories closed, some were actually packed up and shipped to low-wage countries such as China, Guatemala, and countries in Eastern Europe.

> American wages were stagnant, but Americans *felt* wealthy as long as their home continued to "appreciate" in value. Instead of earning more money, Americans began using their credit cards to keep on shopping. And rather than pay off their credit cards, Americans used their homes as ATMs and refinanced their homes to pay off their credit-card debt.

The fairy tale ended in 2007. Houses dropped in value and were soon worth less than the mortgage. People lost their jobs because spending dried up. Many lost their homes.

In 1913, President Woodrow Wilson signed a bill creating the Federal Reserve Bank of the United States. Did President Wilson sign willingly…or was he coerced by the "power somewhere so organized" as to allow the creation of the Federal Reserve Bank of the United States?

Is this what Amschel Mayer Rothschild meant when he said:

> *"Give me control of a nation's money and I care not who makes the laws."*

I have asked myself many times: Is this why there is no financial education in our schools? Is this why our schools advise students to work hard, save money, get out of debt, and invest in a government-sponsored retirement plan?

Debt Is Good

The average person believes debt is bad. And debt *is* bad for most financially uneducated people. This is why they listen to financial "experts" who say, "Get out of debt. Cut up your credit cards and save, save, save!"

If a person had a basic financial education, they would have some financial intelligence, be able to stand on the edge of the coin, and look at the other side of the coin…the side where debt is good, and debt makes you rich, and debt can be tax-free wealth.

Turning Debt into Gold

For centuries, alchemists attempted to turn lead into gold.

Over a thousand years ago, the Roman government began to mix lead into some of their gold and silver coins. This deception may have accelerated the fall of the Roman Empire.

In 1971 President Richard Nixon became a modern-day alchemist when he took the U.S. dollar off the gold standard, and basically turned debt into gold.

Today, the best and brightest graduates of our finest business schools work as employees for investment banks such as Goldman Sachs and Citigroup, turning debt into gold. These "A" students, most without any real-life financial education, continue—even after the crash of 2007—to package debt as assets. They wrap this debt in pretty paper and tie it with a ribbon, using words such as derivatives or CDOs (Collateralized Debt Obligations), CMOs (Collateralized Mortgage Obligations)...terms few average people use or understand. And they sell this debt to professional investors, pension funds, insurance companies, and governments. Many of these so-called "professional investors" who purchased these derivatives are "A"-student employees in the E quadrant, not the I quadrant. Most have nothing at risk, no "skin in the game" or personal financial responsibility if they are wrong. If they lose billions, they still collect their paycheck, bonus, and retirement benefits.

Warren Buffett has called these types of derivatives "weapons of mass financial destruction." Today there are over $1.2 quadrillion of these weapons of mass destruction, time bombs, that will one day go off and destroy the world as we know it.

In spite of his warning, Warren Buffett's company, Moody's, was collecting high fees to rate subprime debt as AAA, the highest-quality, investment-grade debt. Rating subprime debt as AAA amounted to (in my opinion) taking a pig's ear and selling it to smart people as the proverbial silk purse.

"A" students from our finest schools were on both sides of the transactions, buying and selling toxic debt, believing it to be as good as gold. Again, I find myself asking: Is this a truly amazing story in mass global stupidity—or a story in legalized corruption?

This situation is a reminder that it's very important to look at *both* sides of the coin.

The good news is that as long as the world is on the debt standard, the people who know how to use debt will become richer. Unfortunately, many of those who do not will become poorer.

That's why, in 1973, rich dad advised me to take classes in real estate investing. When I asked him why I should invest in real estate, he answered, "Because you must learn to use debt if you want to become rich."

As you know, handling debt can be like handling a hand grenade. Both must be handled carefully. As millions of people found out after 2007, debt can financially kill you. If you are not willing to study and learn how to *use* debt, it may be best to follow the popular advice to get out of debt.

Saving Money Is Stupid

As strange as it may sound to most people, saving money is stupid and getting into debt is smart. As long as governments are printing trillions of counterfeit dollars, why save them?

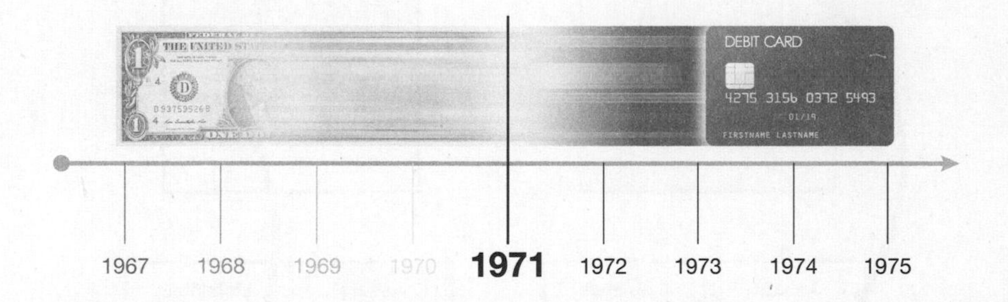

Remember: After 1971, the U.S. dollar and debt became the same thing. They are both debt. *If* governments stop printing money and begin raising interest rates, then it *may* be wise to save money…maybe.

Using Debt to Become Poorer

Today, debt is money. People have been using debt as money for years. The reason so many people got into financial trouble is because they used debt as money to buy liabilities rather than assets. For example, millions are in financial trouble because they used student loans to pay for their education, secured a mortgage to buy their house, accepted financing on a car loan, and used their credit cards to go shopping. These are examples of people using debt as money to become poorer.

When someone says, "I don't have money to invest," it is because they don't know how to use debt as money…they don't know how to use debt to create more money.

Debt Makes Bankers Rich

When you look at a bank's financial statement, your savings are the bank's liability and your mortgage is your bank's asset.

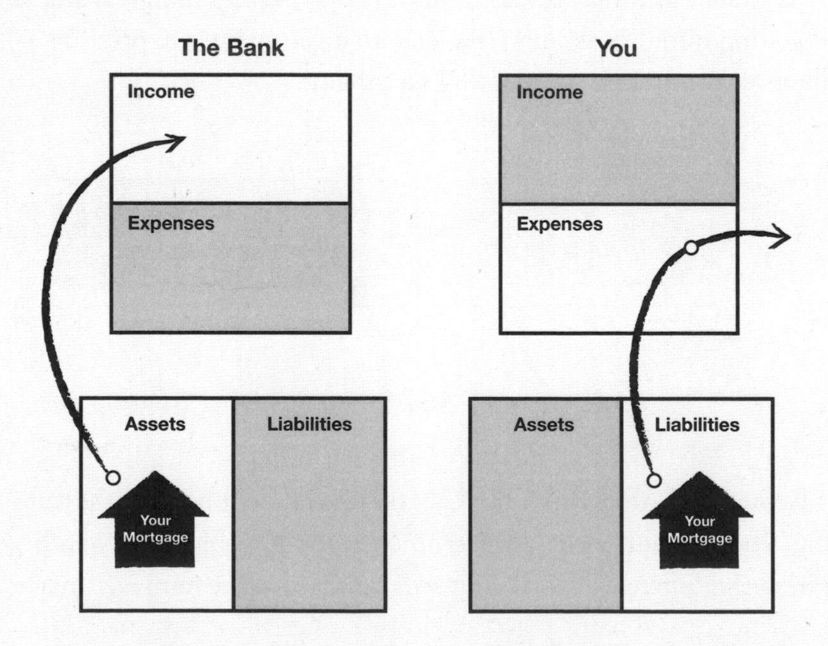

Remember, the way you can distinguish assets from liabilities is to ask: "Which direction is the cash flowing?"

Your bank is paying you interest on your savings, so your savings is the bank's liability because your interest is taking money from your banker's pocket. Your mortgage, or any debt, is the bank's asset because your mortgage puts money in your bank's pockets.

Rich Dad Lesson

"Your debt makes bankers rich. Your savings makes your banker poorer."

In fact, your banker really does not need your savings. Banks can print their own money through the fractional reserves process.

Remember the rules of Monopoly: *"The Bank* never goes broke. *If the Bank runs out of money, the Banker may issue as much as needed by writing on any ordinary paper."*

You may have noticed that banks have incentive programs to use their credit cards. Every time I am in the airport, the airlines are always asking me to sign up for their credit card so I can get bonus points or miles forgetting into debt. I have yet to see bankers offering me bonus miles for saving money. The only reason banks want your savings and checking accounts is to get your *debt* business.

Use Debt to Acquire Assets

Since dollars are taxed and debt is tax free, which makes more sense to learn to use?

In 2007, the banks of the world began printing trillions of dollars. They were following the rules of *Monopoly*, printing trillions of dollars electronically, to prevent a collapse of the debt bubble, a bubble that had been inflating since 1971, the year Nixon turned the dollar into debt. Every time money is printed taxes go up, inflation causes food and energy prices to go up…as savings and the purchasing power of the dollar go down.

As inflation goes up and the dollar goes down in value, does it make sense to save dollars? As the dollar declines in purchasing power, does it make sense to go back to school only to work harder for more of it? As inflation goes up, doesn't it make more sense to learn to use debt to acquire assets—assets that are likely to go up in value with inflation and provide cash flow?

To me, it makes more sense to learn to use debt than to get out of debt.

My Story

Today, I use 100 percent debt financing as often as possible to acquire real estate assets, assets that put money in my pocket. It sounds simple on paper, but in reality it can be tough. It took me a while to establish a track record as a real estate investor and prove to the banks that I understood real estate and property management. This is why I recommend taking real estate investment courses. Why work for money when you can use debt, increase your cash flow, and become wealthier?

Kim and I started small, with single-family rental properties. We learned from our mistakes, studied so we'd become smarter, and then applied what we learned to our next investment. One we felt confident—and had a few cash-flowing properties in our portfolio—we stepped up our game and looked at small apartment complexes.

Today, my personal debt is in the hundreds of millions of dollars, but it's debt that makes me richer not poorer, debt that puts more money—passive income from cash flow—in my pocket every month.

I can hear some of you saying, "Hundreds of millions in debt! You've just been lucky. Some day you're going to lose it all."

Could I lose everything? Absolutely. That is why I take my education seriously. As I've explained earlier in this book, each quadrant is a classroom. Rather than learn to become a professional investor in the I quadrant, most people have been trained by our schools and our media to blindly turn their investment money over to total strangers, hoping and praying they will they will return it to them. It's almost Pavlovian, this training and conditioning. My rich dad trained me to be an entrepreneur so I could make my money work for me. I do not turn my money over to strangers. In my opinion, that's risky and stupid.

The Other Side of the Coin

Using debt is one of the reasons I don't need a job. And why I don't need to save money, have a 401(k), or count on Social Security or Medicare to take care of me. My situation today is a result of investing time and effort into the life-long learning process of financial education—and then putting what I learned into practice. Not every investment was a windfall. There are always ups and downs in the process. And always lessons I could learn from the mistakes I made. That's how the process works for all of us.

My game *CASHFLOW 101* is the only board game that teaches players to use debt to get rich, to use debt to produce income. As in real life, if you misuse debt in the game, you will be soon go broke. The good news is, you will go bust using play money and play debt. And the lesson will cost you nothing but your time.

If a parent will begin teaching their child during their first window of learning, from birth to age 12, using *CASHFLOW For Kids*, then using *CASHFLOW 101* and *202* between ages 12 to 24, their child will better prepared for real life before they leave home. Their child will also have a financial headstart even most rich kids don't have.

Rich Dad Lesson

"Since all money is now debt, financial education must include lessons on debt, both good and bad."

I recommend parents create a ritual, family financial education night, at least once a month. By playing games and discussing real world financial events at home, the relationship between parent and child will grow stronger and both parent and child will be better prepared for the uncertainties of the world ahead. One of the many jobs of a parent is to prepare your child for the opportunities of tomorrow.

As the Cone of Learning illustrates, simulation is the next best thing to doing the real thing. By playing the *CASHFLOW* games many times, you can learn to use debt, before doing the real thing with real debt and real investments. As the saying goes, "Practice makes perfect." By using a game as a teaching tool while your child builds their financial neural pathways you will increase their financial intelligence and connect the dots to their financial future.

Leaders in Need of Education

In my opinion, the global economic crisis is a crisis of leadership and a crisis of education in individuals who are very smart people, but lack real world financial education. Most of our leaders are "A" students who became "B" students, bureaucrats. Very few are "C" students, true capitalists like Steve Jobs, Thomas Edison, and Henry Ford.

Our current leaders are attempting to use more debt to solve the problem of too much debt. Our leaders are begging for more bailout money, more QE—Quantitative Easing, aka printing more and more counterfeit money. They see tax hikes and increased spending as solutions. This, from my point of view, is financial suicide.

Many people want to believe debt is the problem. The problem is not debt. The problem is the lack of financial education. If our leaders were better educated, they would know how to use debt to make us richer as a nation and a people, rather than poorer.

> ***Conspiracy and Prophecy***
>
> *Two of my books on the subjects of money and investing are* Conspiracy of the Rich, *about how our wealth is stolen via our monetary system, and* Rich Dad's Prophecy, *published in 2002, about my prediction that the biggest stock market crash in history is coming within the next decade.*

Today, I believe we are experiencing the biggest financial crisis in world history, a crisis far bigger than the Great Depression of 1929. I am afraid this crisis will not end well. If history once again repeats itself, we may be headed for a financial collapse. For thousands of years, every government that has used fraud—by adding lead into coins or using the printing press to solve its financial problems—has destroyed the very economy it promised to save.

This is why financial education that increases your financial intelligence is crucial. If you can see the other side of the coin, you and your child will be better prepared to make intelligent choices about money. You can be among the financially educated who will thrive while the masses struggle to survive.

Question: Am I against the system?

Answer: I am not against the banking system. I am a student of the system, using it to my benefit. The giant banking system does a lot of good and a lot of harm. I choose to use it for good.

Question: Do I recommend getting into debt?

Answer: It depends. And most people are already in debt. Every time you use money, you are using debt. Each time our governments print money and bail out banks, retirement plans, or entire countries, we are getting deeper into debt. The answer to this question is tide to understanding bad debt and good debt—as well as your level of financial education on how to use debt to make you rich.

Since 1971, the U.S. dollar has lost 90 percent of its purchasing power. It will not take much longer to lose the last 10 percent.

You have already taken the first step in investing in your financial education by reading this book. You are learning about money, learning about the power of debt, and the power of taxes. So many people use debt out of ignorance, and in doing so unintentionally enslave themselves, their families, and their country to debt and taxes.

While I want to be wrong and I hope for the best, I doubt our political leaders, Republican or Democrat, can solve the problems we face. The problem is simply too massive for one country, much less one political party to solve. Besides, I suspect there are people who are quite happy with the problem. And, perhaps, quite happy with the fact that there's little if any financial education in our schools. Intentional or unintentional, it is the lack of financial education that has pushed billions of people to the edge…living lives filled with fear and worry and uncertainty.

Unfortunately, our leaders cannot protect us from this global crisis. But parents can protect their children from the incompetence of our leaders. Because, like it or not, debt is the new money. We can use debt to become poorer or use it to be richer. The choice is ours.

Action Step for Parents

Teach your child that there are two kinds of debt: good debt and bad debt.

Bad debt makes you poor and good debt can make you rich. Discuss different types of debt: credit card debt, your mortgage, student loan debt, and an auto loan.

If it's age-appropriate, you can discuss interest and interest rates—and how interest impacts debt the cost of what you finance. Your child should also know that good debt can be tax-free—and can be used to make you rich. This means the more good debt you use, the more money you make and the less you pay in taxes.

Other topics for a family finance discussion might be: interest on credit card statements, your mortgage loan interest rate…as well as news coverage that discusses interest rates.

CASHFLOW 101 and *202* are the only games that teach the power of debt. Games offer the opportunity to test what you learn about using debt with play money. This means you can practice, making lots of mistakes, losing lots of money, and getting smarter along the way about the power of debt.

If your child leaves home understanding the power of debt, they may never fall into the trap of too much bad debt and they may even become extremely wealth using good debt.

How and Why Taxes Make the Rich Richer.

Part Two | Chapter Thirteen

ANOTHER POINT OF VIEW ON TAXES

Every time voters demand to "tax the rich," it is the poor and middle class who pay more in taxes, not the rich. Taxes are often viewed as punitive, onerous—that one thing, besides death, that we just can't escape. In fact, the other side of the coin on the tax code is that it includes a very long list of tax incentives, incentives from the government for those in the private sector to address specific economic needs and receive tax advantages for doing it.

Making the Case

William J.H. Boetcker (1873-1962), an American religious leader and public speaker, is perhaps best remembered for his authorship of a pamphlet titled *The Ten Cannots* that emphasizes individual freedom and responsibility. They are, with my emphasis added:

- You cannot bring about prosperity by discouraging thrift.
- You cannot strengthen the weak by weakening the strong.
- You cannot help little men by tearing down big men.
- You cannot lift the wage earner by pulling down the wage payer.
- **You cannot help the poor by destroying the rich.**
- You cannot establish sound security on borrowed money.

- You cannot further the brotherhood of man by inciting class hatred.
- You cannot keep out of trouble by spending more than you earn.
- You cannot build character and courage by destroying men's initiative and independence.
- **And you cannot help men permanently by doing for them what they can and should do for themselves.**

Taxes Favor Capitalists

In Economics 101, there are three things a person can bring to market.

1. Labor
2. Property
3. Capital

Most students, even "A" students, go to school to learn a trade and sell their labor. They go to school to get a job. Few students go to school to learn to sell or develop their property or sell their capital.

In Rich Dad terms, people who sell their labor are on the left side of the CASHFLOW quadrant. People who sell property and capital operate from the right side of the CASHFLOW quadrant.

Repeating from the opening section of this book, here are the tax rates per quadrant:

TAX PERCENTAGES PAID PER QUADRANT

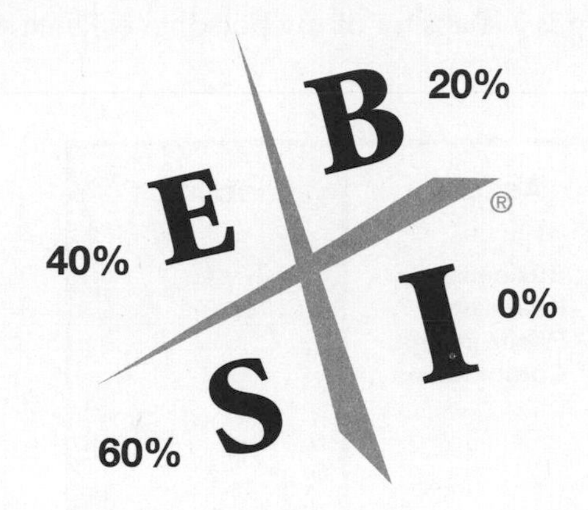

A progressive income tax applies to the E and S quadrants with those in the S quadrant paying the highest percentages. In the E and S quadrants, the more you earn, the more you pay in taxes.

In the B and I quadrants, percentages go the other way. The I quadrant pays the least in taxes. On the right side, the more you earn, the less you pay in taxes.

Again, the difference is that people in the E and S quadrants sell their labor. People in the B and I quadrants sell their property and capital and *hire* labor. You may recall from *Rich Dad Poor Dad* that rich dad's lesson #1 is, "The Rich Don't Work for Money."

When parents say to their child, "Go to school and get good grades so you can get a good job," parents are advising their child to sell their labor, to work hard for money.

In high school, every time my grades were low, my teacher threatened, "If you don't get good grades, you won't get a good job." I would say, "Good. I don't want a job." In economic terms, I had no plans to sell my labor.

This does not mean the rich do not work hard. They just work hard for something else. They work hard to acquire assets, that put more money in their pockets and allow them to keep (thanks to better tax rates) more of what they earn.

The Government Needs Help

The government needs a lot of help so it offers tax incentives as stimulus packages to those in the B and I quadrants. These are legal government tax loopholes.

The following is a snapshot of my personal balance sheet.

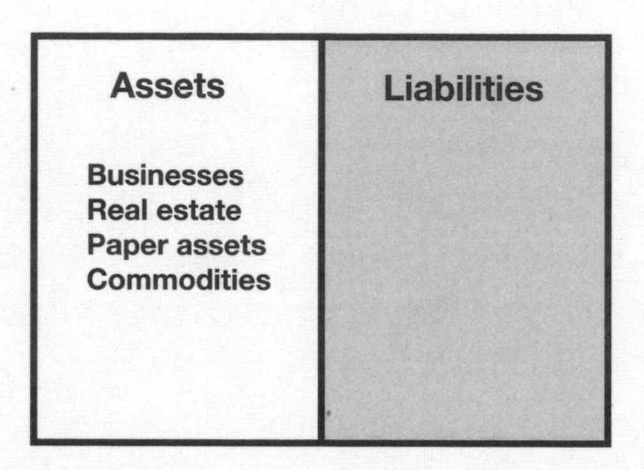

Assets
Liabilities
Businesses
Real estate
Paper assets
Commodities

My Story

Since 1973, I have worked to create or acquire assets that sell property and capital. I have not wanted a job selling my labor.

The U.S. tax code has over 5,000 pages dedicated to "loopholes" which are not really "loop holes." They are intentional tax incentives and stimulus plans. I will describe, as simply as possible, the loopholes I use.

My Taxes Made Simple

- **Business:** The tax code offers me tax incentives to provide jobs. The more jobs I provide, the more I can make and the less I pay in taxes. From the government's perspective, the more people working the more government is collecting in taxes.

- **Real Estate:** The tax code wants me to provide housing. The more housing I provide, the more money I make and the less I pay in taxes.

- **Debt:** One advantage of real estate is debt. Debt is capital. And, today the dollar is debt. If I stop borrowing, the economy slows. That is why the government wants me to get into debt. That is why interest rates on debt have continued to go down during the financial crisis. The deeper in debt I get, the more money I make and the less I pay in taxes.
- **Stocks:** While stocks are good for most people, I do not invest in stocks. While stocks have made a few people very rich, they have also made many people poorer. When you invest in stocks, you place your money with employees and managerial capitalists, rather than entrepreneurs, or true capitalists. The primary reason I choose not to invest in stocks is simply because there are not enough tax incentives and far too much risk for me.
- **Commodities:** I invest in oil production, not oil company stocks. The more money I make, the less I pay in taxes. The government wants investors to keep producing oil for two reasons:

  1. to keep the price of oil down
  2. to reduce dependence upon foreign oil

If you look at the board of the *CASHFLOW* Game, you will notice two tracks. One track is a circle called the Rat Race. People in the Rat Race invest in stocks, bonds, and mutual funds.

The second track on that same game board is the Fast Track. In real life, there really is a Fast Track. The Fast Track is where the rich invest. On the Fast Track, investors choose more sophisticated investment vehicles like Limited Partnerships and Private Placement Memorandums. This is where I chose to invest my money. The advantage I have is I know the entrepreneur, a true capitalist who is the founder of the company as well as the person who runs the company. When I invest as a "partner," the entrepreneur will take my call.

If I invest in stocks, I will probably never know the CEO, who is in most cases an employee, a managerial capitalist, not an entrepreneur or true capitalist.

Simply said, stock holders invest in *shares* of a company. Most public companies have millions of shares. A partner invests in *percentages* of the company. In many cases, partners receive tax breaks. Shareholders do not.

There Are Many Tax Incentives and Stimuli

There are many tax incentives in the tax code. I have only listed the ones I use. The lesson here is that, the tax code is an incentive and stimulus plan for capitalists on the right side of the CASHFLOW quadrant who provide jobs, housing, use capital (debt), and produce essential commodities such as food and oil. There are many other tax incentives.

Rich Dad Lesson

"There are many CPAs and tax attorneys, but very few smart ones."

Before investing for tax incentives, always, *always* seek professional advice from tax accountants and tax attorneys.

If you would like to learn more about tax incentives, my personal tax advisor, Tom Wheelwright C.P.A., has written a Rich Dad Advisor book, *Tax-Free Wealth*. It would be a good book for you to read, and one you may want to share with your tax advisors as well.

Who Pays the Highest Taxes?

The tax code punishes those on the left side of the CASHFLOW quadrant with higher taxes. The people who pay the highest taxes are:

- People who have a job
- People who have only one house
- People who save money
- People who have a 401(k) retirement plan

These people generally pay ordinary income tax on everything. The more they earn, the higher their taxes.

> **Question:** Why do people pay more taxes on a 401(k) plan? What about the tax-free money your employer matches with your contribution?
>
> **Answer:** It all depends upon your point of view. First of all, the money your employer supposedly gives to you is your money anyway. He did not donate it. He just did not pay it to you, and then he let's you think he is giving you extra money. Second of all, the reason financial planners say, "When you retire, your taxes will go down" is because most people plan to retire on less money than they earned prior to retirement. If your income is higher when you retire, then the income from your 401(k) will be taxed at the higher level, since income from a 401(k) is ordinary income.

Earlier in the book, I wrote about how the financially educated are always working to transform their *ordinary income* into *portfolio* and *passive income.*

Friend and Rich Dad Advisor, Andy Tanner has a very interesting, entertaining, and disturbing book titled, *401(k)aos.* If you have a 401(k), you may want to read his book.

Financial Education in School

The financial education being taught in school is: "Go to school, get a job, work hard, save money, buy a house, get out of debt, and invest in a 401(k)." *From a tax point of view, this is subprime financial education.*

If you follow that kind of financial education, you will turn your children into tax slaves for the rest of their lives. They will work for capitalists, trading time for money, rather than becoming a capitalist.

Tax Education for Your Kids

Millions of people believe in the principle of "taking from the rich and giving to the poor." This is the basis of taxation. This is also the basis of the Robin Hood theory of economics, also known as socialism.

When President Nixon took the U.S. dollar off the gold standard, two things were guaranteed to happen:

1. an increase in taxes

2. an increase in inflation

When the government prints money, they do so by issuing government bonds, Treasury bills, Treasury notes, municipal bonds, and other instruments you and I would call IOUs. All bonds are debt, and all debt comes with a percentage of interest paid with the repayment of principal.

Keeping the numbers simple, if a government offers a bond for $1 million and the interest is 10 percent per year, then someone has to pay that $100,000 a year in interest. In many cases, that person is you or me, taxpayers.

The U.S. national debt is now over $16 trillion and climbing. You do not have to be a Nobel Prize-winning economist to know that this is a *lot* of interest and a *lot* of taxes. Today, an increasing percentage of our tax dollars are flowing to banks and countries such as China, creditors that hold our debt and expect to be repaid.

Inflation goes up when governments print money because that new money dilutes the existing financial pool and the result is that the purchasing power of the dollar goes down. You can look at the chart of gold pictured below to gain some idea of how much money the Federal Reserve has been printing.

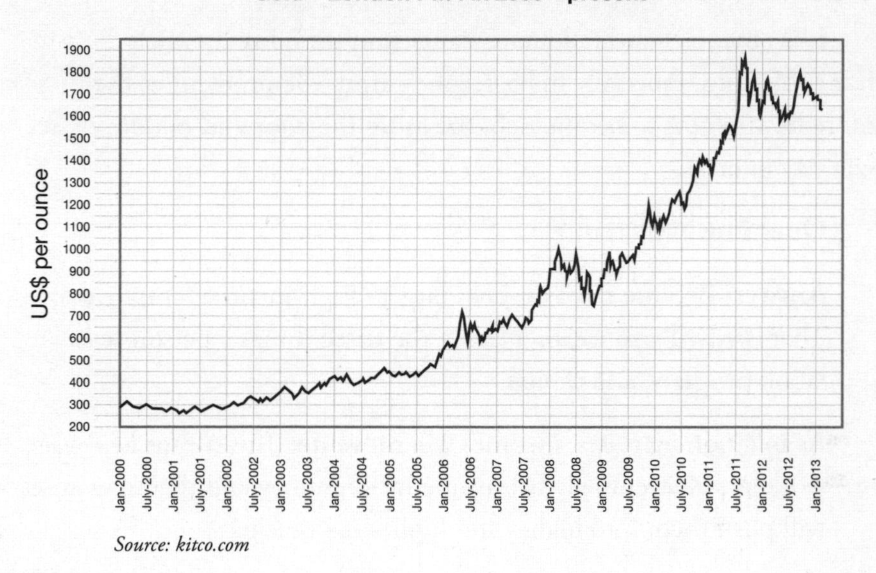

Source: kitco.com

You can also see it in the price of oil. This is what happens when the Fed prints more money.

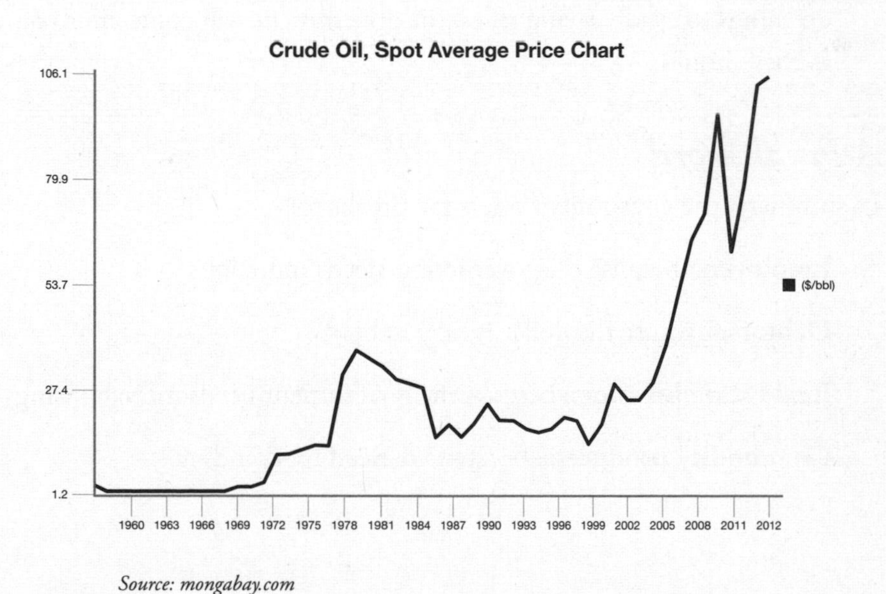

Source: mongabay.com

Obama's Second Term

It is obvious that President Obama is in the "Tax the Rich" frame of mind, especially in his second term. The problem is, the more he attempts to tax the rich, the more the poor and middle classes will pay in taxes.

Question: Why is this?

Answer: Because most tax laws target "high-income" employees. That is why I wrote earlier about the three things a person sells: labor, property, and capital.

As inflation increases, incomes will move up. This means low-wage workers will eventually be earning more money and their pay raises will push them into higher and higher tax brackets.

While the President will score a few victories, the fundamental principles of capitalism will hold. If a person continues to act as a smart business-person and does what smart business people do, the government will welcome you as a partner, and offer you tax incentives to do things the government is not able to do. If you only do things to evade paying taxes, the government will come after you, as they should.

A Final Word

In summary, the government offers tax breaks to:

Employers: because the government needs more jobs

Debtors: because the dollar is now debt

Real Estate Investors: because the government needs more housing

Commodity producers: because we need food and oil

If private citizens did not do what the government needs done, we would have communism, an economic system where the government controls the economy.

This is why General Motors, aka Government Motors cannot produce an economical electrical car; Solyndra, Obama's darling, could not produce solar panels.

Rich Dad Lesson

Taxes are your single largest expense.

True financial education must include lessons on taxes, who pays them, and why some people are offered tax breaks.

Ask yourself these questions: Why is government housing some of the most dangerous housing in the world? Why is the U.S. Postal Service going out of business? Why is Medicare corrupt, expensive, and inefficient? Why are our governments going bankrupt? And, to get to the heart of the messages in this book: Why are our schools failing to educate our children with the information they need to make responsible and smart choices with their money?

Ask yourself this question: If the government took over the airlines, would you continue to fly? That's one of the reasons why governments offer tax incentives.

Action Step for Parents

Teach your child to look at taxes from two points of view.

While it's true that taxes can make some people poor, they can also make others rich.

It's a matter of point of view. So often taxes are viewed a punitive…a burden that very often is a family's single largest expense. The rich see taxes as an incentive program that the government offers businesses and individuals that do work that the government wants or needs done. Some of the kinds of things that merit incentives are the creation of jobs, supplying affordable housing, and energy-related initiatives.

Other conversations and learning opportunities related to taxes can be explored when you child is old enough to understand that you file a tax return in each year. Review a copy of your tax return with you child…showing them where both income and expenses are recorded. Also point out the section that details deductions. Also show your child a pay stub or summary of the deductions from your paycheck. It will help them see how programs like Social Security are funded and how income is taxed—with the government taking its tax from the gross wages and the difference between those gross, total, wages and take home pay.

I encourage you to teach your child the *three* sides of the coin of taxes and help them to understand the differences.

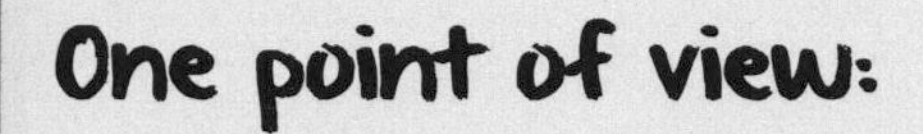

"Sticks and stones may break my bones but words will never hurt me."

Another point of view:

"Words can do more damage than sticks and stones."

Part Two | Chapter Fourteen

ANOTHER POINT OF VIEW ON WORDS

In Sunday School, an important lesson is:

"And the Word became flesh and dwelt among us."

—John 1:14

Words Become Flesh

In real life, words do become flesh. And each economic class has words that reflect it and define it: Rich people use rich words, middle-class people use middle-class words, and poor people use poor words. It's said that "what you think about you bring about." I believe that the same is true for what we say and the words we use.

Favorite words of poor people are, "I can't afford it." Rich people say, "How can I afford it?" Simply said, if you want to change your life, change your words.

Making the Case

Money Talks

Rich dad often said, "Money talks and BS walks." He taught us that money has its own language, a language that's not taught in schools. "If you want to be rich," he advised, "take the time to learn the language of money."

Rich dad also said, "When it comes to money, there is a lot of BS walking around." Millions are in a financial crisis because they listened to a lot of financial BS. Rather than teach kids the language of money, schools focus on the language of schoolteachers, a language that uses words such as verbs, calculus, nouns, history, chemistry, and physics.

Those words are important, but they fail to prepare students for the real world of money.

As Albert Einstein said:

> *"The difference between stupidity and genius is that genius has its limits."*

This financial crisis is a crisis of unlimited stupidity.

Words Can Hurt

There is an childhood rhyme that goes: "Sticks and stones may break my bones, but words will never hurt me."

Nothing could be further from the truth. Few things affect a child's future more than words. Words are incredibly powerful.

- Words can hurt
- Words can heal
- Words can make them rich
- Words can make them poor
- Words can encourage
- Words can discourage
- Words can carry lies
- Words can carry truth
- Words can cause pain

The Power of Words

Many financial problems begin with words. Many people get into financial trouble due to bad financial advice, financial BS or Blue Sky, from those they believe have their best interests at heart. Many times that's just not the case.

What is *Blue Sky*? Blue Sky is when salesmen (or women) say anything to make a sale. If the customer wants to hear their money will grow in a mutual fund, the salesman will say, "Mutual Funds have returned 8% per year on average." They may *not* tell you those gains occurred during the boom years between 1970 and 2000. They may use words and information that support their sales pitch—and omit what doesn't. And hope that the customer is not financially savvy enough to notice.

One reason many government pension funds are in serious trouble is because they based future projections on the stock market going up 8% on average. Talk about financial BS. Many government employees will be hurt because they did not understand the words of money.

Other examples of financial Blue Sky are:

"Your house is an asset."

"Diversification is a way to reduce risk."

"Invest for the long-term in a well-diversified portfolio of stocks, bonds, and mutual funds."

Many people mistake these words for financial education. They are not. In most cases these words are sales pitches, disguised as financial education. When a real estate broker says to you, "Your house is an asset and your biggest investment," he is probably saying to himself, "Buy this house. I need the commission."

If a financial planner advises you to "Invest for the long-term," they might just as well be saying, "Send me a check every month. I need the commission. By the time you retire, I'll be long gone."

When financial planners advise you to "diversify," they are really advising you to "de-worsify." They are really saying, "Buy different products because I do not know which ones will do well and which ones will fail. (But I get a commission on all of them.)"

The worst thing is, even when people believe they are diversifying, most aren't. When the average investor diversifies, they tend to diversify within the same asset class. They may buy high-growth mutual funds, emerging market mutual funds, and bond mutual funds—all within the same asset class. Technically, they are not really diversified, because all the investments are in the same investment vehicle, mutual funds.

When a banker advises you to "Save money," they are also saying, "So that I can give you a credit card and maybe a home loan." Remember, banks do not make money on savings. They make money on debt.

Financial Advice vs. Financial Education

Financial problems begin when *financial advice*, a sale pitch or BS, is confused with *financial education*. Many people think *advice* and education mean the same thing, but they don't.

- Asking for advice means, "Tell me what to do."
- Seeking education means, "Tell me what to study so I can learn what I need to do."

The difference between *education* and *advice* may seem like a small point, but little differences can often have a significant impact over a person's lifetime. If all you've been taught to do is hand your money over to salespeople, you are a *customer*, not a *financially educated person*.

When Bernie Madoff's Ponzi scheme was revealed, many people took huge financial hits. Much worse than losing money, perhaps, was that they gained very little in the way of financial education.

Rich dad encouraged Mike and me to make honest mistakes with our money. He said, "If you make the mistake, you will learn from that mistake. If your financial advisor makes the mistake, *you* are no smarter than the day you handed over your money."

Tell Me What to Do with My Money

One of the questions I am asked again and again is, "I have $10,000. What should I do with it?"

My reply: "The first thing I would do is keep quiet. Don't let the world know you have money to invest and don't know what to do with it. If you ask financial advisors what to do with your money, their answer is usually the same, 'Turn your money over to me.'"

Employee Retirement Plans

Employee retirement plans are even worse. When a new employee is hired, the Human Resources director hands them a form and says, "Choose a mutual fund for your retirement fund contributions."

It might be better to just advise the employee, "Go to Las Vegas and have a good time with your money. You might win. At least there, if you win, you'll keep 100% of your money."

In an earlier chapter I talked about John Bogle, the founder of Vanguard. He cautions investors that in a mutual fund they put up 100% of the investment, take 100% of the risk, but get only 20% of the gain, if there are any gains. The mutual fund, via fees and other charges listed in the fine print, keeps 80% of any gains you may make.

Worst of all, even if you lose money, you may have to pay taxes on capital gains—gains you never received. How does this happen? Let's say a fund has 2 million shares of XYZ Company that it purchased 10 years ago. For purposes of this example, let's say the stock went up from $10 a share to $50 a share. Then you buy the mutual fund. Two days later, the market crashes, the mutual fund must sell XYZ to raise capital to survive. You, the new shareholder, must pay the capital gains tax on the $40 gain, a gain you never enjoyed or saw the return on.

The stock market might be called a government-sanctioned Ponzi scheme. The early guys get their money and the new guys pay the taxes. That is why financial advisors say, "Invest for the long term and diversify." Blue Sky…again.

To be fair, anytime a person invests for capital gains, buying low and selling high, the transaction could be viewed as a Ponzi scheme. The reason so many people believe investing is risky is because most people invest for capital gains. When real estate "flippers" flopped after the real estate market crashed, they were investing for capital gains. Today, millions are buying gold and silver, hoping the prices keep going up. That, too, is investing for capital gains.

The Greater Fool Theory of Investing

In the world of investing, there is a theory known as "The greater fool theory of investing." Anytime a person invests for capital gains, they are waiting for the "greater fool" to come along, a person more foolish than they are…a person willing to pay more for something—shares of stock, a real estate property, or a silver coin. At the risk of repeating myself: This is why most people think investing is risky. When people invest for capital gains, which the majority of investors do, they are the greater fool, hoping for a fool bigger than they are.

This is why words are so important. Later in this chapter, I will go into the difference between investing for *capital gains* (waiting for the greater fool) and investing for *cash flow*.

My Story

The Goose that Lays Golden Eggs

When explaining the differences between capital gains and cash flow to a young person, I often use Aesop's fairy tale of *The Goose that Laid the Golden Eggs*. A person who invests for capital gains will sell the goose. A person who invests for cash flow, on the other hand, will nurture and take care of the goose, and sell the golden eggs.

The irony is that you pay much lower taxes, sometimes zero percent, with golden eggs. You pay a higher percentage in taxes, eating roast goose.

Since most financial experts are sales people, not real investors, they sell geese.

And since most adults do not know the difference between the words *capital gains* and *cash flow*, they believe investing is buying and selling geese. Most do not know how to invest for golden eggs. The irony is that it's likely an investor will pay lower taxes, sometimes zero percent, on the sale of golden eggs. They retain the production (the goose) that delivers a steady stream of products (the golden eggs) for sale.

This is why words—and the learning the language of money—are an important part of your child's education.

The Grand Financial Plan

It's always been surprising to me that, when it comes to money, most people are waiting to be told what to do. I've come to believe it's because they receive no financial education in school. This is exactly what the big banks and financial services industry wants. Your financial ignorance is part of *their* grand financial plan.

Most people seek financial advice from brokers, salespeople such as stock, real estate, and insurance brokers as well as financial planners—people who profit from giving financial *advice* rather than financial *education*.

That is why rich dad often said:

> *"The reason they are called* brokers *is because they are broker than you."*

Warren Buffett says:

> *"Wall Street is the only place that people ride to in a Rolls Royce to get advice from those who take the subway."*

Believe it or not, it takes up to two years to get a license in massage therapy. It takes about two months to become a financial advisor.

That is why it is important for parents to begin their child's financial education early. A child needs to know the difference between financial advice and financial education, the difference between being *told what to do with their money* versus knowing what to do with their money.

Financial Vocabulary

If you were planning to work in Germany, it would help to learn the German language. If you want to be a medical doctor, you will need to learn the language of medicine. If you want to play football, you'll need to learn the language of football. When I went to school to learn to be a ship's officer, I had to learn the language of the navigation. And when I entered flight school, my education began by learning the language of aviation.

The Language of Money

Rich dad taught his son me the language of money, starting at nine. I taught the language of money to Kim. That is how Kim and I retired early in life, so we could then get on with our life work as advocates of financial education

Kim and I created the *CASHFLOW* games so parents could learn and teach the language of money to their children.

The good news is, there are only seven basic words of money to learn. Once you master those seven words, your financial vocabulary will grow, you will think differently, and your view of the world will change. By playing *CASHFLOW,* your child will learn the difference between the goose and golden eggs, between *capital gains* and *cash flow*. If they understand the differences between *just those two* financial terms, they will tip the scales and put the odds of a more secure financial future in their favor. If they learn all seven basic financial terms, who knows where they will go in life? They may never need a job. They may choose to take a job for the experience, but not the need for a paycheck. They may become employers rather than employees. They may become real capitalists, rather than managerial capitalists.

Your Report Card in Real Life

Pictured below is the financial statement from the *CASHFLOW* game. The *real* game of *CASHFLOW* is played on the financial statement. Your financial statement is your report card in the real world, the report card a banker will ask you for. By playing the game repeatedly, you and your child will begin to master the seven basic words of money, the foundation of a financial vocabulary.

PROFESSION

PLAYER

GOAL: Get out of the Rat Race and onto the Fast Track by building up your **Passive Income** to be **greater** than your **Total Expenses**

INCOME STATEMENT

INCOME

Description	Cash Flow
Salary:	
Interest/Dividends:	
Real Estate/Business:	

AUDITOR

(Person on your right)

Passive Income: $
(Cash Flow from Interest/Dividends + Real Estate/Business)

Total Income: $

EXPENSES

Taxes:	
Home Mortgage Payment:	
School Loan Payment:	
Car Loan Payment:	
Credit Card Payment:	
Retail Payment:	
Other Expenses:	
Child Expenses:	
Loan Payment:	

Number of Children:
(Begin game with 0 Children)
Per Child Expense: $

Total Expenses: $

Monthly Cash Flow (PAYDAY): $
(Total Income - Total Expenses)

BALANCE SHEET

ASSETS

Savings:		
Stocks/Funds/CDs:	# of Shares:	Cost/Share:
Real Estate/Business:	Down Pay:	Cost:

LIABILITIES

Home Mortgage:	
School Loans:	
Car Loans:	
Credit Cards:	
Retail Debt:	
Real Estate/Business:	Mortgage/Liability:
Loan:	

G101CTI8.v12

The foundation of a financial vocabulary begins with the words *income*, *expenses*, *assets*, and *liabilities*, the key components of a financial statement.

If a person does not understand one or more of these basic words of money, their lives can be damaged financially. For example, millions are in trouble today simply because they were told, "Your house is an asset." For most people, their home is a liability. Others are in trouble because they were told, "Get a job," but did not understand the three different types of income—ordinary, portfolio, and passive income. Income from a job is considered ordinary income and taxed at the highest rates.

The English language has more than 1 million words. The average person has command of somewhere between 10,000 and 20,000 words, which means there is always room for increased intelligence related to vocabulary and the language of money.

The Seven Words of Money

The good news is that the seven basic, most important words of money are ones that may already be familiar to you. All of them are taught in the *CASHFLOW* games. The words are:

Income: As we've already covered, there are three basic types of income: ordinary, portfolio, and passive. This is an example of how your financial vocabulary will grow from learning and understanding the basic words.

Expense: Expenses, or liabilities, take money from your pocket. The number one expense for most people is taxes. Other typical expenses are housing, food, clothing, medical care, education and entertainment,

Assets: Assets put money in your pocket. There are four basic assets or asset classes:

Business

Many of the richest people in the world built B-quadrant business—people like Steve Jobs, Bill Gates, Larry Ellison, Richard Branson, and Larry Page. Building a B-quadrant business is extremely difficult and requires the highest levels of financial education. If you're successful, the payoffs are literally out of this world.

B-quadrant businesses require the entrepreneur to learn multiple languages. For example, an entrepreneur might need to speak the languages of law, accounting, engineering, marketing, sales, IT, leadership, and more. They do not have to be fluent in all these languages. They just need to speak and understand some the important words of each profession that supports the success of a business.

In most cases, schools teach kids to be specialists, learning more and more about less and less. Entrepreneurs need to be generalists, which means they need to speak a little of many different professional languages.

One reason why "A" students do not make good entrepreneurs is that they tend to hang out with other specialists. For example, teachers hang out with teachers, and doctors spend time with other doctors. My poor dad spent 90% of his working hours with teachers. My rich dad spent 90% of his time working with "A" students such as bankers, accountants, lawyers, architects, contractors, and MBAs.

After college, many "A" students go on to graduate and professional schools, such as med school, law school, or dental school. After graduation, they often join other doctors, lawyers, or dentists in business. They become more specialized, more isolated, less able to communicate with other people and professions.

Some of the advantages of owning a B-quadrant business are the opportunities for significant wealth, global scale and reach, and tax advantages. The biggest advantage is becoming multi-lingual, speaking the languages of many different professions.

Real estate

Real estate is the second-most challenging asset class. Real estate is about debt, and debt has a language of its own. Real estate requires both property management and people skills.

The biggest advantages of real estate are debt and taxes. The disadvantage is property management. In other words, getting the loan is the easy part. Managing the property well and profitably is the hard part. Property management speaks a different language and is where most novice real estate investors get into trouble.

The beauty of being a professional real estate investor is you can invest for *both* capital gains and cash flow—and pay little, if anything, in taxes. (More about that in upcoming chapters.)

Paper Assets

Paper is the asset class of the masses. The advantage to paper assets is that amateurs can get in easily. This is because paper assets such as stocks, mutual funds, bonds, and ETFs are "scaleable," Which means a new investor can start with $100 as easily as $100,000.

There are limited tax advantages for paper-asset investors. For example, if a person invests in real estate via a paper asset like a REIT (Real Estate Investment Trust), they lose the tax and debt advantages of true real estate investors. The same is true for investing in commodities via paper assets like ETFs (Exchange Traded Funds).

If you're familiar with The Rich Dad Company you know that we do not sell investments. In the marketplace you'll find many organizations that offer financial programs, but they're often programs that train you to use their financial services and buy their financial products. In other words, very often their financial programs are nothing more than a disguised sales pitch, or Blue Sky…also called a "lead generator."

There is nothing wrong with selling and sales pitches. This is capitalism, and I support capitalism. In a true environment of capitalism the words of caution are *caveat emptor*, Latin for "buyer beware." This drives home the point of why financial *education* is more important than financial *advice*. True education should make you more aware of the world around you.

Commodities

Commodities are the staples of life. This category includes oil, coal, gold, silver, and food such as corn, soybeans, pork bellies, and so on. Each commodity has its own language.

There are large tax advantages for commodities such as oil and food.

As long as governments are printing money, I save gold and silver rather than counterfeit money.

Which Asset Class Is Best for You?

Simply put, if you want to be an entrepreneur, the first two assets—business and real estate—are probably best for you. You will gain great real life experience becoming a professional in those two asset classes. Those asset classes require tremendous financial education, resilience, and dedication.

If you do not want to be an entrepreneur, then paper assets and commodities are probably better for you.

Paper assets and commodities, like gold and silver coins, are great for people with limited entrepreneurial skills. In financial terms, paper assets as well as gold and silver are very "liquid." This means that purchases and sales can be done instantaneously and electronically, 24/7, all over the world.

And you don't need good people skills to invest in paper or gold and silver. Many "A" students tend to do well with paper assets and commodities like gold and silver because the investor skills in these two asset classes are similar to classroom skills. You can sit in front of a computer screen and trade the world—without having to interact with other people. A very different environment and skill set than the leadership and interpersonal skills that an entrepreneur must develop.

Liabilities: Simply said, liabilities, such as a mortgage, school loan, credit card debt, and car payments, take money from your pocket on a regular basis. Most people acquire liabilities that cost them money.

The objective of the *CASHFLOW* game is to teach you to acquire liabilities that *make* you money.

For example, when I buy a rental property, the liabilities such as taxes, maintenance, and mortgage are paid for from the rent revenue of the tenants. The profits flow to me, the investor, but only if I am a competent entrepreneur.

Debt: Debt can be a liability. Debt can also be an asset. If I lend someone $10 at 5% interest, that debt is my asset and the borrower's liability.

The *CASHFLOW 101* and *202* games are the only games I'm aware of that teach the use of debt and other types of financial leverage, such as options, calls, puts, and straddles. Learning to use debt or options to become rich is an incredible unfair advantage.

Cash flow: According to rich dad, the words *cash* and *flow* are the most important financial words of all. Until you learn to *see* cash flowing on a financial statement, you may have a difficult time determining assets from liabilities, and expenses from income.

I believe *Rich Dad Poor Dad* was a success because I used simple diagrams so readers could "see" cash flowing.

For example:

Cash flow pattern of a poor person:

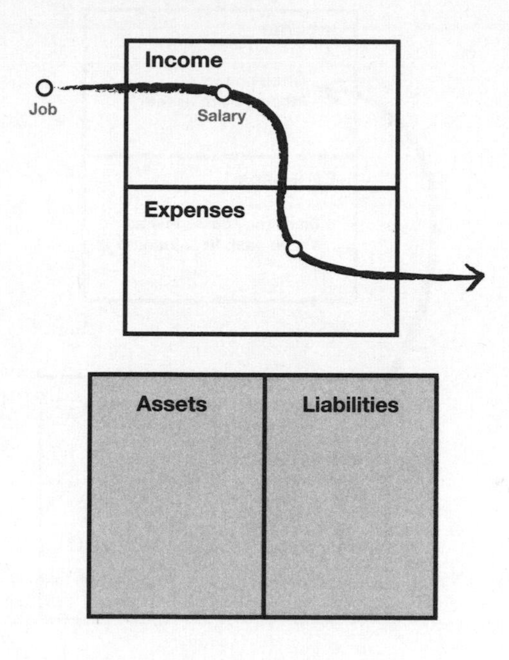

Cash flow pattern of middle class person:

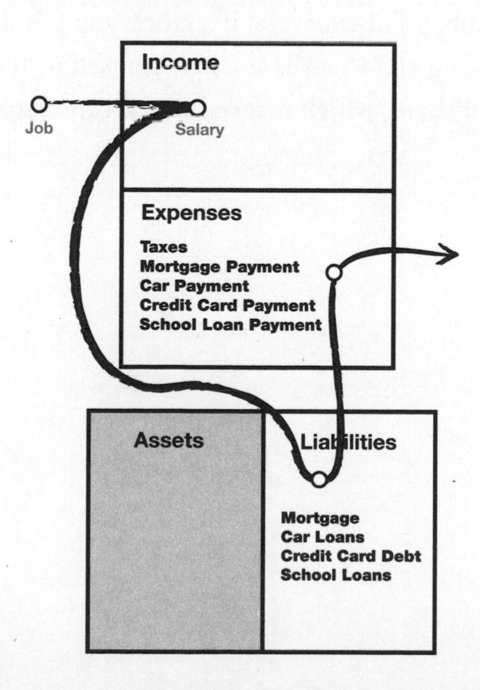

Cash flow pattern of a rich person:

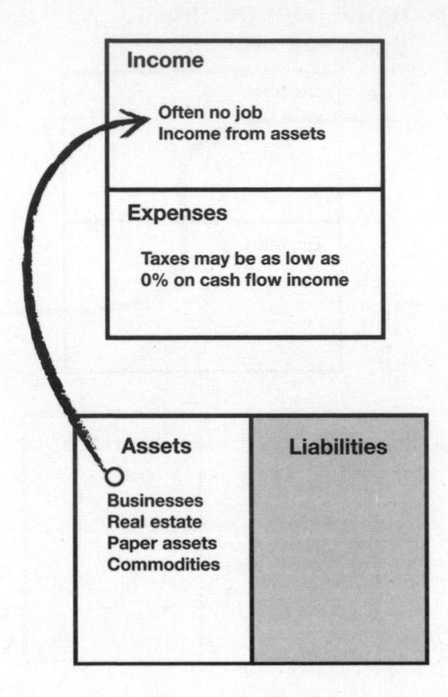

Capital Gains: Capital gains occur when the value of an asset increases in value. For example, if a stock you purchased for $10 a share is trading at $15 a share when you sell it, there is a capital gain of $5 per share, which is taxed at the capital gains tax rate.

The transaction looks like this:

	$15.00	sale price per share
-	$10.00	less purchase price per share
	$5.00	profit in capital gains
-	$0.75	less capital gains tax due… at average of 15%
-	$0.18	less additional 3.5% for Obamacare tax due
	$4.07	**actual net cash flow**

If the transaction were 100 shares of stock…your capital gains would be $500, your approximate tax liability would be $100 ($92.50)—or nearly one fifth of your profit.

	$1,500	sale price per share
-	$1,000	less purchase price per share
	$500	profit in capital gains
-	$75	less capital gains tax due… at average of 15%
-	$17.50	less additional 3.5% for Obamacare tax due
	$407.50	**actual net cash flow**

To review: Investing for capital gains is buying and selling the goose.

Investing for cash flow is investing in the goose that lays golden eggs…and then selling the eggs.

Money Talks

If you understand what money is saying to you, your financial intelligence goes up.

The word *debt* can be both good and bad. If someone owes you money, that is good. If you owe someone else money, and cannot pay it back, that is bad. Seeing both sides increases your intelligence.

F. Scott Fitzgerald said it best:

"The test of a first-rate intelligence is
the ability to hold two opposed ideas in the mind at the same time,
and still retain the ability to function."

Trillion-Dollar Trouble

In 2000 the US national debt was $5.5 trillion. By 2013 it had grown to $16.5 trillion. What's the next stop—$20 trillion?

To give you an idea of just how much a trillion dollars is, imagine this: If you had started spending one million dollars every single day when 2000-plus years ago, you *still* would not have spent one trillion dollars. Another example of how to comprehend what a trillion dollars represents is: If started spending one dollar every single second, it would take you more than 31,000 years to spend one trillion dollars.

The U.S. government has accumulated debt of over $16.5 trillion and it's expected that debt will top $20 trillion in the years ahead. This is debt burden that your child will be expected to carry. In my opinion, this state of affairs speaks to the level of "first-rate intelligence" among our leaders in Washington.

Your Child's Future

Compare the seven basic words of money with the seven basic concepts of traditional school.

Words of Academic Education	**Words of Financial Education**
Go to school	Income
Get a job	Expense
Work hard	Assets
Save money	Liabilities
Get out of debt	Debt
Buy a house	Cash flow
Fund a retirement plan	Capital gains

Given the four 800-pound gorillas facing children today, which child will have a better chance of doing well? The child with only the language of school or the child who also learns the language of money?

Einstein's Words to Students:

In the words of Albert Einstein:

"Education is what remains after one has forgotten what one has learned in school."

That's his way of saying that for many people education just "goes in one ear and out the other."

I studied calculus for three years. I have never used calculus in real life and would not know how to solve any problem today using calculus.

Most students leave school with this as their plan: "I'm going to get a high-paying job with good benefits, save money, live below my means, buy a house, get out of debt, and invest in my retirement plan." Those words become flesh, become actualized or real as they run into the 800-pound gorillas.

If your child fully understands the definitions of the seven basic words of money, they will have a solid foundation on which their financial vocabulary can grow. Remember, words are the basis of financial intelligence.

Rich Dad Lesson

Rich dad said, "The financial statement is the center of the world of money, just as the sun is the center of the solar system."

He also said, "If a father has a weak financial statement, the entire family suffers. If a business has a weak financial statement, the employees suffer. And if country has a weak financial statement, the citizens suffer."

Words Become Flesh

When children play the *CASHFLOW* games, they will see that they use their body, mind, and emotions when they play the game. Each time they buy or sell something, they are mentally, physically, and emotionally transforming seven basic words of money into flesh.

And it's like riding a bicycle: Once you learn to ride, you can ride forever. The same is true for the basic, fundamental understanding of the key words of money.

Words, Definitions, and Relationships

In playing the *CASHFLOW* game, players learn more than just the definition of the words. They are learning the *relationships* between the words. For example, if a person buys an asset, they will immediately see how assets increase their income. If they buy a liability, they'll see their income goes down. Understanding the relationships between words and transactions is much more powerful than simply memorizing definitions.

Today, the financial statements of the United States, Japan, England, and France are gravely ill, riddled with economic cancer. The best way to protect you and your family from this deadly disease is to have healthy *personal* financial statements.

Action Step for Parents

Discuss the power of words and why the words we use are important

My rich dad forbade his son and me from saying, "I can't afford it." Rich dad said, "Poor people say "I can't afford more it than rich people." In my family, "I can't afford it" was used repeatedly.

Words have the power to build people up...or tear them down. They can inspire and empower; they can be devastate and demoralize. The magic of words if that they are free—and we have the power to choose the words we use.

Expanding your child's vocabulary related to money can start at a young age and will continue throughout his or her lifetime. As you play the games that introduce new words—words like assets, liabilities, cash flow, capital gains take the time to find the definitions and understand what they mean. Encourage your child to use the new words in sentences in everyday conversation.

As they grow older, keep a financial dictionary nearby and choose a Word of the Day. Look up the word, discuss the definition, and use the word in conversation at least three times during the day.

As the years go by, the language of money will become a part of your family vocabulary.

Q: Who Does God Love More?

A: The Rich?
The Middle Class?
Or the Poor?

Part Two | Chapter Fifteen

ANOTHER POINT OF VIEW ON GOD AND MONEY

This quote, by Mohammad, makes me stop and think…

"A man's true worth is the good he does in this world."

I think that God looks at what we do with the talents and gifts he gives us and whether or not we use them to do good things. So, who does God love more? Most likely it's those who share their gifts—talents, time, or treasure—with the world.

Making the Case

The Bible says a lot about money, wealth, debt, bankers, generosity, and greed. In fact, it's said that the Bible contains more verses about money than about any other subject.

The Bible verses that resonate with a person has a lot to do with which side of the coin they are on, and how they see themselves and the world.

- Poor people tend to listen to verses on the evil of money.
- Middle class people tend to follow verses on being content and grateful for the money they have.
- Rich people tend to follow verses on how God rewards the rich and punishes the poor.

Bible Verses for the Poor

Here are a few that come to mind:

"Jesus answered, 'If you want to be perfect, go, sell your possessions and give to the poor, and you will have treasure in heaven. Then come, follow me.'

"When the young man heard this, he went away sad, because he had great wealth.

"Then Jesus said to his disciples, 'I tell you the truth, it is hard for a rich man to enter the kingdom of heaven. Again I tell you, it is easier for a camel to go through the eye of a needle than for a rich man to enter the kingdom of God.'"

– Matthew 19:21-26

"Now listen, you rich people, weep and wail because of the misery that is coming on you. Your wealth has rotted, and moths have eaten your clothes. Your gold and silver are corroded. Their corrosion will testify against you and eat your flesh like fire. You have hoarded wealth in the last days.

"Look! The wages you failed to pay the workers who mowed your fields are crying out against you. The cries of the harvesters have reached the ears of the Lord Almighty.

"You have lived on earth in luxury and self-indulgence. You have fattened yourselves in the day of slaughter. You have condemned and murdered the righteous man, who was not opposing you."

– James 5:1-6

Bible Verses for the Middle Class

"If they obey and serve Him, they will spend the rest of their days in prosperity and their years in contentment."

– Job 36:11

"The fear of the Lord leads to life; then one rests content, untouched by trouble."

– Proverbs 19:23

Bible Verses for the Rich

"What use is money in the hand of a fool, since he has no desire to get wisdom?"

– Proverbs 17:16

The Parable of the Talents

Note: A *talent* was a large sum of money. Today it might be $100,000 or even more.

"For it is like a man going on a journey who summoned his slaves and entrusted his property to them. To one he gave five talents, to another two, and to another one, each according to his ability. Then he went on his journey.

"The one who had received five talents went off right away and put his money to work and gained five more.

"In the same way, the one who had two gained two more.

"But the one who had received one talent went out and dug a hole in the ground and hid his master's money in it.

"After a long time, the master of those slaves came and settled his accounts with them.

"The one who had received the five talents came and brought five more, saying, 'Sir, you entrusted me with five talents. See, I have gained five more.'

"His master answered, 'Well done, good and faithful slave! You have been faithful in a few things. I will put you in charge of many things. Enter into the joy of your master.'

"The one with the two talents also came and said, 'Sir, you entrusted two talents to me. See, I have gained two more.'

"His master answered, 'Well done, good and faithful slave! You have been faithful with a few things. I will put you in charge of many things. Enter into the joy of your master.'

"Then the one who had received the one talent came and said, 'Sir, I knew that you were a hard man, harvesting where you did not sow and gathering where you did not scatter seed, so I was afraid, and I went and hid your talent in the ground. See, you have what is yours.'

"But his master answered, 'Evil and lazy slave! So you knew that I harvest where I didn't sow and gather where I didn't scatter? Then you should have deposited my money with the bankers, and on my return I would have received my money back with interest! Therefore take the talent from him and give it to the one who has ten.

"For the one who has will be given more, and he will have more than enough. But the one who does not have, even what he has will be taken from him.

"And throw that worthless slave into the outer darkness, where there will be weeping and gnashing of teeth.'"

– Matthew 25:14-30

The Question

Which verses most resonate for you—verses for the rich, the poor, or the middle class?

My Story

Although I am not very religious, my spiritual and religious education has served me well. This education has given me life and guidance during some very tough times in my personal life, in war, and in business.

When I mention "god" in this section, I do not mean a specific religion's god. I mean a spiritual being, not a human being. I believe in a spiritual god. I use GOD as an acronym for "General Overall Director."

I like what Steve Jobs said:

"Heaven has many doors."

I also like what Mark Twain said:

"I don't like to commit myself about heaven and hell—you see, I have friends in both places."

And I especially like Joel Osteen's comment:

"I'm going to let God be the judge of who goes to heaven and hell."

I also support personal religious freedom, which includes not believing in a God. I do not like people imposing their religious beliefs on me, and I have no plans to impose my beliefs on you.

New Preacher in Town

My religious education began when I was 10 years old. A new preacher came to town. He was young, single, handsome, and from Texas. He wore cowboy boots, jeans, and always had his guitar slung across his back, ready to play and sing. When he spoke, he taught lessons on life, rather than preaching of hell and damnation.

The kids loved him. He was like the Pied Piper. Young people began to come to church without being dragged by their parents.

The "church ladies" were disturbed. He was gone in less than 18 months. During those 18 months, for the first time in my life, I looked forward to going to church. I learned a lot about God, money, religion, and spirituality.

Reverend Ichabod Arrives

The young pastor was replaced by "Reverend Ichabod." The kids named him after Ichabod Crane in Washington Irving's short story, *The Legend of Sleepy Hollow*, first published in 1820.

"Reverend Ichabod" was tall and skinny with a pointed nose. The kids felt he was mean, continually preaching about God's wrath. Although he was skinny, he ate a lot, much like the Ichabod in the Sleepy Hollow story.

Once his family arrived, the church seemed to have a potluck dinner every week. We kids believed he held potluck dinners because he was cheap, feeding his family of six kids and his own unbelievable appetite to test the generosity of the congregation.

His sermons always had something to say about money, greed, the rich, the goodness of the poor, and giving more to the church. He often quoted these Bible verses:

"It is easier for a camel to pass through the eye of a needle than for a rich man to enter the kingdom of God."

and

"For the love of money is the root of all evil."

Spiritual vs. Religious Education

It did not take long for us kids to realize the difference between spiritual education and religious education.

The young preacher with the guitar wanted Biblical lessons to be used as a guide to life. He spoke to our spirits.

"Reverend Ichabod" taught religious education with fear. He was dogmatic. He was into right and wrong, good and bad. To him, life was black or white, with no shade of gray. He had little tolerance for other religions. He was a more powerful speaker than the young preacher. Church attendance went up, but the people attending began to change.

Same Religion, Different Messages

- The young preacher spoke of the love of God.
  Revered Ichabod spoke of the fear of God.
- The young preacher spoke about money as the result of generosity. Revered Ichabod spoke about money as the result of greed.
- The young preacher spoke about God inside us.
  Revered Ichabod spoke about the God outside of us.

Learning about both sides of the religious coin was a great education. After six months, I stopped going to Reverend Ichabod's church. I did not like his side of the coin and went in search of a new spiritual teacher.

Spiritual Education

The young preacher focused spiritual education more than religious education. In addition to teaching us about the Bible and Jesus, he spent time teaching us about the spiritual power inside each of us.

He often said, "We have the power to create our own heaven or hell here on earth." I do not know if it is true, but it has been a useful belief. He also taught us, "God has already given us that power. It is up to us to find and use that power in us."

This lesson about God inside of us really bothered some of those "church ladies," which is one reason why the young preacher didn't stay around very long. I do not know why this upset them, but it did.

In Vietnam, I witnessed many times the spiritual power inside of us that the young preacher spoke about. As a friend said, "I am alive today because dead men kept fighting."

A number of times, we took the guns and rockets off our gunship and became a medical evacuation helicopter. We performed far more dangerous and courageous deeds saving lives than we did in taking lives. As my crew chief said, "We seem to do our best work when we care more about others than when we care about ourselves."

In Business

I continue to use the young preacher's lesson in business. If not for his lessons, I might not have survived my journey from the E-S to the B-I side of the CASHFLOW quadrant. There are many evil, greedy, and desperate people who will do anything for money. The world is filled with modern day Judases, like the disciple who betrayed Jesus for 30 pieces of silver. You have probably met a Judas or two in your life.

Modern Day Judases

My life changed when Rich Dad Poor Dad became a best-selling book around the world. The moment fame and money came rolling in, so did the lawsuits—from friends and business partners, modern-day Judases. That is why Chapter 5 and Lesson 4 of *Rich Dad Poor Dad*, "The History and Power of Corporations", is an important chapter to read if you are rich or are planning to be rich. Lesson 4 is about the rich protect themselves from the Judases of the world via asset protection vehicles known as "legal entities."

Rich Dad Lesson

Rich dad often said: "I don't think god cares if you are rich or poor. God loves you any way. But if you want to be rich, then choose your church and your preacher carefully."

My poor dad always said, "My house and my car are in my name." My rich dad always said, "I want nothing in my name." He kept his wealth in legal entities that protected him from lawsuits from friends, partners, and Judases.

Friend, attorney, and Rich Dad advisor, Garrett Sutton goes into more detail how the rich protect themselves from modern day Judases in his book, *Run Your Own Corporation.*

I state this as a reminder that getting rich does not mean your problems are over. In many ways, new problems begin. Going through the court system and defending yourself, your business, and your money is a modern day hell.

There is an old saying that goes, "When going through hell, keep going."

Millions in Hell

After the crash of 2007, millions of people entered their personal financial hell. Rather than keep going, many are stuck in hell. Many are blaming the rich for their financial problems.

Many young people are also in financial hell, burdened with school loans and low-paying jobs. If they do not make personal changes, many will be in financial hell for life, even though they're highly educated.

Albert Einstein has these spiritual words of wisdom:

> *"Imagination is more important than knowledge. Knowledge is limited to all we now know and understand, while imagination embraces the entire world and all there ever will be to know and understand."*

A Lesson from Hell

In looking back, I've realized that I've needed four different types of education to get through hell on earth. They are:

1. Academic education
2. Professional education
3. Financial education
4. Spiritual education

Action Step for Parents

Discuss the role religion and faith plays in your home…and how your beliefs affect how you think about money.

Many powerful lessons are found within religious beliefs. And whether a person believes in god or follows a specific religion or not, the references and lessons offer other points of view on money and the roles it plays in our lives.

Consider discussing generosity related to god and money. Talk with your child about choices and how, with every dollar that's earned, you have the choice to spend it, invest it or tithe. Discuss the concepts of honesty and truthfulness, as they relate to life and business dealings…and your religious believes. Talk with your child about spiritual money and importance of giving back.

Part Three

GIVE YOUR CHILD AN UNFAIR ADVANTAGE

The true purpose of:

1. **Banks**
2. **Stock Exchanges**
3. **Insurance Companies**
4. **Government Tax Departments**
5. **Pension Funds**

Part Three
INTRODUCTION

There are many benefits to a financial education. And the financial education that you as parents take on, in the home, will give your child these three unfair advantages in life:

1. Make more money
2. Keep more money
3. Protect more money

Legalized Plunder

In the 1850s, the French political economist, Frederic Bastiat, stated:

> *"Everyone wants to live at the expense of the state.*
> *They forget that the state lives at the expense of everyone."*

Bastiat also stated that the privileged classes use the government for "legalized plunder." Today, the legalized plunder of the rich is known by terms like "pork, military contracts, bridges to nowhere, and shovel-ready projects." The rich have the power to influence the laws of the land. That is why there are so many lobbyists offering the President, Senators, and Congressmen "special deals" for support of their special interests.

The biggest corporations, from banks and pharmaceutical companies to farm conglomerates and oil companies, have the power to influence laws, all in the name of helping the people. The 401(k) and Roth IRA retirement programs in the United States are examples of "legalized plunder." This, in my opinion, is why there is no financial education in schools.

The only financial education allowed in schools, it seems, supports teaching kids to "Save money and invest in a 401(k) filled with stocks, bonds, and mutual funds." These directives send money straight into the treasuries of the richest banks and people in the world. Again, I am not saying this is bad. From a position on the edge of the coin where I can see both sides of it, I get the complete picture. When cash flows into these giant investment banks, my partners and I borrow that money to invest in our own private projects such as apartment houses and oil wells.

Bastiat said the legalized plunder by the rich encourages the lower classes to revolt and use *socialist* legalized plunder in retaliation against the rich. Examples of socialized legal plunder are programs such as Social Security, food stamps, welfare, Medicare and now Obamacare. It is the legalized plunder by big corporations that caused the rise of labor unions. Today, the biggest labor unions are not factory laborers but unionized government workers. Among the largest unions in America are the teachers' unions, including the NEA, the National Education Association. This organization is not focused on your child's education. The NEA focuses on making more money to pay for its lobbyists in Washington.

Bastiat recommended that both capitalists and socialists cease all legalized plunder. Like most academics, he lived in a fantasy world, a dream state. He accurately forecasted that legalized plunder for any group, if perverted, would be turned and used against the group it was to defend.

In other words, when capitalists use legalized plunder to make themselves richer, they lose. This is why Lehman Brothers, big banks, Wall Street, and many GSEs (Government Sponsored Enterprises such as Fannie Mae and Freddie Mac) got in trouble and had to be taken over by the government. As you may recall, this takeover took place after the executives, the *managerial capitalists*, helped themselves to hundreds of millions of dollars in pay and bonuses.

This plunder of socialists, via programs such as Social Security, Medicare, and government pensions, is a contributing factor to the insolvency these programs face.

Caught between these giants of legalized plunder are the ordinary citizens, working without the protection of government and giant pools of money.

When giant corporations such as Walmart or Home Depot come to town, many small family businesses die. Managerial capitalists, trained by the finest schools in the world, run these large companies, companies that have replaced the "Mom and Pop" shops that thrived in small towns across the country and around the world. Rather than the warmth of a family-owned business, we see aloof corporate management. Rather than the spirit of "we're all in this together," the feeling becomes "everyone for himself." Rather than high-paying jobs, these corporate giants create a new class of working people, the working poor. Instead of wages going up, wages are coming down. And the more wages fall, the more people depend upon government support for financial and medical survival.

There is an old saying that goes, "When elephants fight, small animals get trampled."

If you are not financially educated, the odds are you will be trampled, no matter how hard or how long you work.

Railroads vs. Oil

During the depression of the 1870s, Tom Scott, owner of the Pennsylvania Railroad Company, began building his own oil pipeline in Pennsylvania. This upset John D. Rockefeller, who had a monopoly on oil pipelines. Rockefeller retaliated by closing one of his refineries in Pittsburgh. The result was a huge financial blow to Scott.

Scott and Rockefeller both lost money, but workers on both sides lost too. They lost their jobs.

Scott fired workers and slashed the wages of those he kept. In retaliation, angry workers set fire to his railroad yards and Scott's empire came tumbling down. The depression of the 1870s got worse as more workers and families struggled financially.

Today, free trade agreements have succeeded in sending an estimated 2.5 million American jobs outside the country to nations that may or may not have labor laws, minimum wage standards, health care benefits, and worker compensation laws.

The winners are corporate giants such as Walmart, General Electric, Microsoft, and Apple.

The losers are American workers who have little choice but to shop at Walmart or Amazon, buying low-priced products from GE and Microsoft. Apple uses its own stores, as well as other retailers, to move its products.

This is why your child's financial education is more important today.

This is why most American parents want their young child to get good grades so they can find jobs with one of the corporate giants, or become an attorney or a doctor.

Even if they find that high-paying job in the E quadrant or become a well-paid professional in the S quadrant, without financial education it's likely that your child will have a significant percent of their money taken, via legalized plunder, over their lifetime.

As the global economy worsens, the legalized plunder will only increase. Our courts are filled with lawsuits, people suing other people and claiming they are entitled to more money. Drug-related crime and violence, kidnapping, and home invasions are a fact of modern life—and not because people want to be crooks. For many people a life of crime seems like their only option. There is also a rise in white-collar crime. I have lost more money to white-collar criminals than I have to street criminals.

The Presidential election of 2012 was a reflection of the "legalized plunder" going on in the world. On one side you had the rich, demanding that spending for social programs be cut and that the defense budget remain untouched. On the other side you had the poor, demanding more government money for unemployment benefits, Medicare, and Social Security.

As Basitat states there is legalized plunder on both sides. Repeating his words:

"Everyone wants to live at the expense of the state.
They forget that the state lives at the expense of everyone."

In other words, we are no longer capitalists. Today we are a more socialist nation, depending on the government to take care of our personal needs.

As former British Prime Minister Margaret Thatcher said:

"...and Socialist governments traditionally do make a financial mess. They [socialists] always run out of other people's money. It's quite a characteristic of them."

Part Three of this book focuses on the importance of giving your child a Financial Unfair Advantage—and how to do that. Financial education is the best defense when elephants are fighting.

Who Wants to Be a Millionaire?

Part Three | Chapter Sixteen

THE 10 UNFAIR ADVANTAGES OF A FINANCIAL EDUCATION

This chapter will summarize the first two parts of this book by reviewing the 10 unfair advantages of a financial education and how they can impact your child's life. Reviewing these 10 unfair advantages will better prepare you to understand the fourth and final part of this book, Be the Fed.

Making the Case

What I refer to as an unfair advantage is the competitive edge that you gain through financial education. These are lessons that you, as parents, can apply and benefit from as well. The examples of life-long learning that you set in your home and within your family will bring your child a lifetime of rewards and put them on a path to a rich life.

Unfair Advantage #1:

The Ability to Transform Your Money and Your Life

As you now know, there are three types of income. They are:

- Ordinary
- Portfolio
- Passive

Most people leave school and work for ordinary income, the highest taxed of the three incomes.

When a person saves money, in a savings account, CD, or in a 401(k), they are working for ordinary income. It requires financial intelligence to be able to convert ordinary income into portfolio or passive income.

A review, in simple terms, of most typical earning patterns:

- **The poor work for ordinary income.**
- **The middle class work primarily for portfolio income.** This includes capital gains, increases in value on their home, stock market investments, and retirement accounts.
- **The rich work for passive income.** This means cash flowing in, whether they work or not.

When I was a kid, I used to watch the TV show *The Beverly Hillbillies*. The sit-com was about a poor man who took a shot at a rabbit and struck oil. That 'black gold' made them rich and they moved to Beverly Hills and learned to adjust to a rich and glamorous lifestyle.

Having passive income is like striking oil in your back yard. The money keeps flowing as long as the oil (or asset) keeps flowing. If you drill more wells, more oil or money flows in to your pockets.

I like to interpret the story of the goose that laid the golden egg as a fairytale about portfolio and passive income. If you eat the goose, it's portfolio income…capital gains. If you keep the goose, you will have more and more golden eggs or passive income, in the form of cash flow.

Question: Why is knowing how to transform your income important?

Answer: Because after 1971, money was no longer backed by gold. Today central banks around the world are printing trillions of dollars, which means your money is worth less and less.

Being able to transform your money means you are better able to keep up with the devaluation of the money you earn.

When a young adult learns to transform their income, they transform their lives from poor to middle class to rich. Rather than work for money, they might strike oil in their brains. That is what Steve Jobs, Walt Disney, and Thomas Edison did.

The word education comes from the word *educe*. Educe means *to draw out*, not put in. Unfortunately, our school system is not interested in drawing out your child's financial genius. They want to keep putting more stuff *into* your child. And, in most cases, this "stuff" programs your child for life as an employee.

Unfair Advantage #2:

The Ability to Be More Generous

The primary reason there is so much greed in the world can be found in Maslow's Hierarchy of Needs, at the second level: Safety.

With a strong financial education, your child has a better chance of reaching Maslow's fifth level, Self-Actualization. At Self-Actualization, the child becomes more generous, giving rather than taking.

As long as they feel insecure financially or uncertain at level two, the child will remain needy, which often leads to becoming greedy.

Rich Dad Lesson

Governments today are actively devaluing the purchasing power of their money by printing more money. Governments want to make the products produced in their country less expensive. If wages go up and money stays strong, products become more expensive on the global markets, and exports slow down.

Lower wages means we can export more products which, in turn, keeps more workers employed. Poorer, but employed.

This is why your child needs to know how to transform their I income, especially ordinary income into portfolio or passive income.

The King of Rock and Roll

When I was a kid, a few stories of Elvis Presley's generosity made the news. In one story, a woman had admired his diamond. With a smile, he took off his ring and gave it to her.

He clearly believed in sharing his blessings with others and gave to many people and many charities. His beneficiary choices were diverse and showed no preference for age, race, or creed. He saw only the need. There is a film titled *200 Cadillacs* that documents his generosity.

According to Maslow's Hierarchy of Needs, Elvis reached the top of the pyramid. He reached the top by sharing his gifts, his talents as an entertainer and the more he gave, the more he received.

There is a saying my Mormon friends taught me: "God does not need to receive but humans need to give." This may be why the Mormon faith is so powerful. They not only preach tithing, they practice tithing. It is a requirement.

The word *tithe* comes from the same word as ten, and it means to give back 10% of what you earn.

Many people say, "I'll tithe when I have the money." The reason they do not have the money is because they do not tithe.

Unfair Advantage #3:

Lower taxes

The more generous you are, the lower your taxes. That may be a bit of an oversimplification, but it's accurate in principle.

As stated in Parts One and Two of this book, the tax laws are guidelines from the government. If you do what the government wants done, the government offers tax incentives or a tax stimulus.

Most people have only one house. The government offers tax breaks for those who provide housing. Along the same lines, the government offers tax breaks for people who create jobs. Most people leave school looking for a job.

Most people work hard to stay out of debt. The government offers tax breaks for those who use debt. This is because the dollar is now debt. If people stop using debt, the economy slows down. Most people consume commodities such as food and oil. The government offers tax breaks for those who *produce* food and oil.

Who Pays the Most in Taxes?

Do you remember this diagram of the CASHFLOW quadrant from the beginning of this book? It shows income tax rates for each quadrant.

TAX PERCENTAGES PAID PER QUADRANT

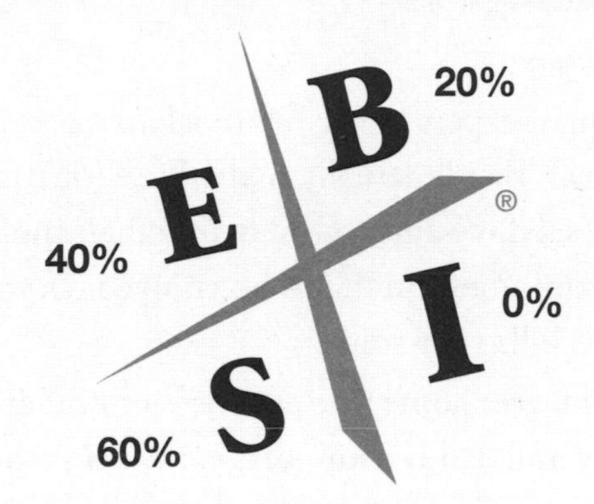

Financial education can give your child an unfair advantage over taxes, if they are more generous and use their resources and wealth to support the economy and assist the government with what the country needs…housing, jobs, specific products or services.

Unfair Advantage #4:

Use Debt to Become Richer

After 1971, the dollar became debt, an IOU from the American taxpayer.

As parents you know first hand that our schools do not teach students about money or debt. Most kids leave college, deeply in debt with school loans and credit cards. After they are married, they go deeper in debt with mortgages, car payments, and consumer debt.

With financial education, your child will learn that there is good debt and bad debt. Good debt makes people richer and bad debt makes them poorer.

Since debt is the new money, a financial education will teach kids to become richer using debt. They will not have to live their lives saying, "I can't afford it" or "I don't have any money."

In learning to use debt to acquire assets such as real estate, a child learns to be more generous in choosing a type of investment that serves a need in society—like providing affordable housing. When they do that, they earn passive income and pay less and less in taxes.

Unfair Advantage #5:

Expand Your Means

Most every quasi-expert in the financial arena recommends, "Live below your means." That is actually bad advice for those with financial education. Besides, who wants to live below their means? There are too many wonderful things in life to be enjoyed. In my opinion, living below your means kills your spirit.

When a child leaves home, the expenses of life hit them in the face. Without mommy and daddy's support, expenses such as rent, food, clothing, transportation, and entertainment overwhelm them—and their paycheck. If they go on a trip or go shopping or an emergency arises, they fall back on their credit cards. Now they have an additional expense: high-interest credit card payments.

If they get married, that could mean two incomes, and two can live as cheaply as one—that is, until the first baby comes along. When the child arrives, their one-bedroom apartment becomes too small and discussions about buying their first home become more intense.

Without financial education, they believe, "Our home is an asset and our biggest investment." With that bit of financial deception spread by the banks and real estate agents, the young couple takes the leap and buys their first home, often more home than they can afford.

With a new home, expenses increase. They now need furniture, appliances, and a car. If an emergency arises, like a leaky roof or car problems, the swipe of a credit card solves the problem.

They tell themselves, "We need to live below our means" and then work hard to become debt free. Being debt free of *consumer* debt is a good idea. The problem is that, without financial education, few people have any idea that using debt to acquire cash-flowing assets could expand their means.

Without a financial education, most kids leave home and enter the same Rat Race their parents are in. I talk with parents all over the world and I know they want more for their kids.

The Rat Race

As the saying goes, "The problem with the Rat Race is, the rats are winning."

Many financial planners recommend starting a college fund for your child's education. In the United States they are called 529 Plans. While the idea, the *context*, is good, the government requires that the content in the 529 Plan be primarily mutual funds, the most expensive and inefficient way to save money. This is another example of Basitat's legalized plunder, another example of how big corporations create laws that send more money into their pockets.

How to Beat the Rats

Rather than do as the rats tell you to do, learn how to beat the rats. The way to beat the rats is by *expanding your means* rather than *living below your means.*

Teaching your child to expand their means gives your child an unfair advantage.

How I Expand My Means

I love cars. If I had more garages, I would have more cars. The problem is, cars are liabilities. My solution to buying more cars is to expand my means by first buying an asset and then letting the cash flow from the asset pay for my liabilities.

I will use a simple example I have written about in a previous book.

Years ago, a rare Porsche convertible came up for sale. The price was $50,000. I had the money. My problem was, if I bought the Porsche, I would be buying a liability and losing my $50,000. When I talked with Kim about it she didn't tell me not to buy the Porsche. She simply said, "Buy an asset that buys the Porsche."

I gave the dealer $5,000 to hold the Porsche for 90 days.

It took me awhile, but I finally found a mini-storage business in Texas and bought it with the $50,000 cash and a loan from the bank. The cash flow from the mini-storage rentals more than covered the monthly payments on my Porsche.

Money and Happiness

"The person who said, 'Money does not make you happy' was manic-depressive," said rich dad.

Today, I have the Porsche, and it's paid off. Once it was paid off, I used the cash flow from the mini-storage to buy other toys. A few years ago, we sold the mini-storage and invested the gains, tax-deferred, into an apartment complex. Rather than making us poorer, the Porsche made us richer. I used the same process when I bought my Bentley.

This is an example of *expanding your means and having your assets buy your liabilities*. Kim and I follow this process religiously.

Another example is our beach house. Before buying our beach house in Hawaii, we spent a few years buying more apartment houses. The cash flow from the apartment houses, our assets, pays for our beach house, a liability. Rather than liabilities making us poorer, creating assets to buy our liabilities makes us richer.

Living below your means does not make most people happy. The luxuries of life are to be enjoyed. Rather than live below your means, teach your child to go for the good life and become richer. Let their dreams of life's luxuries give them the ambition and incentives to move forward.

If your child adopts this process early, they will beat the rats and the Rat Race. All it takes is a little financial education to learn to have your assets buy your liabilities, which can be a powerful unfair advantage.

In other words, even liabilities make you richer if you buy assets that pay for your liabilities.

Unfair Advantage #6:

Increase Your Emotional Intelligence

When I purchased my Porsche by first buying real estate that generated cash flow, I was playing *Monopoly*® in real life. Starting with small green houses, Kim and I slowly began buying bigger properties, properties like the mini-storage.

The reason most people will not follow that process is because they lack emotional intelligence.

Earlier in this book, I introduced a list of Gardner's Multiple Intelligences. As a review, I'm listing them here.

1. **Verbal-linguistic**
2. **Logical-mathematical**
3. **Body-kinesthetic**
4. **Spatial**
5. **Musical**
6. **Interpersonal**
7. **Intrapersonal**

> ***Why Money Doesn't Make You Rich***
>
> *It seems impossible for multimillionaire athletes to go broke. However,* Sports Illustrated *found that after two years of retirement, 78 percent of NFL players are bankrupt or under financial stress. How can that be possible?*
>
> *There are many contributing factors to the suddenly wealthy becoming suddenly living hand-to-mouth again. Horrific spending habits, bad investments, generosity and child support can put the wealthiest athlete into the poor house.*
>
> *And it's not just the NFL: Within five years of retirement, an estimated 60% of former NBA players are broke.*

Emotional Intelligence is often called the "success intelligence."

One indication of high emotional intelligence is *delayed gratification*. One reason why so many people struggle financially is because they cannot delay their gratification. Most people would run out and buy the Porsche or Prius on credit, using bad debt.

By teaching your child to buy assets first and then use their assets to buy their liabilities, you are increasing the child's success intelligence.

Unfair Advantage #7:
Understand the Different Paths to Wealth

There are many paths to becoming a millionaire. A few are:

- You can marry for money, but we all know what kind of person does that.
- You can win the lottery. The lottery is for losers because without the millions of losers, there would be no winners.
- You can win the game show, *Who Wants to Be a Millionaire?* Whoever designed this game show must be an "A" student. Only an "A" student would think that knowing the right answers would make you rich. Very few people become rich by knowing the right answers. Most people become millionaires by making mistakes first and learning from those mistakes—many, many mistakes.
- You can become a professional athlete. The problem is that many professional athletes are bankrupt five years after retirement. If they lose their millions, it's hard to make their money back as they get older.
- You can become a millionaire by being financially intelligent.

Different Types of Millionaires

Many people claim to be millionaires. When I hear this, my first question is: "What kind of millionaire are you?" The following are the different types of millionaires.

- **The net-worth millionaire**

  Before the subprime crisis in 2007, there were many net-worth millionaires. For example, their house appraised at $3 million and they owed $1.7 million. This means their net worth was $1.3 million—making them a net-worth millionaire.

After the crash, their home is now worth half the value or $1.5 million, which means they are no longer millionaires because their home is worth less than the mortgage.

Many stock investors are in this category. They have millions in stock, but very little cash flow from their investments. They are millionaires only on paper.

- **The high-income millionaire**
  Many CEOs, doctors, lawyers, professional athletes, movie stars, and entertainers are high-income millionaires. This means they earn more than $1 million a year. The problem for this type of millionaire is taxes. Most are in the highest tax brackets of all.

- **The inheritance millionaire**
  This group is often called the "lucky-sperm club." They were born into a rich family. The problem for this group is hanging on to the money. Many family fortunes are gone by the third generation. The grandparent who created the fortune passed on the money, but failed to pass on the knowledge needed to preserve and grow that money.

- **The cash-flow millionaire**
  A cash-flow millionaire is a person who earns a million dollars or more from their investments…without working. One of the great things about being a cash-flow millionaire is that both debt and taxes work in your favor. Debt and taxes work against the other types of millionaires.

I knew my best chance to be a millionaire was to be as a cash-flow millionaire. I knew I had no exceptional academic, singing, acting, or athletic talents. Starting at the age of nine, I knew I had to find my own way to success. That is why I loved the game of *Monopoly*. I knew I could do that. Starting small with little green houses, building both my asset column and my confidence, I play the game of *Monopoly* today in real life.

When discussing money with your child, it is important to discuss the different types of millionaires and which type might be best for them. The possibility of becoming a millionaire may inspire them to learn, study, and work to achieve their dream. Their dreams are important because, as rich dad said, "Your genius is found in your dreams."

You can give your child an unfair advantage by inspiring them to pursue their dreams, rather than a steady job. Remember that the word *inspire* comes from the word *spirit*. If you ignite your child's spirit, their genius may emerge.

Unfair Advantage #8:

Protect Your Assets

Many people in the poor and middle classes are proud to say, "My house is in my name," or "My car is in my name." It's called the *pride of ownership*.

The rich, on the other hand, want nothing in their name. The rich protect their assets through legal entities with names like S Corporations, LLCs (Limited Liability Companies), and C Corporations, just to name a few.

The rich use these legal entitles to protect themselves from two types of predators and their two strategies:

1. **Government (taxes)**
2. **People (lawsuits)**

If you or your child is planning on becoming rich, it's important to have legal entities in place—before you are rich. If you are rich, but do not have these entities in place, you could lose everything.

Protection from Predators

There are two types of predators.

One is the government. Without an entity to protect you, you will pay more and more in taxes. The other is people…human hyenas, predators on two legs.

As I shared earlier in this book, my life was peaceful until fame and fortune put me in the spotlight. My high visibility (coupled with my propensity for calling things as I see them) brought unwanted attention and made my wife and me deep-pocket targets. Since 2000, we have been sued several times.

The lesson here is this: If you want your child to be rich, teach them about asset protection before they become rich. As the saying goes, "You cannot buy accident insurance after you have an accident."

Unfair Advantage #9:

Retire Young

Warren Buffett has warned that the coming retirement crisis will be a bigger crisis than the subprime mortgage crisis.

As baby boomers around the world retire, they may encounter a perfect storm of lies, incompetence, and deception that will turn their golden years into a black abyss. The Central Banks of the world may be called on to bail out retirement plans.

For the millions who do retire, their problem will likely be too much time and not enough money. In other words, they know how much retirement money they have, but they do not know how long they will live. With inflation on the rise, many will run out of money sooner than expected.

The best plan for your child's option of 'early retirement' is to start financial education at an early age. Starting while they're young and instilling the lessons and value of life-long learning will give your child the unfair advantage of an early retirement, if that's what they want to do. Financial education is a critical step in preparing for the future—a future that gives your child freedom and choices as they travel through life. Given a foundation of education on money and investing, your children may not have to work all their lives like so many baby boomers will soon be doing.

In 1994, Kim and I retired. She was 37 and I was 47. One reason we retired early was to test our investments. In the event that we were wrong and our investments failed, we were still young enough to recover from our mistakes. Instead of failing, our investment strategies did extremely well, especially after the subprime crash stress-test of 2007.

The retirement scenario on the horizon isn't a pretty one. Forty-nine out of 50 states have government pension plans that are underfunded. On top of this mess, Social Security and Medicare are going broke.

By the year 2020, the retirement crisis will emerge as a worldwide crisis. The golden years for baby boomers will not be so golden. In the near future, there could be three to four generations of a family living under one roof.

Unfair Advantage #10:

Use the Law of Compensation

The Law of Compensation states: My compensation goes up as my experience goes up. In other words, the smarter and more competent I become, the more I earn. For example, in professional sports, rookies start off with lower pay. If they continue to get better with experience, their pay goes up. If they do not get better, they are often cut from the team.

One reason why this financial crisis will be a long-term crisis is because millions of unemployed young people are failing to gain valuable professional experience. This crisis is creating a lost generation because they are unemployed in their third window of learning, ages 24 to 36.

You can give your child an unfair advantage by teaching them to seek mentors and to be willing to work for free in exchange for experience. That is what I did. I learned more working for rich dad for free than I did in school. I believe that working for free is the reason I am financially free today.

You would be surprised by how many successful people are willing to teach the next generation. Successful people know that the more they give, the more they receive. Most unsuccessful people do not know that, or don't believe that it's true. Today there are many fine mentorship programs available for young people.

The primary skills I learned from rich dad were the skills for the B and I quadrants. The basic skills are:

- Know how to raise capital
- Know how to lead people
- Know how to design businesses
- Know how to use debt to make more money

My Story

In 1974, I took a job with the Xerox Corporation in Honolulu to learn to sell. It was my first real job as an adult. For two years I struggled to overcome my shyness and my fear of rejection, all the while worrying that I'd be fired. After four years, I was consistently in the top five sales representatives for Xerox in Honolulu. Although I was making a lot of money, I knew it was time for me to move from the E quadrant to the B quadrant and start a business that was taking shape in my mind. It was my nylon-and-Velcro® surfer wallet business, a venture that made a lot of money at first, but then failed. Although the failure hurt and the financial loss was extreme, I knew I was gaining experience in the B and I quadrants. I was 28 years old and in my third window of learning when I left Xerox for the B quadrant. It was a leap of faith, a leap I have made many times since. Most entrepreneurs are experts at leaps of faith.

Work to Learn

I worked at Xerox to learn to sell. As a rookie capitalist, I knew my primary job was to learn how to raise capital. Today, that is still my primary job. If you ask any entrepreneur, they will tell you the same thing. Their primary job is to raise capital from customers, investors, and from employees' labor.

Donald Trump and I recommend a network-marketing business to gain the same skills and experience. We know that if you can sell, handle rejection, and develop your leadership skills, you have an excellent chance for success in the B and I quadrants. The Law of Compensation applies to the network marketing industry. But most people quit too early, and fail to learn anything significant form the experience.

Today, the Law of Compensation still holds true. For me, the years struggling in the classrooms of the B and I quadrants have paid off. My unfair advantage was that my rich dad spent years preparing me for the process. You can do the same for your child.

Two Professions

Today it is more important than ever that your child have at least two professions—one for them and one for their money. For me, my profession is teaching, but teaching in the B quadrant as opposed to the E quadrant where you'll find most teachers. My money's professions in the I quadrant are in businesses, real estate, intellectual property, oil, gold, and silver.

Other People's Talents

Leadership skills are important for entrepreneurs. I learned a lot about leadership in military school, in the Maine Corps, on sports teams, and in my businesses.

Your child can gain leadership skills in many ways. They learn these skills every time they participate in a group activity. The first thing they must learn is to be a good follower…before they can be a good leader. Too many people, especially those in the S quadrant, want to be good leaders but they are terrible followers.

Many A students lack this skill, which is why they tend to become doctors and lawyers in the S quadrant.

Other People's Money

If you know how to use debt—aka OPM (Other People's Money)—to buy your assets, your returns can be infinite. This will be covered in more detail in Part Four of this book, titled Be The Fed. As you may know, the government offers significant tax breaks if you use OPM. That's another unfair advantage that financial education can give your kids.

This use of OPM is done all over the world. The biggest businesses and tallest buildings are all built with OPM. Simply said, the capitalists of the world use OPM to get rich.

Remember, the cash flow looks like this:

When Es and Ss deposit money in a savings bank, investment bank, or insurance company, the financial institution then move that money. While Es and Ss are advised to *park* their money, Bs and Is are always moving their money. That's because parked money, money that isn't actively working for you, is a liability to Bs and Is.

The Es and Ss of the world are the OP, the Other People who provide the labor and provide the money, through their savings accounts and retirement plans. When you advise your child to "go to school, get a job, save money, and invest in a retirement plan," you are advising your child to be the OP employed and used by Bs and Is.

The purpose of the education system is to produce OP. If you don't want your child to be the OP in the world of money, then it is up to you as parents to give their child a financial education at home.

In Conclusion

Quadrants Are Classrooms

Remember that each quadrant is a different classroom teaching different skills. Teach your child about the quadrants early so they can prepare for their future classrooms.

Quadrants Are More Important than Professions

Also remember that the quadrant is more important than the profession. Although I never dreamed of being a teacher, especially when I was flunking out of school, I am a teacher today. But, I am a teacher in the B and I quadrants, not the E and S quadrants. The difference is, I make as much money as I want, pay very little (legally) in taxes, and do not need a paycheck or a pension.

By giving your child these 10 Unfair Advantages, they gain other advantages in life.

Financial Advantages of a Financial Education:

- Earn more money
- Keep more of your money
- Protect more of your money

Spiritual Advantages of a Financial Education:

- More peace of mind
- More generosity
- More control over your life

Now, on to graduate school. That's Part Four: Be The Fed.

Action Step for Parents

Explain to your child why learning about money will give them an unfair advantage in life.

Education is not about equality. Education is not about being fair. One reason parents put such importance on their child's education is because they know that it has the power to give their child advantages in life. Financial education is an important part of that and teaching your child about money gives him or her a special, unfair advantage. They will be learning things that most kids don't learn,things that aren't taught in schools.

Take the time to explain the different types of income and why understand the differences among them are important. If it's age-appropriate, you can help them to connect the dots between ordinary income and taxes, as discussed in the Action Step in Chapter Thirteen.

Since very few schools have any financial education, if you as a parent have the opportunity to turn your home into a classroom, creating your Wealth Education Nights as an environment that welcomes questions and looks for the lesson in each of life's challenges or setbacks.

In creating an active learning environment in your home you are giving your child a huge—and unfair—advantage. With a strong financial education, your child will have the freedom to follow their dreams. You open the door to the possibility that they may never need a job or a paycheck.

Part Four

GRADUATE SCHOOL FOR CAPITALISTS

Why Not Print Your Own Money?

Part Four

INTRODUCTION

The dream of many entrepreneurs is start a business and "take it public." Taking it public means selling shares of the business, via a stock offering, to the public. This is what Steve Jobs and Mark Zuckerberg did when Apple and Facebook went public. When they took their companies public they started up the printing presses, printing millions of shares of stock in their own companies. They became billionaires.

For many entrepreneurs, selling shares of their companies to the public is their *graduation* from graduate school. Your graduation present is that you can now—legally—print your own money. This also means you may not need to borrow money. You can print more money by issuing more shares of stock in your company and selling those share to the public. It's like getting your PhD in Capitalism.

March 9, 2004 was one of the happiest days of my life. A company I started with a few friends went public on the Toronto Stock Exchange. The company was a mining company in China with a proven body of gold ore valued at five billion dollars.

Although my dream was realized, my education continued. Once the Chinese government realized how much gold we had discovered, the game began. During our negotiations, a high-level government official let us know that we had to make a few people "happy" if we wanted to stay in business. After five years of unsuccessful negotiations we were faced with a choice: do something illegal or sell. We sold our shares and walked away from a business we had been building since 1997.

I do not blame the Chinese government or the Chinese people. Bureaucratic corruption is found in countries all over the world. Corruption exists anywhere money is changing hands.

My experience in China reminds me of what my rich dad said, "Bureaucrats only know how to spend money. They do not know how to make money. If they knew how to make money, they would be capitalists." He also said, "In capitalist countries, capitalists are rich. In socialist and communist countries, bureaucrats are rich."

In the United States, many bureaucrats are becoming rich. This is not a good sign. It is a sign of growing corruption due, in my opinion, to failures in our educational system.

In the opening sections of this book, I quoted from Dr. Frank Luntz's book *What American's Really Want...Really:*

"So how to equip a generation of American's for success in entrepreneurship. Forget about MBAs. Most business schools teach you how to be successful in a big corporation (a bureaucrat) rather than how to start your own company."

Again, his research found:

- 81% of Americans say universities and high schools should actively develop entrepreneurial skills in students.
- 70% say the success and health of our economy depend upon it.

I agree with Dr. Luntz. Most teachers are employees. How can they teach kids about entrepreneurship? If the teacher does come from the world of business, it's most likely that they are a managerial capitalist, a bureaucrat who never started a business from the ground up, much less took it public through a stock offering.

My concern is that our schools are mass-producing more and more bureaucrats with advanced degrees. If this continues, not only will corruption increase but more entrepreneurs may choose to leave the country.

This is why I believe financial education for your child is important. We need entrepreneurs. We need people who grow up to start businesses, create jobs, and learn how to print their own money.

Ways to Print Your Own Money

Starting a business and selling it to the public is one way to print your own money.

Another popular way is called *technical trading* in the stock market, using trading strategies such as *shorts, call* and *put options, collars,* and *straddles*. A few of these strategies are taught in the *CASHFLOW 202* game. As with any new investment plan or strategy, I always recommend education and practice—lots of practice—before doing the real thing.

You do not have to be in the stock market to print money. Every time I write a book, I am printing my own money. I print even more money when I license the international rights to publishers who translate and print my books in other languages. That money arrives on a regular schedule—via royalty check—from every corner of the world.

There are ways a child can begin developing their own neural pathways for printing money. Here are five simple examples:

1. When a child sets up a lemonade stand and exchanges lemonade for money, the child prints their own money—a form of money known as *lemonade for sale*.

2. When a group of children get together to put on a theatrical play, the tickets they sell are another way of printing their own money.

3. If a garage band produces a hit CD, the sale of the CDs is their way of printing their own money. When they go on tour and sell tickets, they're printing more money.

4. When a person creates an *app* for a smart phone or tablet device and receives revenue—money each and every time it's downloaded—their app is their way of printing money.

5. Selling Girl Scout Cookies is an important lesson in printing money…and thinking like a generous capitalist.

My point is this: Printing your own money can be taught and encouraged at home. You do not need government bureaucrats to teach your child this lesson. Besides, having an *academic-bureaucrat (employee)* teach entrepreneurship would be like me trying to teach your child to be a brain surgeon. The results could be brain *damaging*.

There are many ways a parent can teach their child to print their own money and they range from the very simple to very complex. A person is limited only by his or her imagination.

A study guide, *Awaken Your Child's Financial Genius*, has been created to complement this book. That guidebook will assist you in the process of teaching your child the lessons of money and how to be a capitalist who knows how to print their own money. Once your child learns to print their own money, they may never need a job. If they work, it will be because they want to work. That's an incredible gift that any parent can give their child.

You can give your child a massive head start at home just by encouraging them to set up a lemonade stand or get a job at McDonalds. McDonalds is a great place to learn to be an entrepreneur who will, one day, print his or her own money.

A Great Business School

Many people make jokes about "flipping hamburgers" at McDonalds. That is because most people are in the E quadrant.

McDonald's is one of the best business schools for those who want to earn their money in the S or B quadrants.

When a young person asks me how they can gain real world business experience, I suggest they take a part-time job at McDonalds and learn their systems. McDonalds, arguably, has the best business systems in the world.

I suggest they work at every position possible, from cashier to cook, janitor, and if possible, shift manager. In a small retail space, a young person can gain a well-rounded, "hands-on" business experience, in many different departments, that will prepare them to run their own business.

Working at McDonalds will give them experience in 80% of the different components that make up a business. If they work for a traditional business they may gain experience in one department such as accounting, and not gain experience in other departments.

If they look at McDonalds from an E-quadrant mindset, the pay will be terrible. If they look at their job at McDonalds from the S- or B-quadrant mindset, they will see their work experience as priceless.

For you health fanatics, I'm not recommending the food at McDonalds, I'm recommending their business systems. As my rich dad said, "Most of us can make a better hamburger than McDonalds, but very few of us can build a better business."

Remember my rich dad's lesson, "It's not the profession…it's the quadrant." Today, I am a teacher in the B and I quadrants, which is why I make more money than most teachers. Teaching in the B and I quadrants is how I print my own money.

The fourth and final Part of this book focuses on how financial education can teach you and your child to "be the Fed," to print your own money, pay less in taxes, do more good, be more generous, and protect yourself and your family—rather than be crushed by rising inflation, higher taxes, and more poverty in the looming financial turbulence.

Why the Rich Don't Work for Money

Part Four | Chapter Seventeen
BE THE FED

Prior to the 2007 crash, I suspect that relatively few people were aware of the Fed, the Federal Reserve Bank of the United States. Prior to 2007, the Fed was an obscure institution that wielded silent power over the United States and the world economy. Although many people have now *heard* of the Fed, its role and how it functions remains a mystery to many.

The defined purpose of the Fed is "to promote effectively the goals of maximum employment, stable prices, and moderate long-term interest rates."

Obviously, the Fed is having trouble doing its job. One reason we have multi-trillion-dollar deficits is because the Fed is failing. Rather than solve the underlying problems, the Fed prints more and more money.

Making the Case

Today, even homeless people are aware of the Fed, and "End the Fed" signs have appeared in many campgrounds filled with homeless people. During the Occupy Wall Street movement that began on September 17, 2011 in Zuccotti Park near Wall Street in New York City, there were many signs demanding the Fed be shut down. Today many people know that the Federal Reserve Bank is not federal, is not a bank, and has no reserves. It's not even American, owned instead by the richest people and banks in the world. The Fed has the power to print money, even though Fed Chairman Ben Bernanke denies that it does that.

What the Fed does is write checks, out of thin air, to buy U.S. Treasury bonds and other assets to keep the economy from collapsing. The money then flows to the biggest banks and into the economy. The Fed then collects interest on the bonds, interest paid by taxpayers. What happens to the money the Fed collects? That's the trillion-dollar question.

In 2009, Ron Paul, former Presidential candidate and U.S. Representative from Texas, wrote a book titled, *End the Fed*. He has been a critic and opponent of the Fed for years. Paul views the Fed as a quasi-criminal organization, a cartel made up of the biggest private banks in the world. While I agree with Ron Paul and believe the world would be better without central banks like the Fed, I choose not to spend my time in protest. I would rather increase my financial intelligence and look at the Fed from the edge of the coin, the vantage point that lets me see both sides. In looking at both sides, I can see how the Fed has done a lot of good, in spite of what many view as harm.

Although I understand both sides of the argument, I am encouraged to see the heightened level of awareness that has even homeless people now protesting the Fed.

When I was in high school, during the 1960s, President Lyndon B. Johnson launched his Great Society programs that led to the creation of Medicare, Medicaid, and the Older Americans Act. The Great Society was designed to save the poor. The Great Society programs expanded under Republican Presidents Richard Nixon and Gerald Ford, with its greatest expansion during the term of President George W. Bush. Facing re-election challenges, President Bush passed Medicare Part D, the Medicare Prescription Drug, Improvement, and Modernization Act. This allowed Medicare + Choice to add prescription drug coverage and became known as Medicare Advantage (MA) plans. Medicare may be the most expensive of all U.S. social programs to date. That decision made the pharmaceutical companies and elderly voters happy and Bush won his second term.

My Story

Now we have Obamacare, which may prove to be the worst of all Presidential policies. I think many would agree that Obamacare is about more than just healthcare. It's about money and power. There are laws written into the plan that have nothing to do with healthcare and everything to do with passing on more power to government at the expense of even greater invasion into our private lives. It isn't surprising that, in recent months, the words socialism and communism are heard more and more often in mainstream media.

Saving the Middle Class

During the Presidential race of 2012, the campaign rhetoric of both President Obama and Mitt Romney promised to "save the middle class." I asked myself: "What happened to saving the poor?"

Has the Fed made life easier for the poor and the middle class, or harder? One thing seems certain: The Fed has definitely made life much better for the rich.

Unfortunately, very few politicians have the courage to take on the Fed. Rather than take on the Fed, our political leaders talk about "QE" or "Quantitative Easing." That's Fed-talk for "printing money."

Going Over the Cliff

In the final weeks of 2012, the U.S. government was locked in a battle between Republicans and Democrats. The news was filled with stories about "Going over the Fiscal Cliff." One side talked about cutting spending and the other side talked about taxing the rich. In my opinion, the reason they cannot agree is because they know they cannot solve our problems. Politicians know they lack the power. They may know what to do, but they lack the guts to do it.

So lawmakers, "kicking the can" once again, put bandages on America's financial wounds, and the problem is pushed on to the next generation of lawmakers and Americans. That is what Franklin Delano Roosevelt did. He created Social Security and other socialist programs during the last Depression. His solutions, along with President Lyndon B. Johnson's Medicare program, are now today's problems. Like it or not, we began going over the 'fiscal cliff' a long time ago.

During the last depression, tent cities of homeless families were known as "Hoovervilles," named after President Herbert Hoover. If history is any guide, more quantitative easing, printing money to solve our problems, will mean millions more will be homeless.

While I agree with Ron Paul to "End the Fed," I choose to use my rich dad's financial education, which is: *Be* the Fed. As my rich dad often said, "The best way to help the poor is to not be one of them." He also said, "The more you try to help poor people, the more poor people are created." Instead of governments printing more and more money, rich dad believed in teaching people to fish—to print their own money.

In the following chapter you will learn how to be the Fed, rather than end the Fed.

Action Step for Parents

Teach your child ways to print their own money.

One advantage to being poor and then working for rich dad (who paid me nothing) was that I had to learn to use my head when it came to figuring out ways to get my own money.

It's said that "Poverty leads to creativity." And, as I've told the story in *Rich Dad Poor Dad*, I began "making money" by melting old toothpaste tubes and making lead nickels. At the Merchant Marine Academy, I made extra money taking old sails from sailboats and sewing colorful nylon wallets. Since leather wallets rotted when exposed to the elements, nylon wallets were well received by sailors.

My point is, not having money caused me to become creative in finding ways to print my own money. I do the same today with books I write, games I develop, and our educational businesses like The Rich Dad Company as well as with investments in rental properties and oil. With your help, your child can do the same.

Graduate School for Capitalists

Part Four | Chapter Eighteen

HOW I PRINT MY OWN MONEY

The following is the process I use to print my own money. I have done my best to make it as simple as possible. I am afraid I have not done a good job, since it is not a simple process.

I ask you to do your best to follow my explanation. If you do not fully understand it, don't worry; most people don't. If you want to understand it further, I suggest you get together with a friend, someone who also wants to learn, and read my words and discuss the process.

When I want to learn something new, I get together with friends and we discuss different subjects of interest as a group. As they say: "Two minds are better than one." And if you want to learn to print your own money, more minds are better than one.

Collaboration is how I learn best. And that's why I surround myself with a team of smart and experienced Advisors.

Unfortunately, in school, that's called cheating.

Making the Case

It never seems to fail that, when I explain the *Be the Fed* process, someone will stand up and say, "You can't do that." My reply is always the same: "Maybe you can't do it, but I can. I do it everyday." In more precise terms: I have created vehicles—investments, intellectual property, and assets—that put money in my pocket, month after month and year after year, whether I continue to work or not. That's "being the Fed"...or printing your own money.

Needless to say, not *everyone* can actually *be the Fed*, but there are certain steps that anyone can take to improve their financial status.

A few suggestions:

1. Be an entrepreneur: Own your own business
2. Build a team of advisors, attorneys, accountants, and other entrepreneurs
3. Understand how to use debt
4. Understand tax laws
5. Develop high emotional intelligence
6. Set high standards for legal, ethical, and moral character and practices
7. Be a real estate investor
8. Be a commodities investor
9. Dedicate time to financial education and putting what you learn to work
10. Develop strong communication and people skills

My Story

Let me tell you how I created my own Fed...

Returning from Vietnam in 1973, I didn't know if I could make it in rich dad's world. I had at least a basic understanding of the 10 requirements listed above, his guidelines for what was important in his world. I knew job security and a steady paycheck were *not* on his list. And I understood why. At age 25, I knew the process was not going to be an easy one.

Although I did not like school, I did want to learn to be a capitalist. That was my advantage. I wanted to learn—and as you, the *desire* to learn is the key to learning.

In financial terms, the phrase "in kind" means "to pay back with the same." Years ago, it meant paying back the interest with calves. Today it means paying back the interest with money.

When commodities are used for money, *barter* is the word that describes the exchange process.

2. Reserve Money

The second type of money was reserve money. When a merchant traveled across the desert to buy goods from foreign lands, rather than carry gold, which was dangerous, the merchant would deposit his gold or cattle with a *banker*, someone they trusted for safekeeping.

The trusted person would issue a note stating that there was gold or cattle in his safekeeping. The merchant would travel across the desert and pay for his purchases with this note, which was known for a time as *reserve currency*.

3. Fractional Reserve Money

It was not long before the banker who was entrusted with the valuables realized that the merchant did not really need or want his gold or his valuables.

Most of the banker's customers were happier with *notes*, the pieces of paper or IOUs, from the trusted banker. Notes were lighter, foldable, traveled better, and posed less of a risk than the transport of bags of gold.

A light went on in the banker's head and he began lending out *fractional reserve notes*. That meant that if a banker had $1,000 in gold in its coffers (from depositors) he might lend out $10,000 in fractional reserve notes to other borrowers and charge interest, in kind. With the introduction of fractional reserve money, banks began printing money.

When this happened, the money supply expanded, and so did prosperity. In this example, the *fractional reserve* was 10. That meant there were 10 dollars in circulation for every one dollar of gold in the bank.

Everyone was happy…unless, of course, all the savers wanted their money back at the same time. Today, when all the savers want their money back at the same time, it is called a run on the bank.

In 2008 after Lehman Brothers failed, President George Bush signed TARP, the Troubled Assets Relief Program, into law. He was doing his best to prevent a massive, panic–driven run on the banks.

This is how the global economy got into trillions of dollars in debt. Governments all over the world had printed trillions of dollars, yen, euros, and pesos to prevent a global run on the banking system. The bankers were caught lending out money they did not have.

4. Fiat Money

In 1971, when President Richard Nixon took the dollar off the gold standard, the dollar became fiat money. This is the type of money that fuels the world economy today. Fiat money is money a government declares to be money. The definition of the word *fiat* is "it shall be done."

In simple terms, the government runs a printing press and turns a piece of paper into money. Today, it can be done with an electronic pulse. They don't even need paper.

With fiat money, two things happen when more money is printed:

- Taxes go up
- Inflation goes up

Printing money is, essentially, a double tax on the poor and middle class. That's why the gap between the rich and everyone else grows wider. This is also why the first chapter of *Rich Dad Poor Dad* states, "The rich do not work for money." Why would anyone work for *fiat money*?

Printing fiat money can be good for the U.S. economy…for a little while. Fiat money keeps wages low, and keeps the products we produce less expensive so we can export more. If governments did *not* devalue their fiat money, products would become more and more expensive, unemployment would rise, and social unrest would brew. Fiat money also means the government pays off its debt with cheaper dollars. And it means the government collects more in taxes as incomes rise into higher tax brackets, even though the *value* of money is going down.

When I left the Marine Corps in 1973, $25,000 a year was considered a good middle-class income. Today it's considered poverty-level income.

If we keep printing fiat money, it may not be long before $250,000 will be the poverty-level income and a loaf of bread will cost $50. It has happened many times in history. People make more money, move into higher tax brackets paying more in taxes...only to become poorer.

This is why *becoming the Fed* is important. You want to print as much money as possible, your own fiat money, pay as little in taxes as legally possible, acquire more and more assets. These assets will produce more fiat money, and eventually revert back to commodity money, or gold and silver.

This is the process the rich use. This process is the reasons why the rich are getting richer as the poor and middle class continue to struggle and become poorer and poorer. The rich do not work for (fiat) money, but the poor and middle class do.

Could I Become the Fed?

After leaving the Marine Corps, I worked at Xerox learning to sell during the day and started businesses at night and on weekends. I was doing my best to achieve step one on the list of milestones to becoming the Fed, to become an entrepreneur. I knew that if I became an entrepreneur in the B quadrant, I could make much more money than if I was in the E or S quadrants.

My life was a series of successes and failures. My first big success was the nylon and Velcro® surfer-wallet business, a business that soon failed, leaving me nearly a million dollars in debt. I paid off the debt by going into the rock 'n' roll industry, producing licensed products for bands such as Duran Duran, Pink Floyd, and the Police. My rapid success in rock 'n' roll was soon followed by failure. Although I knew that each failure was making me smarter, the pain of failure was excruciating.

This is why emotional intelligence and spiritual education are vital to the process of learning. Many times I wanted to quit and many times I wanted to cheat, lie, or steal, but I stayed on the path and faced each day and every problem as one more chance to become smarter, gain more experience, and develop my legal, ethical, and moral character.

Eventually I made it. But I may not have without my wife Kim and great friends. Much like fight school, it is a transformational process. Today I *own* my own Fed.

The following is what I do to Be the Fed:

Why Banks Love Debtors

In the modern banking system, for every $1 you put in the bank as savings, the bank is allowed to lend out $4. When I invest in real estate, I help the bank lend money to me. Remember, your $1 in savings is the bank's liability. When I borrow money, my $4 in debt is the bank's asset.

Where did the additional $4 come from? It came out of thin air. It's how the smaller banks print money. It's the fractional reserve system. The system allows banks to lend more money than they have on deposit, but they must keep a fraction of it, in this case one quarter of total deposits, hence: fractional reserves. If no one is borrowing, the banks do not want your savings because your savings cost the bank money. At the peak of the financial crisis, savers were pouring money into the banks. When banks could not lend, a few banks began charging savers interest to keep their money safe.

1. **I print my own fiat money**

   In 1996, Kim and I started The Rich Dad Company. We raised $250,000 from investors. Once the company was up and running, we paid the investors back with interest (in kind).

   Today, the business prints its own (fiat) money by operating in over 55 countries with gross revenues in the millions of dollars providing jobs all over the world.

All money coming in is an *infinite return*, since all the money we originally invested into the business, our investors' money and ours, has been repaid. An infinite return is the same as printing money, just as the Fed does. Every year, we design new products and, once again, more money comes in. If The Rich Dad Company were shut down, the cash would still flow in from our international book and game licensees.

> ***You Can't Do That.***
>
> *Whenever I explain how we print our own money I encounter someone who says: "You can't do that." Or, "You can't do that in my country."*
>
> *I assure them it is done in every country of the world. My response is: "Maybe* you *can't, but somebody in your country is doing it. This is the way the laws work in almost every country in the free world. The next time you see a large office building, or hotel, or residential project remind yourself that the people who own those big buildings are doing it." How are they doing it?*

2. **I invest in real estate using fractional reserve money**
   Real estate is a great investment because bankers love real estate. It is much easier to get a real estate loan than a business loan. Investing in real estate is fractional-reserve money. For every dollar I invest in real estate, like apartment buildings or commercial properties, the bank will loan me another five dollars. So the ratio is 1:4.

I call fractional reserve money a *one-to-five* lift because I have expanded my personal money supply by 500 percent. Some call it *leverage*. Some call it *OPM*. Some call it debt, a four-letter word that for some is a very good word.

Our objective is to get our dollar, our fiat money, back. That means we go from a 1:4 equity-to-debt ratio to a ratio of 0:5. An 0:5 ratio means that none of my money is in the property and it is debt that is financed, 100%, with the bank's money. By borrowing our $1, we shift from fractional reserve money to pure fiat money. The real estate property is printing our money with 100% of the bank's money. Having none of our money in the investment, we again achieve an infinite return, which is in effect printing 100% fiat money.

The Law of Compensation

In 1973, after taking a three-day real estate seminar, I purchased my first property for $18,500. I put 10% down, or $1,850, using my credit card. That was my first 100%-financed investment.

By 2005, Kim and I and our partners Ken McElroy and Ross McAllister were putting together our first multi-million dollar, 100%-financed investment. Kim and I put up $1 million as our down payment. We improved the property and added new apartments. The rents went up and, on the basis of the additional income generated, the bank refinanced our loan on the property. (In small real state investments, banks lend money according to the investor's financial strength. On larger real estate investments, banks lend money on the financial strength of the property, more so than the investor). With the new loan on the property, Kim and I received our $1 million investment back, tax free, because it was debt. (If it were ordinary income, we would have paid approximately $500,000 in state and federal taxes.)

Today, we still own the property. It is 100% bank-financed and we still receive our monthly cash flow income, which is taxed at the lower passive-income tax rate. The bank is our partner that has provided 100% of money invested, but we receive 100% of the appreciation, amortization, and depreciation. The bank gave us our $1-million-dollar investment back, which we re-invested, into another apartment project and then repeated the process. This is why I love banks. They are the best partners, providing

How Money Changes Quadrants

When I make money in the B quadrant, I immediately invest more in the I quadrant. I do this to further minimize taxes on the B-quadrant income.

If I spent my money from the B Quadrant, I would not be as wealthy and I'd pay higher taxes.

For example, if I make $100,000 in the B quadrant, I will either invest in a real estate project or an oil and gas project. Not only do I acquire more assets, I gain more cash flow and, again, reduce my taxes.

that you are a good partner to them. The tax department is also a great partner because we are doing what the government wants done, which is employing people, using debt, and providing housing.

The core principles in my first investment in 1973 and in the investments Kim and I do today are the same. Only the number of zeros in the amount of the transactions has changed. This is an example of The Law of Compensation in action, the law that states as education an experience goes up your compensation goes up as well.

As long as we have our own money in the investment, the cash flow we receive is fractional-reserve money. The moment all of our money is pulled out, via financing using 100% debt, the cash flow we receive is pure printed money. We are the Fed.

The Velocity of Money

Most people, especially Es and Ss park their money in savings, insurance policies, or in retirement accounts. Bs and Is borrow that money and keep the money moving by acquiring assets, then getting the money out of the asset to invest in another asset, over and over again.

Their motivation is that they receive more and more income and pay less and less in taxes. This is because they do what the government wants done. They create jobs, housing, food, fuel, and use debt to make more money.

In simple terms: Es and Ss park their money. The Bs and Is keep money moving. In financial terms, keeping money moving means acquiring more assets is known as "the velocity of money."

Banks Are the Best Partners

When it comes to investment partners, banks are the best. Banks put up most or all of the money and let me keep all the profits—as well as the tax advantages like amortization, appreciation, and depreciation. Most partners want to share in the profits and tax advantages, but banks don't.

If the words amortization, appreciation, and depreciation are new terms that are not you in your financial vocabulary, flip to the Glossary at the back of this book. Also make a note to talk with you tax preparer or a tax professional to explain these important terms in greater detail.

3: I convert cash flow to commodity money

Many so-called experts call gold a barbaric relic of the past. They are correct. It is a relic that has survived thousands of years.

Many people are buying gold and silver to convert their fiat money into commodity money. The problem is that in doing so they do not acquire assets that produce cash flow. Their fiat money goes straight into hiding…as barbaric relic of the past. It doesn't do much good for society or the economy, as it sits in a safe doing nothing.

By being the Fed, I print my own fiat money and acquire assets such as businesses, real estate, and oil wells—assets that serve society, as well as produce cash flow. With our extra money we purchase gold and silver. We don't save fiat, counterfeit, money.

Since the U.S. dollar is no longer real money, but instead a currency that is going down in value, it makes no sense to me to save dollars. If we need dollars—cash—then gold and silver are liquid and can be converted quickly and easily back into dollars.

By being the Fed I've reversed the history of money. I start with fiat money and get back to commodity money.

Two Dads

I was fortunate to have two father figures in my life. They were my best teachers. I learned more from them than I learned in school. From my poor dad I learned the importance and value of study. From my rich dad, I learned the power of generosity.

Starting at age nine, by playing *Monopoly*, my education in the world of "C" students—the students of capitalism—began. It's a world that many "A" students, the academics, or "B" students, the bureaucracy, rarely see.

On thing that's become crystal clear to me as I've gotten older: In the big picture, life is not about grades. Life is about what you choose to study.

Action Tip for Parents

Explore and experience the real-life world of money with your kids.

As a parent, it is important to teach your child to take action and learn by doing.

And when it comes to learning about money, great ways to do this is to take trips into the real world. Money is a part of nearly every decision we make: what to have for dinner, where to gas up the car, and how to pay for dental care.

Here are a few examples:

- Take your child grocery shopping...and discuss the family budget and what it costs to feed your family.
- Take them to a real estate office...to look at an investment property and discuss how to evaluate an investment opportunity.
- Take them to a coin shop that sells gold and silver coins...and explain how the prices are determined and why gold and silver can be good investments.
- Take them to a financial planner's office or a stock brokerage... and let them listen in on the conversation.
- Use real-life family situations and problems as learning opportunities.

In my poor dad's home, money problems were never discussed nor were financial mistakes admitted. For my poor dad, to admit you had problems or made mistakes meant he was stupid or a failure. In other words, he brought his culture from school into our home. In my rich dad's home, money problems and even mistakes related to money were learning opportunities.

When real money problems or mistakes occur in your home, take the time to discuss and bring in new information, from this book or other resources and seek wisdom from the other side of the coin.

By seeking wisdom from the other side of the coin, you are teaching your children to increase their intelligence in all aspects of life.

My poor dad believed that knowing the right answer was enough. For him, knowing that Columbus discovered America in 1492 was enough. My rich dad believed knowledge was action, what you knew you could do. My rich dad would rather learn to be Columbus than memorize the date he set sail.

As the Cone of Learning reminds us, *doing the real thing* and *simulation*—both action-oriented and experiential ways of learning—are not only more fun but more memorable.

When real money problems or mistakes occur in your home, take the time to discuss them and seek out new information, from this book or other resources, which will help you to look at the problem from the other side of the coin. By seeking wisdom from *every* side of the coin and multiple points of view you are teaching your child to increase his or her intelligence in all aspects of life.

Who Is Teaching Your Child to Fish?

Final Thoughts

A home is a classroom…a child's most important place of learning. The foundations for life are built at home. Unfortunately, millions of children grow up in homes that are not healthy or supportive environments. Many kids are raised in environments of abuse, drugs, lies, hate, prejudice, and addictions. And these are rich kids. Poor kids grow up in an even tougher environment of poverty.

I wrote this book for parents because parents are a child's most important teacher. Even if a parent is uneducated, that parent can still encourage learning. Even if a parent has suffered abuse or neglect, that parent can still hold their child and make them feel safe and loved. Love is a gift we all have to give and it doesn't cost any money. And it can find its way into every home, rich or poor.

This book is the most important book I have ever written because I knew only parents who truly loved their child and were concerned about his or her education—and their future—would read it. I did my best to keep things simple.

I cannot emphasize strongly enough the importance of understanding the three sides of every coin, the importance of seeing things from multiple perspectives and being open to other points of view. Parents can increase their child's intelligence by teaching them how to see a bigger picture, more than a right or wrong world.

I've emphasized the importance of generosity over greed and attempted to explain how the U.S. tax code actually rewards generosity. I've shared my belief that education is a life-long process, rather than a grade at the end of a semester, and that learning from our mistakes is how we're designed to learn.

Keeping Pace with Change

There are many causes for the financial crises the world faces. The lack of financial education in our schools is only one of them. Another important cause of this economic turmoil is a concept known as *accelerating acceleration*, or the acceleration of change. Said another way, one reason schools fail students is simply because the school system cannot keep pace with change. Our current education system was founded in the Agrarian Age, marginally updated for the Industrial Age, and sorely lacking, in my opinion, in its ability to serve today's kids living in a fast-paced, ever-changing Information-Age world.

In a world of accelerating acceleration, what is new today may be obsolete in less than two years. The good news is that most children are programmed to keep up with this accelerating acceleration. The flip side of that coin is that most schools and teachers are not. It shouldn't be surprising that many students are diagnosed with ADD, or Attention Deficit Disorders. In many cases, I think, ADD may be nothing more than a new name for boredom.

These facts of academic life make a parent's role as teacher more important than ever. And this begs the question: How do parents keep their child engaged in learning?

One answer is games. Kids sit for hours engaged in games—on computers, game consoles, tablets and smart phones. I learned some of the most significant lessons about business and investing by playing *Monopoly* for hours. Many companies, The Rich Dad Company included, are investing in tools and products that will deliver education in formats that work for today's kids. I believe that kids *want* to learn. Every day they discover new and exciting things in the world around them…ideas, and innovations and people that fascinate them. Our job as teachers and parents is to make learning fun, engaging and experiential—so the lessons translate into real life and are relevant, real and useful.

The bottom line is that your child can learn more at home than at school. And you, as a parent, can turn your home into the world's greatest classroom by opening your child's mind to all that life has to offer. In helping them find their special genius—and supporting their dreams—you are giving them a priceless gift.

Will iPhones and iPads ever replace teachers or traditional schools? I don't think so. But for now, a proactive parent can supplement and accelerate their child's learning via mobile devices and content designed for the learning speed of kids. The good news is that, in a world of soaring college tuition costs and student loan debt, this electronic way of learning offers a affordable alternative to the traditional education model.

An Information-Age World

In this Information Age, the emperor of education truly does have no clothes. And, thanks to the innovations of modern-day entrepreneurs, quality education can be affordable and accessible. And, like the era when Henry Ford made the automobile affordable for almost everyone, today's true capitalists are doing that with education.

Entrepreneurs such as Steve Jobs and Bill Gates have turned every home—rich or poor, first world or third world—into a first-rate university. A world of information is accessible at lightning speed with the touch of a button or the tap of a key. Technology has changed the world and in my opinion is the biggest change in the history of the world. Never before has a world like this existed, a world without limits or boundaries. And it is open to your child.

Oprah Winfrey found her genius on television. Thomas Edison found his genius in his laboratory. Tiger Woods found his genius on the golf course. And The Beatles found their genius in a nightclub. These geniuses never finished school.

It's not inconceivable that, just as gun powder and the cannon brought down the castle walls of kings and queens six hundred years ago, mobile devices will bring down the hallowed walls of education as we know it today. Rather than governments telling us what to learn, your child will choose what they want to learn from anywhere in the world. Just as Steve Jobs dropped out of Reed College so he could start dropping in on classes and choose what he wanted to learn, your child can follow their heart and, later in life, the spirit within them that drives their passion and dreams. Maybe that path will lead to becoming an entrepreneur whose business "prints money," an investor who puts his or her money to work for them…rather than an employee in a world of high unemployment and low wages, working hard for money all their lives.

Fortunately or unfortunately, this may mean greater global chaos as the old is replaced by the new. Schools are slow to change. Teachers' unions do not want change. They want the status quo, which may be good for them, but bad for your child and the taxpayers.

The world changed in 1971. When President Nixon took the world off the gold standard, the rules of money changed. Sadly, perhaps criminally, our schools have not adapted to that change. Today our schools continue to teach kids to save money, even when money is no longer money. Schools advise students to get out debt, while the rich use debt to become richer. Schools teach kids that "Your home is an asset," even after the crash in the real estate market decimated the financial foundations of millions of families. And schools program you child to view taxes as a person's "highest expense" rather than opportunities and incentives. I believe the keys to the future are in the hands of parents, the classroom of the home enhanced by technology, and the genius in their child. In other words, the future of the world is truly in our homes, our hearts, and the minds of our children. We are all, I believe, at the precipice of the greatest human transformation in world history.

Will there be chaos? Yes. Will there be violence? Probably. Will there be fear? Of course. Will there be new entrepreneurs who choose to take on the future and all the opportunities it offers? Absolutely.

Question: What can a parent do?

Answer: Use time at home with your child wisely. Keep in mind the three windows of learning, the concept of multiple intelligences, the Cone of Learning, the power of games, and Maslow's Hierarchy of Needs. Remember that even the first, smallest steps toward creating a home environment that celebrates learning and applying what you learn puts you and your child on the path toward taking greater control over your financial future.

> It's important that a parent make the home learning environment one in which it's okay to make mistakes, try new things, ask questions and admit that you might not know all the answers but that you can learn together. Foster an environment that's open to change and modification…in this fast-paced world of accelerating acceleration.

Most important, perhaps, is setting an example for you child by being someone who has an open mind, someone who can stand on the edge of a coin—an idea, an issue, a statement…whatever it is that you're thinking about or talking about—and see it from *both* sides. That's intelligence—and the kind of intelligence that can impact your financial future and, truly, accelerate your child's life.

Too many people leave school seeing the world from a right-or-wrong, black-or-white point of view. Many believe there is only one right answer in the test of life. In reality, life is a multiple-choice test, a test where every choice might be right.

One reason I wrote this book is to expand a parent's view of the world, allowing them to see the different sides of every coin. Seeing the other side to any issue increases a person's intelligence. It also means people who live in right-or-wrong, black-or-white worlds, may be highly educated, but less intelligent.

For example, when it comes to money, people who say, "Tax the rich" are unable to see the other side of the coin. They fail to see that when governments raise taxes, they raise taxes on people who say, "Tax the rich." They do not raise taxes on the rich.

In another example, when people say, "The rich are greedy," they often fail to see their own greed and how the rich might be generous. And when a parent advises his or her child to, "Go to school to get a job," they could, more intelligently, advise their child to learn to provide jobs.

One of the biggest problem I see with education is that our schools teach kids to work for money, rather than teach kids how to have money work for them.

Rather than teach kids how to have money work for them, schools advise kids to turn their money over to banks, mutual fund companies, real estate agents, and retirement funds—the very people who caused this crisis. I am not saying the financial services industry is good or bad. I am saying that a lack of financial education is at the core of the crisis.

All children have a natural interest, attraction, and curiosity about money. Why not use this natural interest in money to stimulate the genius in your child?

The General Education Board

In 1902, John D. Rockefeller founded the General Education Board. It appears that he created the board to take over the education system of the United States. I've often thought that this may be why our schools do not teach financial education.
It seems the reason why capitalists like John D. Rockefeller, JP Morgan, Cornelius Vanderbilt, Washington Duke, and Leland Stanford, often called Robber Barons, took over education was to watch for the best and brightest children of the poor and middle class families. They'd teach them, then hire them as employees, managerial capitalists, to run their corporations. It seems apparent that these Robber Barons did not want students to know much about money, lest they inspire a generation of entrepreneurs versus the steady stream of employees that the Robber Barons needed as employees and managers.

Selling Your Soul

"As long as you need money, a part of your soul is always for sale." –*Anonymous*

Politicians prey on the poor by offer entitlement programs, such as Social Security, Medicare, and now Obamacare to get for votes.

Corporate executives, like food industry managers, who sell fat, sugar, and salt to an obese population to keep their high-paying jobs, bonuses, and pensions.

Bankers offer credit cards, mutual funds, and student loans to people without any financial education to make fees, interest, and commissions.

Why "A" and "B" Students Work for "C" Students

In simple terms, "A" students are the academics, specialists like lawyers, doctors, accountants, teachers, engineers, and journalists. The "B" students, students of bureaucracy, are often management students. Both "A" and "B" students study only one side of the coin.

On the other hand, "C" students, true capitalists, must be students of *all three sides* of a coin. And that is why "A" students, and many "B" students, work for "C" students.

"I'm Entitled."

It seems obvious to me that the lack of financial education is a primary reason for the growing entitlement mentality. From elected officials and public servants to unionized workers, military personnel, corporate employees and poor…more and more people are jumping on the entitlement bandwagon with the belief that the world owes them a living. And as the purchasing power of the dollar continues to decline, many of the once-productive and self-sufficient people in the middle class may join the ranks of the poor.

The Emperor of Education Is Naked

From my perspective, I believe that—we are faced with an education crisis and an entitlement crisis—more than an *economic* crisis.

When you look at the trillions in unfunded liabilities such as Social Security, Medicare, and corporate and government pensions, it is obvious we have a people crisis caused by a dysfunctional and obsolete educational system. The United States and the world will probably print trillions in money—money backed by little more than faith—attempting to give people fish, rather than teaching them to fish. And all the while refusing to admit that the Emperor of Education is naked.

All coins have three sides. Teaching your child to fish means teaching your child about the three sides to every coin. It is a life-long educational process that has the power to transform a child from poor, or middle class, to a global entrepreneur who shares new ideas and products and services with the world.

A parent's role in a child's education is more important today than ever before. This is why I personally thank you for caring enough about your child's financial future and financial education to do all that you can to give them an unfair advantage. For many of you, I expect this means stepping out of your comfort zone, opening your mind to other points of view, and making the commitment yourself to become more financially educated.

Every child has the potential
to grow into a rich person,
a poor person, or a middle-class person.

Parents have the power to influence
which one their child becomes.

Thank you for reading this book. And thank you for taking an active role in your child's financial education.

Financial education has the power to transform lives.

The Greatest Love of All

"I believe the children are our future

Teach them well and let them lead the way

Show them all the beauty they possess inside

Give them a sense of pride..."

from the song, ***The Greatest Love of All***
written by Michael Masser and Linda Creed

EPILOGUE

Obama Meets Jobs

"A" Student Meets "C" Student

As Steve Jobs was struggling with cancer, in the fall of 2010, he had a 45-minute meeting with President Barack Obama.

The following are excerpts from the book *Steve Jobs*, by Walter Issacson:

"The administration needed to be a lot more business-friendly. He (Steve) described how easy it was to build a factory in China, and said that it was almost impossible to so these days in America, largely because of regulations and unnecessary costs."

"Jobs attacked America's education system, saying that it was hopelessly antiquated and crippled by union work rules. Until the teachers unions were broken, there was almost no hope for education reform. Teachers should be treated as professionals, he said, not industrial assembly-line workers. Principals should be able to hire and fire them based on how good they were."

"It was absurd," he added, "that American classrooms were still based upon teachers standing at a board and using text books. All books, learning materials, and assessments should be digital and interactive, tailored to each student, and providing feedback in real time."

Thank you, Steve Jobs.

– Robert Kiyosaki

MEET THE LANNON FAMILY

Josh and Lisa Lannon
Haley, age 10, and Jake, age 7

So many families, including ours, expect the school system to teach our children well. We send our children off to school with the highest levels of trust…and then ask ourselves: Is it trust or, at times, just plain ignorance? And while schools teach the basic skills, it's very much an employee-focused curriculum.

Our 9-year-old daughter, Haley, came home from school one day very discouraged. We asked her, "Haley, what's wrong?" She told us that her teacher was having all the kids in her class pick a job. Her teacher had provided career choices for them to choose from. Her classmates were going along with the exercise and picked jobs from the list on the blackboard.

Haley said to us, "When it was my turn, I told the teacher I wanted to own the store."

At first we didn't understand why Haley was so discouraged. Owning the store sounded like a great idea to us.

Then we learned from Haley that one of the jobs was to *work* in the classroom store. When the kids earned money from their jobs, they could buy stuff there. It was like a rewards system. Other occupations on the list were: banker, janitor, police officer, store employee, etc. Haley saw the store and said she wanted to own the store.

The teacher told her this: "No Haley, you have to pick a job to work. We don't have a store owner." So Haley asked the teacher, "Why not? I want to own the store. My parents own a business and they are teaching me about owning businesses."

Haley told us she knew that her teacher was getting mad. Her fellow classmates were snickering and Haley felt like she had done something wrong. Her teacher said "Haley, YOU HAVE TO PICK A JOB." Haley told us that she had become very uncomfortable and that all the kids were looking at her.

We asked Haley, "So what did you do?"

"I picked the police officer," she said. "Why?" we asked.

"Because Mom was a police officer before you built Journey Healing Centers," Haley said in the sweet voice of a nine-year-old.

Haley was upset and we continued to talk about her day at school. Haley told us that she would have worked hard and kept the store looking nice. She knew she could be the store owner and seeing her spirit crushed was tough for us.

But it gave us a great opportunity to talk about the school system and the fact that schools teach kids to be employees. That's the mindset of the school system: choose a profession, then pick a major in college, then get a good job.

We told Haley that at home we will teach differently and we want her to see the both sides of the coin. We want her to understand the school system and what it teaches, but know that there is a bigger picture—and that she can, in real life, own a store if she wants to.

As parents we were incredibly grateful that Haley knew she could tell us about her experience at school.

We told her that picking the police officer was a great second choice. Not only because Mom was one, but because she would learn leadership. She would learn what it's like to enforce the rules, to not always be liked when enforcing those rules, and how to handle it. We talked about how those skills are also important for an entrepreneur.

As a 5th grader—when it's all about being liked and fitting in—Haley's experience was a great opportunity to learn leadership from a different perspective. We told her that it was good to see her hold her ground and question things that didn't make sense to her. Her upset turned into a great learning opportunity for our family.

Our fear is that many parents don't always see the opportunity that upsets like this present...since most were raised with an employee mindset.

Schools are not teaching our children to be entrepreneurs. And they are crushing many dreams and demanding conformity. It's up to us, as parents, to encourage our children to believe that anything it possible, even when a schoolteacher does not agree.

Author's Note: Josh and Lisa Lannon are Rich Dad Advisors as well as good friends. Josh and Lisa are the authors of the Rich Dad Advisor series book *The Social Capitalist.*

MEET THE MCELROY FAMILY

Ken and Laura McElroy
Kyle, age 14, and Kade, age 11

Our two boys, Kyle and Kade, ages 14 and 11, are average kids. They struggle in school with a variety of subjects just like most other kids and working with them to get their schoolwork done can often be a battle.

As parents, we believe that we have the responsibility to teach and guide our children and that it is not the school system's responsibility. It is our responsibility. School systems do not create confident children, and it is not their responsibility to do so. It's the time that parents spend with their children that helps them develop into independent and confident young adults.

My wife Laura and I have discussed ways that we might help our kids learn. Our discussions led to a conversation about the fact that kids don't always know why they're in school. We decided that if we could figure out a way for them to understand the importance of what school teaches them, then perhaps they'd make the connections on how to apply those lessons later in life. We felt certain that the process of learning might come easier for our boys if we could make it fun and help them see and understood the bigger picture.

It has always intrigued me that when our kids had an interest in something they learned very easily. I found that the dots seemed to connect quickly for them on subjects they wanted to learn more about. And I realized that I learned exactly same way: I learned the most when I wanted to learn.

We agreed that one way to make the learning process more meaningful for Kyle and Kade would be to help them create their own business. The process of starting a business would give us the opportunity to teach them how the real world related to the subjects they were studying in school. As a bonus, this strategy would also give them the opportunity to earn their own money.

We could never have imagined how successful this idea would be. Over the course of three years, our kids have started three businesses and the lessons they are learning are invaluable. This new knowledge and financial independence has created confidence in our kids. They no longer look to us as a financial resource for things that they may want. And the most surprising lesson for us, as parents, is how frugal they are with the money they earn. Their dollars seem to last longer because they're dollars that they earned themselves.

One key point in making this entrepreneurial process successful for Kyle and Kade was allowing them to take risks and to make mistakes. Most people are afraid of making mistakes. The freedom to make mistakes and learn from those mistakes creates wisdom, knowledge, and experience. It is an important part of the learning process. Failure should be embraced at all levels and used as a learning tool. Most education systems today teach our top students to be risk-adverse, which can discourage the average student.

Through this process there have been opportunities to teach a number of life lessons—like paying themselves first and the importance of giving back. We educated them about investing in assets versus liabilities and how their money could be used to make more money in the future.

We set up bank accounts for the boys and taught them about how to budget their income and expenses. We taught them about simple and compound interest.

These days the latest smart phones, laptops, designer clothes, $125 sneakers, and video games are a part of daily life at school. Parents must make decisions—as well as set the expectations—that will determine if the "things" kids want or need will be empowering or disabling.

Every child has a special gift, a special genius...but traditional education rarely offers the freedom for these gifts to develop and shine. Involved parents can recognize and nurture each child's special genius and help pave the way for a great life of doing what they enjoy and are passionate about.

Author's Note: Ken McElroy is a Rich Dad Advisor as well as a friend and business partner. Ken is the author of the Rich Dad Advisor series book *ABCs of Real Estate Investing.*

About the Author
Robert Kiyosaki

Best known as the author of *Rich Dad Poor Dad*—the #1 personal finance book of all time—Robert Kiyosaki has challenged and changed the way tens of millions of people around the world think about money. He is an entrepreneur, educator, and investor who believes the world needs more entrepreneurs who will create jobs.

With perspectives on money and investing that often contradict conventional wisdom, Robert has earned an international reputation for straight talk, irreverence, and courage and has become a passionate and outspoken advocate for financial education.

Robert and Kim Kiyosaki are founders of The Rich Dad Company, a financial education company, and creators of the *CASHFLOW*® games. In 2013, the company will leverage the global success of the Rich Dad games in the launch of a new and breakthrough offering in mobile and online gaming.

Robert has been heralded as a visionary who has a gift for simplifying complex concepts—ideas related to money, investing, finance, and economics—and has shared his personal journey to financial freedom in ways that resonate with audiences of all ages and backgrounds. His core principles and messages—like "your house is not an asset" and "Invest for cash flow" and "savers are losers"—have ignited a firestorm of criticism and ridicule… only to have played out on the world economic stage over the past decade in ways that were both unsettling and prophetic.

His point of view is that "old" advice—go to college, get a good job, save money, get out of debt, invest for the long term, and diversify—has become obsolete advice in today's fast-paced Information Age. His Rich Dad philosophies and messages challenge the status quo. His teachings encourage people to become financially educated and to take an active role in investing for their future.

The author of 19 books, including the international blockbuster *Rich Dad Poor Dad*, Robert has been a featured guest with media outlets in every corner of the world—from CNN, the BBC, Fox News, Al Jazeera, GBTV and PBS, to *Larry King Live*, *Oprah*, *Peoples Daily*, *Sydney Morning Herald*, *The Doctors*, *Straits Times*, *Bloomberg*, *NPR*, *USA TODAY*, and hundreds of others—and his books have topped international bestsellers lists for more than a decade. He continues to teach and inspire audiences around the world.

His most recent books include *Unfair Advantage: The Power of Financial Education and Midas Touch*, the second book he has co-authored with Donald Trump.

To learn more, visit RichDad.com

Acknowledgments

As soon as I started writing this book I knew it would be the most important book I've ever written. And over the past two years this book has evolved through four complete rewrites. Like all things in life, it was a process.

A special thanks goes to Mona Gambetta. We have done other books together, but this book tested her patience and our friendship. Never once, throughout the two-year process, did Mona complain. As always, she and the entire Plata Publishing team rallied to bring this book to life and I thank them all.

I also thank the parents who shared their insights and concerns about education and their what is important to them and their children.

I especially thank my sweetheart Kim, for putting up with my absence as a husband during this two-year writing ordeal. Although we live in the same house and have traveled together these past two years, I was not always present.

And most importantly, I thank you, the reader, for being interested in a vital and important subject, the subject of financial education.

Bonus

Book Excerpt

Rich Dad Poor Dad For Teens

The Secrets About Money— That You Don't Learn In School

CONTENTS

Introduction
Your Journey to Financial Freedom Begins Here..1

PART ONE
THE LANGUAGE OF MONEY

Chapter One
A New Way of Learning..11

PART TWO
RICH DAD'S MONEY SECRETS

Chapter Two
The New Rules for Making Money..25

Chapter Three
Work to Learn, Not to Earn..35

Chapter Four
My Money Works for Me..41

Chapter Five
Create Money..45

Chapter Six
It's All About Cash Flow..53

Chapter Seven
Play Games to Learn..63

CONTENTS

PART 3

CREATING YOUR OWN CASH FLOW

Chapter Eight

Moneymaking Opportunities for Teens 77

Chapter Nine

Managing Your Assets 87

Chapter Ten

Managing Your Debt 95

Conclusion

Your Financial Headstart 99

Glossary 103

About the Author 105

Introduction

YOUR JOURNEY TO FINANCIAL FREEDOM BEGINS HERE

Take This Quiz

✔ Do you sometimes feel that what you're learning in school has nothing to do with your life?

Yes ___ **No** ___

✔ Do you feel that school's not really preparing you for the real world?

Yes ___ **No** ___

✔ When you want to buy something that's important to you, do your parents usually say they can't afford it?

Yes ___ **No** ___

✔ Do you secretly worry that you won't be able to live the way you want when you're out on your own?

Yes ___ **No** ___

✔ Do you really want to learn about money, but no one talks about it around your house or at school?

Yes ___ **No** ___

If you answered "yes" to two or more of these questions, this book is for you. I struggled with these situations when I was growing up. I didn't always do well in school. I nearly had to repeat the tenth grade. Now I lead exactly the life I want—a life that includes complete financial freedom.

You may already be struggling to achieve financial freedom and independence in all parts of your life. Even though you might not have to pay rent or put gas in your family's car, there's a chance that you're already thinking about ways to afford your social life.

You may already be saving for something big, like a new computer or a car. If that's the case, this book will help you make your money grow faster and you'll get what you want sooner. You may be struggling to figure out how to pay the high price of going to the movies once a week, or buying CDs, or buying a gift for someone special.

Or, maybe you're one of the many teens whose income is actually *necessary* because your parents aren't able to provide for the whole family. Many adults learned old-fashioned rules for financial security and then were surprised—and defeated—when the rules changed. Unfortunately, many of their children are also suffering as a result.

Rich Dad Poor Dad for Teens: The Secrets About Money—That You Don't Learn in School! covers some really important things I learned when I was growing up. My father taught me to get my education through schoolwork. The father of my best friend Mike gave me a job and taught me about another type of education, one I learned in the real world.

I learned a lot from both dads. They each believed in education but had completely different views on money. One cared about money a lot (Mike's dad) and one didn't care very much about money at all (my dad). One worried about never having enough money (my dad). One thought about money and how to achieve power over it (Mike's dad).

My dad was highly educated, but even so, he used to say that he'd never be rich. He said, "Money doesn't matter." Mike's dad said, "Money is power." My dad always struggled to make ends meet. Mike's dad always had plenty of money. I needed them both to get where I am today. They taught me that there are many ways to be rich. Education is one way to be rich. Financial wealth is another way to be rich.

Rich Dad Poor Dad

In my career I've made enough money in business, real estate, and in paper assets to retire early and fully enjoy the great things life has to offer. I've also written a number of books. My first one, called *Rich Dad Poor Dad*, was about my own personal financial education. In the book, I called my real dad "poor dad," and I called Mike's dad "rich dad." In labeling them this way, I wasn't criticizing either one of them. I was just making a dramatic point about the different ways people think about money and the goals they set.

Rich dad always told me, "If you want to do something—and you *think* you can—chances are, you'll get it done." Rich dad always thought he could be rich, and he did get rich. *Rich Dad Poor Dad* was written to help people who really want to be rich to achieve their financial goals. The book caught on and became very popular. In the book, I offer some views about money that are different from what everyone is used to hearing, but that reflects the realities of today's changing economy—and the messages make sense to people of all kinds of backgrounds and experiences.

Now I travel and share the messages in *Rich Dad Poor Dad* and the other books I've written since then. People often come up to me with questions about how to teach their own kids about money, and so I wrote the book *Rich Kid Smart Kid* to help parents do just that. Now I've decided to write a book especially for teens, and you're holding it in your hands.

Congratulations for picking up this book! *Rich Dad Poor Dad for Teens* will teach you one of the most important subjects that isn't being taught in school: financial literacy. When people talk about literacy, they usually mean knowing how to read well. There's more to the story though. Literacy is about being good at something. I would say it's about being able to speak the language of a certain field. Talking about money requires a whole new language. This book will help you become fluent in the language of money.

There are a lot of ways to be good at something. Being good at money doesn't always come easily. It's something you have to learn and practice. You may study economics in school, or even learn how to balance a checkbook in math class, but that's probably about the extent of financial education in school. And much of what's taught is theoretical instead of a real vocabulary for real-life situations. School is often about studying instead of *practicing*.

This book will pick up where school leaves off. It'll give you the language and understanding you need to feel confident about taking charge of your financial life, whether that means starting your own business or just being able to hold your own in a conversation with someone who might become your financial mentor—your own "rich dad." While some of your friends might be logging major couch time in front of the TV, getting nowhere, you may very well find yourself updating your financial statement, following your stocks online, or brainstorming about business ideas with other friends who, like you, want to own assets instead of liabilities.

Are you nodding your head yes? Or are you saying, "Huh?" to the terms I just mentioned? No matter how much or how little you know this minute, by the time you finish this book, you'll be able to speak the language of money more fluently. You'll begin to understand how money works and how it can work for you. Your journey to financial literacy starts right here, right now.

I actually started to learn about money when I was just nine years old, when Mike's dad, my rich dad, became my mentor. Now I'll share with you what rich dad taught me.

Thinking in Numbers

There are other books that tell you in detail how to open a bank account, balance a checkbook, check a stock price, or get a car loan. But they don't tell you how to *think* about money. Adults often view money as a "necessary evil"—something needed to pay bills, to count and recount, to obsess and worry about. There just never seems to be enough of it. But like it or not, money is something that will always be in your life, so you need to be comfortable with it—not afraid of it like so many adults are. If you're educated about how money works, you gain power over it and can begin building *wealth*.

Financial literacy allows you to not fear money matters, and to see the real value of money. True wealth goes way beyond and is measured by more than cash. Success in life is more than financial success.

This is what I learned when I was growing up, and it's my mission to teach this message to as many young people as I can so that the next generations will be responsible and knowledgeable—and powerful—when it comes to money.

School Is Just the Beginning

Unless you're planning to become a doctor or lawyer or go into a profession that requires a special degree, you may not need to go to any formal training programs after high school or college to earn money if you look for great learning opportunities in a job. In fact, you can be paid to learn in the real world instead of paying high tuition fees to learn in a classroom setting. Your financial education will train you on the job.

Am I saying that education isn't important? Not at all. Education is the foundation of success. I'm saying that school is just one place to learn. We go to school to learn scholastic skills and professional skills. For the most part, we learn financial skills out in the real world.

Remember when you were first learning to ride a bike? Chances are, you started with training wheels and then one day you were ready for a two-wheeler. Perhaps someone held the bike for you until you felt steady—and then let go. You might have wobbled a few times or even fallen off once or twice. But most likely, you got back on the bike and tried until you finally learned to balance, through trial and error and brain power.

Wouldn't it be funny if your parents had taken you to a special bike-riding school? It would have been a waste of their money. There are things you learn in school and other things you learn in life—like how to walk, tie your shoes, ride a bike, and most things that have to do with money.

A new *type* of education is what I'm talking about. The best doctor in the world might have a great medical education, but not know anything when it comes to finances. He or she might save a life on the operating table, but have trouble running an office that makes money.

Amazing, isn't it, to think that you might be getting knowledge that your doctor, or your parents, might not have? Now that's power!

Journal: What Do I Want?

You know about journals. Sometimes you have to keep them in school for English class. But the best journals are the ones that you keep for yourself—where you let your deepest thoughts about real life just spill out. Putting your feelings on paper feels good—and sometimes it helps you express something that was bothering you that you didn't even know was buried deep inside.

Writing about your feelings and experiences with money is one way to help figure out where you are and where you want to go financially. A journal can create a place where you don't have to feel guilty or strange about talking about money. Remember, part of my goal is to help you feel comfortable and powerful with a subject that's often taboo at home or in school. You can start making something that seems abstract feel real by putting your thoughts on paper.

Get yourself a notebook—green (for money) would be a good color!—and different-colored pens to keep nearby as you read this book. Your "Rich Dad Journal" can help you plan your own financial journey as you learn more about mine.

Why not start by writing down all the things that you want? Let your brain buzz with ideas, as if you were creating a birthday wish list. Write in different-colored pens (it helps you be more creative) and draw pictures if you like. Doodling is a good thing!

The list you create doesn't have to be just money-related. Sure, you can write down "car", but you can also write down "make cheerleading squad," "make basketball team," or "get lead in school play." Carry your notebook with you during the day to jot down ideas that come to you. What do you want in your life?

Writing in your journal will also help you chart your progress while reading this book. Keep in mind that you're writing for yourself with no grades and no one judging you. Your journal is a very safe place.

PART ONE

THE LANGUAGE OF MONEY

Chapter One

A NEW WAY OF LEARNING

You Are Smart

First of all, let's get one thing straight: You are smart! I want to make sure you know that from the very beginning. When I was growing up, my dad always told me that everyone is born smart—that every child has a special kind of genius. I love that idea. Even though I didn't always do well in school, I kind of knew the reason didn't have to do with me. I wasn't stupid. I just learned in a different way than the way teachers in school expected me to.

My father taught me to have a good attitude about learning. He taught me to find my best way of learning. If I hadn't done that, I might have flunked out of high school or college. I probably wouldn't have been prepared for my financial life. And I wouldn't have had the confidence to be who I am today.

We all learn differently. The trick is to find the way you learn best. When you do that, you'll discover your own personal genius.

A genius is someone who excels at something. But a genius isn't necessarily good at everything. In fact, a genius usually has a special ability in one area while being pretty average in others.

Did you know that Albert Einstein, who thought up the theory of relativity ($E = mc^2$), never did well in school? He wasn't good at memorizing things, yet he grew up to become one of the greatest mathematical thinkers of all time. His brain focused on ideas rather than facts. Facts, he said, could be found in books, so he never felt the need to keep facts in his head. He wanted his head clear to think creatively.

School asks us to keep facts in our head, but when we're out of school, we usually just need to know where the facts are kept so we can look them up or know whom to call when we need them!

The way our performance is measured in school has very little to do with how intelligent we really are or how successful we can be. The way we perform in school is usually just a measure of how well we take tests. It's not a true measure of the genius you were born with.

Everyone Is Born a Genius

Take out your notebook again and write a list of people you know. Try to get to 20 names. Include people from school, friends, and family members. Put your name at the top of the list. Next to each name write down what that person is good at, no matter what it is. Do you have a friend who can't sit still and is always tapping his foot to some beat that's inside his head? Write that down. Can your sister do the crossword puzzle in ten minutes using a pen without even once glancing at the dictionary? Write that down too. Can you fix almost any computer problem? Put that in the book.

This exercise helps you do a couple of things. It's the first time in your financial journey where you'll be asked to try to see something that you didn't see before—to look at something in a new way. Seeing talents in others you hadn't really recognized leads you to see your own talents. Knowing what your strengths are is one step towards success. Knowing how to detect other people's strengths is a great skill, since creating a solid, reliable team is critical when investing or building a business.

The Myth of IQ and Intelligence

I remember that every once in a while in school, we'd have days when we were given all sorts of tests. The tests were described as "standardized." I was always puzzled by that idea. Every person is unique, so why were we all being evaluated in a cookie-cutter kind of way? The truth is that no two people are alike.

Later I found out that the tests were measuring our IQ, which stands for "intelligence quotient." An IQ number is supposed to represent a person's ability to learn facts, skills, and ideas. But a person's IQ really boils down to this: It's a number that shows the relationship between a person's "mental age" (as measured on a standardized test) and his or her chronological (real) age. Then this number is multiplied by 100 and the result is your IQ. When I was growing up, people thought that an IQ stayed the same for a person's whole life. How limiting! Fortunately, that thinking is changing.

Over the years I've done a lot of reading and research about intelligence, especially about the way people learn. IQ can relate to academics, but it can also relate to other things, like sports. When I was young, I had a high baseball IQ. My friend Andy had a very high academic IQ. Andy had an easier time learning in school because he learned by reading. I learned by doing something first and reading about it later. One formula worked for Andy, and another one worked for me. We each developed our own winning formula.

Everyone Has a Special Learning Style

In those IQ tests in school, only one type of intelligence was being measured: a person's aptitude, or talent, for words. But what if someone is not a word person? I don't especially like to read, so does that mean that I am stuck with a low IQ? Today, the answer is no. In 1983, a psychologist named Howard Gardner published a book called *Frames of Mind*. In it, he describes seven different types of intelligence, not just one. He also argues that people's IQ can change.

Dr. Gardner's list of intelligences, which he also calls learning styles, has created a new road map for learning new skills and information, whether it's rocket science, threading a needle, or financial literacy.

What's Your Learning Style?

Take a look at this list. As you read it, think about what methods best describe your learning style.

This is not a test. I repeat: *This is not a test!* There's no good or bad answer, or high or low score. This is just a way to think about how you learn most comfortably.

On a scale of 1 to 5, circle the number that best describes your learning style.

1 is least like you. 5 is most like you.

♦ **Verbal-linguistic intelligence**

If you always have a book tucked in your backpack, circle 5. This type of intelligence has to do with reading, writing, and language. It's also called being "word smart."

1 2 3 4 5

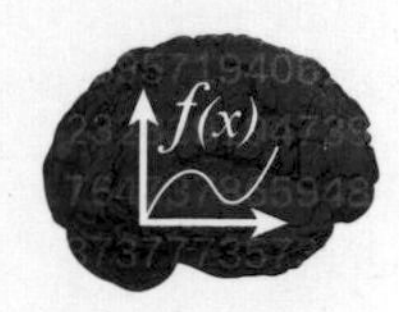

♦ **Numerical intelligence**

If you're one of those people who can do a math problem in your head, circle 5. This intelligence is found in people who easily grasp data and numbers. They're also usually calm and rational thinkers.

1 2 3 4 5

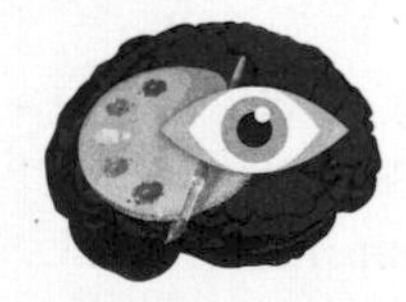

♦ **Spatial intelligence**

If doodling helps you listen in class, or if you're always seeing things that you'd like to photograph, circle 5. This intelligence is used to see patterns, designs, and space—and is found in many artists, architects, and choreographers who can visualize a two- or three-dimensional object or event and make it real.

1 2 3 4 5

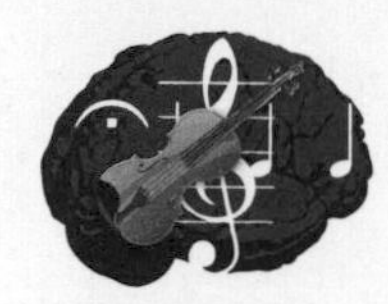

♦ **Musical intelligence**

Are you tapping a pencil or drumming your fingers right now? Head for the number 5. This type of intelligence is especially tuned in to sounds, rhythm, and rhymes.

1 2 3 4 5

♦ **Physical intelligence**

If you love PE in school, or if your room looks like a sporting-goods store, you're physically intelligent—someone with awareness of how to use your body well, like many athletes and dancers.

1 2 3 4 5

♦ **Interpersonal intelligence**

Do friendships seem effortless to you (mark 5) or endlessly complicated (mark 1)? Do you always (or never) know what your friends are thinking—or are you somewhere in between? Mark it down. This intelligence refers to the way someone gets along with other people, which is also called "being people smart."

1 2 3 4 5

♦ **Intrapersonal intelligence**

If interpersonal intelligence is "being people smart," intrapersonal intelligence is "being self-smart," or self-aware. It's also called emotional intelligence, because it relates to the way you handle your emotions, such as fear and anger. Do you understand your own reactions to difficult situations and can you control them? Do you think before you talk back? Are you patient with your own shortcomings, and do you take care of your self-esteem?

1 2 3 4 5

Recently, Dr. Gardner has come up with an eighth intelligence:

♦ **Natural Intelligence**

Natural intelligence describes a person's sensitivity to the world around him or her. If you enjoy being outdoors every weekend or are involved in school or community groups working for the environment, circle 5.

1 2 3 4 5

I've talked a lot with a psychologist who taught innovative learning at Arizona State University about various learning styles and how they help us achieve personal and financial success. Listening to her thoughts, I've added one more intelligence:

♦ **Vision**

Vision is what determines who will be a leader and who will be a follower. Great leaders can see how a situation will play out and take action in response. Winston Churchill, Prime Minister of England during World War II, was one of the world leaders who was against the Nazis from the start. It's as if he could see the terrible things that would happen if they stayed in power. Those of you who see into the future, mark 5.

1 2 3 4 5

Do you notice a pattern to your numbers? Where did you rank yourself highest?

If you ranked yourself a 4 or 5 in verbal-linguistic intelligence, it's likely that you are comfortable with reading and writing as tools for learning. If you ranked yourself a 4 or 5 in physical, musical, or natural intelligences, it's possible that you may have great success in "learning by doing"—using on-the-job training such as internships or being involved in school and community clubs. If you ranked yourself a 4 or 5 in spatial or numerical intelligences, you may benefit from learning through drawing, making charts and diagrams, building models, or working with your hands. If you ranked yourself a 4 or 5 in interpersonal or verbal-linguistic intelligences or vision, you may learn best by talking with friends or grown-ups about their experiences, by debating, or by performing. You'll find your intrapersonal intelligence useful in any type of training, since it will help you maintain your patience and self-esteem in the face of challenges.

It's also possible that you ranked yourself high in several areas. That means that you'll be comfortable with mixing and matching different activities that work with your learning styles.

But what if you didn't rank yourself high in *any area?* Are you doomed? Not at all. This exercise was designed to help you start to think about *how* you think. People who think about the future, who have vision, for example, are likely to become good business leaders. But that doesn't necessarily mean they are *now*. If you don't feel you have vision now, don't panic. You can "pump up" any area if you're determined to exercise your brain, just like rich dad told me to do when I was a kid.

If you're stronger in one area than others, there's a lot you can do to balance out. Here are some suggestions. What other ideas can you come up with?

- **Talk about money** at home and with your friends. *(Verbal-linguistic and interpersonal intelligences)*
- **Read about it!** Lots of magazines about money and finance show how money works in real life, rather than in textbook math problems. The more you learn now about how the experts manage and invest their money, the more inspired you'll be to manage your own. *(Verbal-linguistic and numerical intelligences)*
- **Write about it!** Use your Rich Dad Journal to explore ideas about the role money plays in your life now and in the future. *(Intrapersonal and verbal-linguistic intelligences and vision)*
- **If you get an allowance, take it seriously.** Think of it as part of your income. Make up an invoice for your parents. Figure out ways to earn it and invest it. Manage your own money rather than treating your allowance as a handout. *(Numerical and interpersonal intelligences)*
- **Do your own audit.** Once a week, do an accounting of where your money has gone. *(Numerical intelligence)*
- **Decide to become responsible for your future.** Create a positive attitude about money. Envision the future for yourself. *(Intrapersonal intelligence and vision)*

Finding Your Winning Formula

Unfortunately, the style of learning that is taught in school may not always be the style you are most comfortable with. The ways in which we learn, which might be a combination of learning styles, add up to our winning formula.

Let me return to the example of my friend Andy and me. As I said, I loved to play baseball. I had a high physical intelligence. I also loved to learn about players' statistics. I had a pretty good numerical intelligence. After I had learned all I could about the game from playing it, and had learned all I could about the players from other kids (interpersonal intelligence), I then turned to books to get more information. This style—trying things out first and then reading about them later—has become my winning formula, one that I use to this day.

My friend Andy's winning formula began with books. His strength was verbal-linguistic. He loved to read and study things before he tried them out. He might have made a good manager for a baseball team while I would have made a good player. We were very different, and we each figured out what worked best for us.

Developing Your Financial IQ

Are you beginning to see that any fears or stumbling blocks you may have about money may have to do with how you learn? If verbal-linguistics is not your thing, then, like me, you'll learn by doing and seeing. Later in this book, I'll talk more about learning by doing, and you'll see some concepts explained through pictures and diagrams. Reading this book will also help you develop your intrapersonal intelligence by exploring your goals and fears—and by building your self-esteem.

The road to a high financial IQ is to work on your money skills using the intelligences that work for you—and to work to develop the other intelligences so that your whole brain is working full-steam. Try a few different learning styles on for size. It might not be until the second or third try that you feel you're working with the right combination.

Take out your Rich Dad Journal and make a list of all the activities you do after school and the subjects you do well in. Chances are, you'll see a connection between what you do well and what you enjoy doing. You may also find that there are one or two intelligences from the list that your activities relate to. These are your strengths. The next step will be to find a way to leverage your strengths into financial success by finding financial opportunity.

Rich Dad Q & A

Question:

What do learning styles and winning formulas have to do with getting rich?

Answer:

I'll bet a lot of people who are voted "Most Likely to Succeed" every year in your school yearbook are the people with the best grades. While some of those students will eventually become successful, some of them may not. And it may very well be because they never learned financial intelligence. Many of them will be surpassed in wealth by people like you who are determined to find financial freedom. Discovering your learning style and your personal genius is the first step to having confidence—confidence that allows you to see and pursue opportunities, and to take risks.

Believe It

Tomorrow, listen to yourself as you talk to people throughout the day. How do you sound to others? Determined? Tentative? Do you believe what you are saying? Or do you sound like you don't believe in yourself?

The best way to get what you want is to believe you can get it. Thoughts are powerful. You can make things happen if you set your mind to it.

Here's something you can do to track your belief in yourself: Write down on a piece of paper or index card one statement that describes how you feel about money. It could be something like, "I'll never be rich." Use the piece of paper or index card as your bookmark and check in on your feelings about this statement as you read this book. In the middle of the book, you might write on it, "I will be rich." By the end of the book you might very well cross off the other two sentences and write, "I *am* rich."

All right, you may not really be rich yet. The point I'm making is that turning a thought around can create a mindset that will make something happen. That intention, teamed with the financial education you'll get from this book, is a powerful combination.

Put Your Brain in Motion

Say this sentence: "I can't afford the things I want."
Now say: "How can I afford the things I want?"

One statement stops you from thinking. The other revs your brain and gets you thinking. If you said the first sentence to me, I'd think you'd made up your mind that you won't ever get what you want. But if instead you asked, "How can I afford the things I want?" I would think you were serious about finding solutions. I would view you as positive and forceful.

When rich dad was my mentor, he would say, "My brain gets stronger every day because I use it. The stronger it gets, the more money I make." This book will put your brain in gear.

Bonus

BOOK EXCERPT

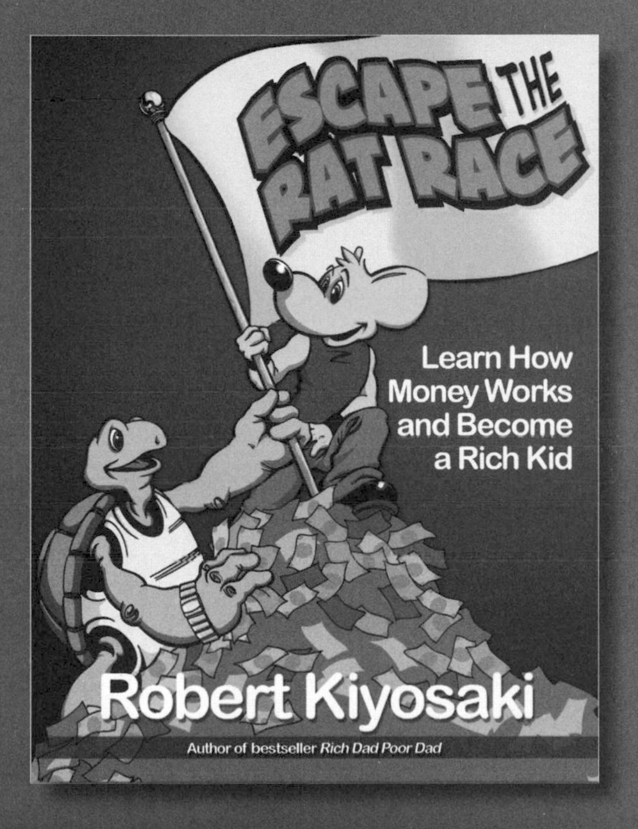

A Color Graphic Novel

Learn How Money Works and Become a Rich Kid

Robert Kiyosaki

Author of bestseller *Rich Dad Poor Dad*

1

Meet Tina, Tim and Red

ESCAPE THE RAT RACE
HOT DOGS
TICKETS
BUMPER CARS
Tim
Red
Tina
HEY DUDE, LET'S GO OVER TO THE ELIMINATOR!
OH MAN, IT'S S'POSED TO BE SO FAST, IT'LL MAKE YOUR EYEBALLS POP OUT!
LET'S DO IT!

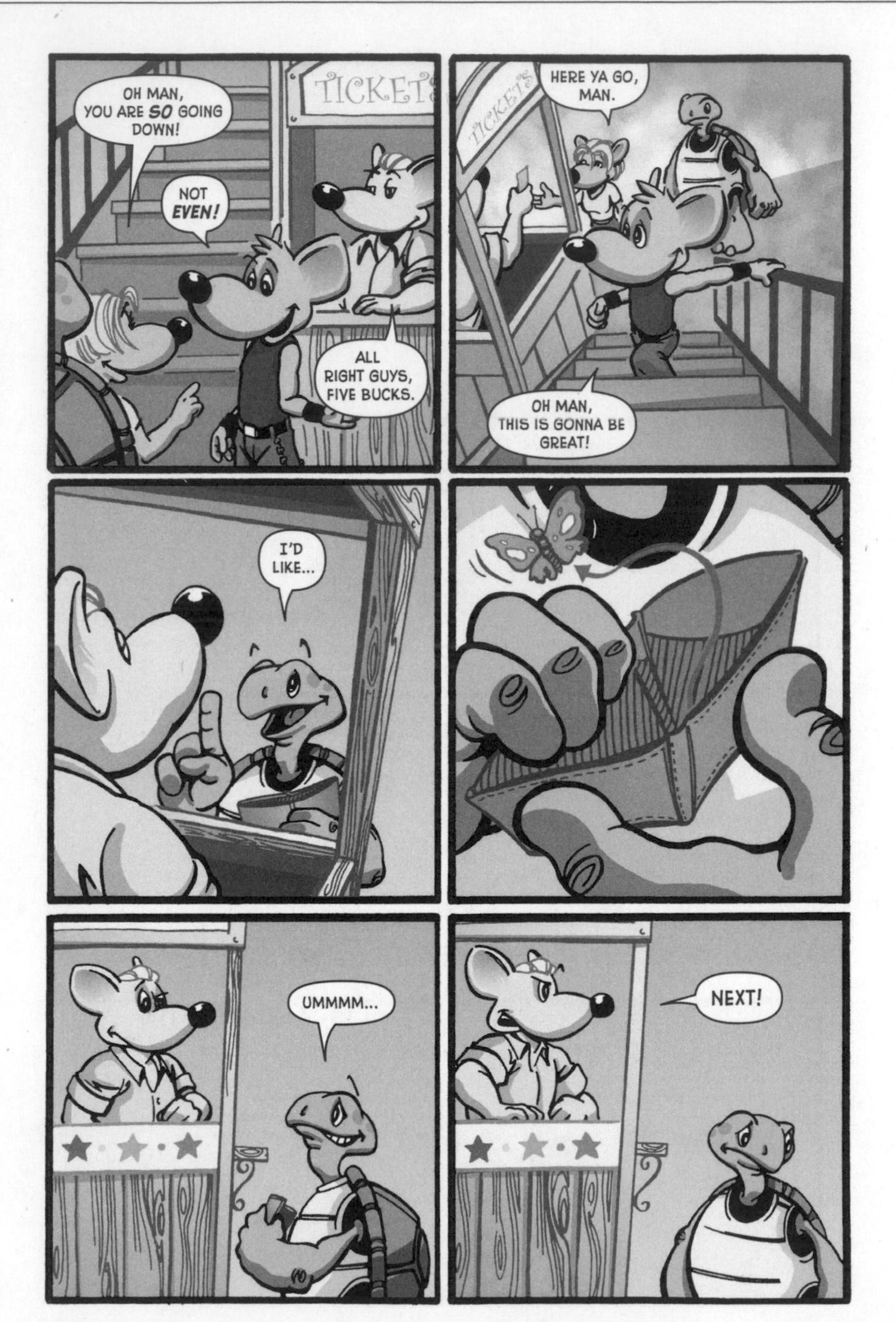
TICKETS
OH MAN, YOU ARE SO GOING DOWN!
NOT EVEN!
ALL RIGHT GUYS, FIVE BUCKS.
TICKETS
HERE YA GO, MAN.
OH MAN, THIS IS GONNA BE GREAT!
I'D LIKE...
UMMMM...
NEXT!

GO AHEAD WITHOUT ME, GUYS. I'LL WAIT HERE.
UGH, THIS STINKS! I'M ALWAYS RUNNING OUT OF MONEY.
RED ALWAYS SEEMS TO HAVE MONEY, AND HE'S GOT A JOB...
HOT DOGS
HELP WANTED
THAT'S IT–I'LL GET A JOB!
IF I HAVE A JOB, I'LL BE MAKING TRUCKLOADS OF MONEY! ALL THE GUYS WILL BE SO JEALOUS, 'CAUSE I'LL BE THE GUY WITH THE BIG BUCKS AND ALL OF THE REALLY COOL STUFF...

WOW, THAT WAS GREAT!
MY TEETH ARE STILL RATTLING!

HEY RED, I THINK I'M GOING TO CATCH UP WITH YOU GUYS LATER.

WELL, I'M HEADING OVER TO THE "RIPPER." YOU COMING RED?
GO AHEAD, I'LL MEET YOU OVER THERE IN A MINUTE.

WHY AREN'T YOU COMING WITH US, MAN? WHAT'S UP?
I CAN'T GO ON ANY MORE RIDES, SINCE I'M OUT OF CASH.

HOT DOGS
HELP WANTED!
SO, I FIGURED SINCE YOUR JOB GIVES YOU ENOUGH MONEY TO GO ON ALL THE RIDES, I THOUGHT MAYBE I'D GET A JOB, TOO. THAT WAY I WON'T HAVE TO WORRY ABOUT MONEY ANYMORE. I'LL BE RICH!

BWAHAHAHAHA!

WHA...WHAT'S SO FUNNY?
WAIT–YOU HONESTLY THINK THAT YOU'RE GONNA GET A JOB AND THEN SUDDENLY BECOME RICH?
WELL... YEAH. I MEAN, YOU'VE GOT A JOB AND YOU'RE ABLE TO GO ON ALL THE RIDES.
YEAH, BUT IT'S NOT MY JOB ALONE THAT MAKES ME MY MONEY.
IT ISN'T?
LOOK, DON'T YOU REMEMBER LAST YEAR WHEN I TOOK THAT SUMMER JOB?
OH YEAH, I DO. YOU WERE TRYING TO BUY THAT BIKE. MAN, YOU WERE EVEN WORKING WEEKENDS.
EXACTLY. I FIGURED IF I GOT THAT SUMMER JOB I'D BE RICH IN NO TIME.
THE PROBLEM WAS, I WORKED ALL SUMMER LONG, BUT NO MATTER HOW HARD I WORKED, I NEVER SEEMED TO HAVE ENOUGH MONEY TO BUY IT--MUCH LESS GET RICH.

BUT, YOU HAVE MONEY NOW... SO, I GUESS YOUR NEW JOB PAYS YOU MORE.
NOPE! SEE, AFTER A SUMMER OF WORKING REALLY HARD, I REALIZED THAT WHAT I WAS DOING OBVIOUSLY WASN'T WORKING.
I REALIZED THERE WERE A LOT OF HARD-WORKING PEOPLE OUT THERE. THEY WORK LONG HOURS, WEEKENDS AND A LOT OF THEM GET PAY RAISES.
PAYROLL
BUT, AT THE END OF THE DAY, MOST OF THEM STILL COMPLAINED ABOUT NOT HAVING ENOUGH MONEY.
SO, IF WORKING REALLY HARD AT A GOOD JOB ISN'T MAKING ALL OF THEM RICH, WHAT MADE ME THINK IT WAS GONNA MAKE ME RICH?
BUT RED, I GOTTA SAY, I DON'T GET IT...IF YOU DON'T GET RICH FROM A JOB, HOW DO YOU GET RICH?

WELL, RATHER THAN JUST ACCEPT THAT I WAS NEVER GOING TO BE RICH, I DECIDED THAT I NEEDED TO LEARN ABOUT MONEY. I NEEDED TO HAVE ***FINANCIAL INTELLIGENCE.***
FINANCIAL INTELLIGENCE?
FINANCIAL INTELLIGENCE IS WHAT SEPARATES THE PEOPLE WHO HAVE MONEY AND KEEP GETTING MORE FROM PEOPLE WHO WISH THEY HAD MONEY AND NEVER SEEM TO HAVE ENOUGH.
UNEMPLOYMENT
TAXES
BILLS
DEBT
INTEREST RATES
FINANCIAL INTELLIGENCE HELPS YOU SEE HOW MONEY WORKS, AND HOW TO MAKE IT WORK FOR YOU-RATHER THAN YOU WORKING FOR IT.
IT'S THE KIND OF INTELLIGENCE THAT SHOWS YOU HOW TO MAKE SURE YOU'RE NEVER WITHOUT MONEY-- AND HOW TO KEEP MONEY FLOWING INTO YOUR POCKETS. ALL WITHOUT YOU HAVING TO WORK AT A JOB IN ORDER TO GET IT.

WOW, THAT SOUNDS REALLY COMPLICATED.
BUT MY GRADES ARE HORRIBLE, AND I'VE NEVER BEEN VERY GOOD IN SCHOOL. NOW I KNOW FOR A FACT THAT I'LL NEVER GET RICH!
I KNOW IT MAY SEEM LIKE THAT AT FIRST, BUT THERE ARE ONLY A FEW BASIC LESSONS YOU NEED TO LEARN. ANYONE CAN DO IT.
THIS IS FINANCIAL EDUCATION. DON'T THINK OF IT AS THE SAME STUFF YOU LEARN IN SCHOOL. THEY DON'T TEACH THIS IN SCHOOL. ANYONE CAN LEARN IT.
UM, WAIT A SEC... YOU MEAN, I DON'T HAVE TO BE REALLY SMART TO GET RICH?
NOPE.
SWEET! NO MORE SCHOOL FOR ME!
WHOA, WHOA DUDE... SLOW DOWN THERE MAN... YOU STILL NEED SCHOOL. IT GIVES YOU OTHER TYPES OF INFORMATION AND SKILLS YOU'LL NEED. IT'S JUST NOT EVERYTHING YOU NEED.
OH. WELL, A GUY CAN HOPE CAN'T HE? SO, HOW EXACTLY DO I BECOME RICH?

FACTS, STATS & SOURCES

An overwhelming **84%** of **students say** they **need financial education.**

Sallie Mae's Study of How Undergraduate Students Use Credit Cards, 2009.

Only 20% of **teachers** feel **comfortable teaching it.**

Results of a National Study by National Endowment for Financial Education, 2009.

41% of U.S. **adults,** or more than 92 million people living in America, gave themselves a **grade of C, D, or F** on their **knowledge of personal finance.**

American Express, *Children Clued In to Recession and Family Finances*, February 16, 2010.

91% of **parents say** they are **committed** to instilling **lessons of financial responsibility** upon their children.

The National Foundation for Credit Counseling and Harris Interactive Inc., Public Relations Research, *The 2009 Consumer Financial Literacy Survey*, March, 2009.

Nearly **72% of the parents** surveyed acknowledged that they are **their children's primary source** of **personal finance education,** and **44%** admit to **needing more guidance** on how to best **teach their children** the skills necessary to become financially responsible and successful adults.

The Hartford Financial Services Group, Inc., *Amid Economic Uncertainty, New National Survey Finds Parents Concerned About Children's Future Financial Independence*, April 14, 2008.

GLOSSARY

GLOSSARY

Rich Dad Definitions

Ages

Agrarian – when the king owned the land, property, and the peasants worked the land

Industrial – from 1500-2000, when the new rich owned production (factories) and peasants became workers (employees)

Information – from 2000 to the present, when the new rich (entrepreneurs) own businesses and create IP, which is intellectual property

Appreciation is an increase in the value of an asset over time. The increase can occur for a number of reasons including increased demand or weakening supply, or as a result of changes in inflation or interest rates. The term appreciation can be used to refer to an increase in any type of asset such as a stock, bond, currency, or real estate. Appreciation is the opposite of depreciation.

Asset is something that puts money in your pocket, whether you work or not.

Canary in the mine a proverbial warning of bad things to come. Because the canary has the ability to detect small concentrations of gas, miners would explore new coal seams with a caged canary. As long as the bird sang, the air supply was safe. A dead canary signaled an immediate evacuation.

Capital is financial resources or assets… the word comes from the word cattle, an early form of 'capital.'

Capitalist is someone who prints his or her own money and an entrepreneur who provides jobs.

Capital gains in basic terms, is buying low and hoping to sell high. Investing for capital gains is also 'gambling'...speculation that the price of something will go up in value.

Cash flow is money flowing into your pocket from an asset.

CBO is the Congressional Budget Office of the United States.

CEO is a Chief Executive Officer.

Commodities were the first type of money—tangibles such as gold, silver, oil, gas, salt, and livestock—and still used today.

Currency is a generally accepted form of money, including coins and paper notes, which is issued by a government and circulated within an economy. It's used as a medium of exchange for goods and services and is the basis for trade and exchange.

Debt

Bad debt is incurring debt to buy doodads (liabilities) and debt that you yourself, not other people, have to pay back.

Good debt is also known as 'leverage,' using other people's money to buy assets. Other people, such as tenants, pay the money back for you.

Debt-to-GDP ratio is a country's national debt—the amount of cash flowing out—as a percentage of the country's Gross Domestic Product, or the amount of cash flowing in. The lower the percentage, the healthier the economy.

Depreciation can be defined in two ways. One is: a decrease in an asset's value caused by unfavorable market conditions. The other is: a method of allocating the cost of a tangible asset over its useful life. Businesses depreciate long-term assets for both tax and accounting purposes. Currency and real estate are two examples of assets that can depreciate or lose value.

Derivative is something that's a product (or by-product) of something else. Orange juice is a derivative of an orange. A more technical definition of derivative is: a security whose price is dependent upon or derived from one or more underlying assets. The derivative itself is merely a contract between two or more parties. Its value is determined by fluctuations in the underlying asset.

Doodads is a term from the CASHFLOW games which means liabilities—non-essential items that we want, but don't necessarily need.

Education comes from the word educe which means 'to draw out.' Our school system seems to define it as putting things—ideas, facts, information—*into* our kids' heads.

Entrepreneurs take risks to solve problems.

ERISA stands for Employee Retirement Income Security Act, a U.S. law passed in 1974 which led to the 401(k). It marked a turning point at which employees were now responsible for their own retirement.

Federal Reserve Bank is an association of global private bankers that control the money supply in the United States. Created in 1913, it is neither federal, nor a bank, nor does it have any reserves.

Fiat currency is paper money printed by the government, backed by nothing except faith in the government that issues it. Fiat currency has always devalued to zero over time as a government prints more and more of it.

Financial statements are our 'report cards' in real life. A financial statement shows how cash flows between a balance sheet (assets and liabilities) and the income statement (income and expenses).

GDP stands for Gross Domestic Product and represents the income of a nation (before expenses).

Genius is the Genie-in-us—what we do that is magical. Our genius is our special gifts and talents...and a child's genius is often found in their dreams.

Golden Rule means, traditionally, that you should "Do unto others as you would have them do unto you." Another definition is: "He who owns the gold makes the rules."

GSE is the acronym for Government Sponsored Enterprises, such as Fannie Mae and Freddie Mac.

HFT stands for High Frequency Trading in the stock market, a computerized trading system which can make over 9,000 trades per minute.

Hyperinflation is a period of rapid inflation that leaves a country's currency virtually worthless.

Income

Ordinary income is generally 'paycheck money' from a salary, commission, or fees and the highest-taxed income. It represents: you working for money.

Portfolio income is also known as 'capital gains' income. Most investors invest by buying low and selling high.

Passive income is also known as 'cash flow,' and it's generally income that's taxed at the lowest rates. Passive income means your money is working for you.

Integrity means whole.

Intellectual property is a new form of wealth, a way of printing your own money.

Investing

Fundamental... *CASHFLOW 101* game

Technical... *CASHFLOW 202* game, using options, puts, and calls for more control

Law of Compensation states that your compensation goes up as experience goes up.

Liabilities are things that take money out of my pocket.

LLC is a Limited Liability Corporation, a legal entity to protect a business or investment.

MBA stands for Master's degree in Business Administration, valued by those who want to climb the corporate ladder.

Money

Commodity – tangibles, real money like gold and silver

Reserve – down payment against a note or credit

Fractional reserve – the ability for banks lend more money than the amount they are holding

Fiat – an IOU, counterfeit money which can be printed in infinite quantities

Multiple Intelligences is Howard Gardner's theory that every person has a unique genius or a unique combination of geniuses. The 7 original geniuses he identified are: verbal, mathematical, spatial, musical, physical, interpersonal, intrapersonal.

Network marketing is a low-risk way to receive sales training in an already-developed business system.

OPM means Other People's Money.

OPT is Other People's Time or Other People's Talents.

Peasant is a person of the land, from the French word *paisant.*

Ponzi scheme is a swindle. Named after Charles Ponzi, the scheme uses money from new investors to give high returns to earlier investors. In time, the entire fraudulent system fails and the later investors lose all their money. (Social Security is often called a government-sponsored Ponzi scheme.)

"Pork" is welfare programs for the rich.

Real estate literally means 'royal land,' from the Spanish word *real* which means 'royal.'

Rich people own property and production. They focus on assets and making money work for them.

Scotoma is a 'blind spot' in which vision is blocked, absent, or deficient.

TARP stands for Troubled Assets Relief Program, and was signed by President George W. Bush in 2008 to provide government stimulus to the economy.

Wealth in Rich Dad terms, is the number of days you can survive without working.

401(k) is a government-sponsored retirement plan, funded by deductions from employees' paychecks and often invested in mutual funds. When withdrawn, 401(k)s are taxed at the highest ordinary-income rate.

Resources

CASHFLOW Quadrant

B-I Triangle

TEAM
LEADERSHIP
Product
Legal
Systems
Communications
Cash Flow
MISSION
®

<table>
<tr><th colspan="3">Cone of Learning</th></tr>
<tr><th>After 2 weeks we tend to remember</th><th></th><th>Nature of Involvement</th></tr>
<tr><td rowspan="3">90% of what we say and do</td><td>Doing the Real Thing</td><td rowspan="5">Active</td></tr>
<tr><td>Simulating the Real Experience</td></tr>
<tr><td>Doing a Dramatic Presentation</td></tr>
<tr><td rowspan="2">70% of what we say</td><td>Giving a Talk</td></tr>
<tr><td>Participating in a Discussion</td></tr>
<tr><td rowspan="4">50% of what we hear and see</td><td>Seeing it Done on Location</td><td rowspan="7">Passive</td></tr>
<tr><td>Watching a Demonstration</td></tr>
<tr><td>Looking at an Exhibit
Watching a Demonstration</td></tr>
<tr><td>Watching a Movie</td></tr>
<tr><td>30% of what we see</td><td>Looking at Pictures</td></tr>
<tr><td>20% of what we hear</td><td>Hearing Words (Lecture)</td></tr>
<tr><td>10% of what we read</td><td>Reading</td></tr>
</table>

Source: Cone of Learning adapted from Dale, (1969)

PROFESSION ____________________ **PLAYER** ____________________

GOAL: Get out of the Rat Race and onto the Fast Track by building up your **Passive Income** to be **greater** than your **Total Expenses**

INCOME STATEMENT

INCOME

Description	Cash Flow
Salary:	
Interest/Dividends:	
Real Estate/Business:	

AUDITOR ____________________

(Person on your right)

Passive Income: $ ____________________
(Cash Flow from Interest/Dividends + Real Estate/Business)

Total Income: $ ____________________

EXPENSES

Taxes:	
Home Mortgage Payment:	
School Loan Payment:	
Car Loan Payment:	
Credit Card Payment:	
Retail Payment:	
Other Expenses:	
Child Expenses:	
Loan Payment:	

Number of Children: ____________________
(Begin game with 0 Children)

Per Child Expense: $ ____________________

Total Expenses: $ ____________________

Monthly Cash Flow (PAYDAY): $ ____________________
(Total Income - Total Expenses)

BALANCE SHEET

ASSETS

Savings:

Stocks/Funds/CDs:	# of Shares:	Cost/Share:

Real Estate/Business:	Down Pay:	Cost:

LIABILITIES

Home Mortgage:	
School Loans:	
Car Loans:	
Credit Cards:	
Retail Debt:	
Real Estate/Business:	**Mortgage/Liability:**
Loan:	

G101CT18.v12

CASHFLOW® for Kids

SNEAK PEEK

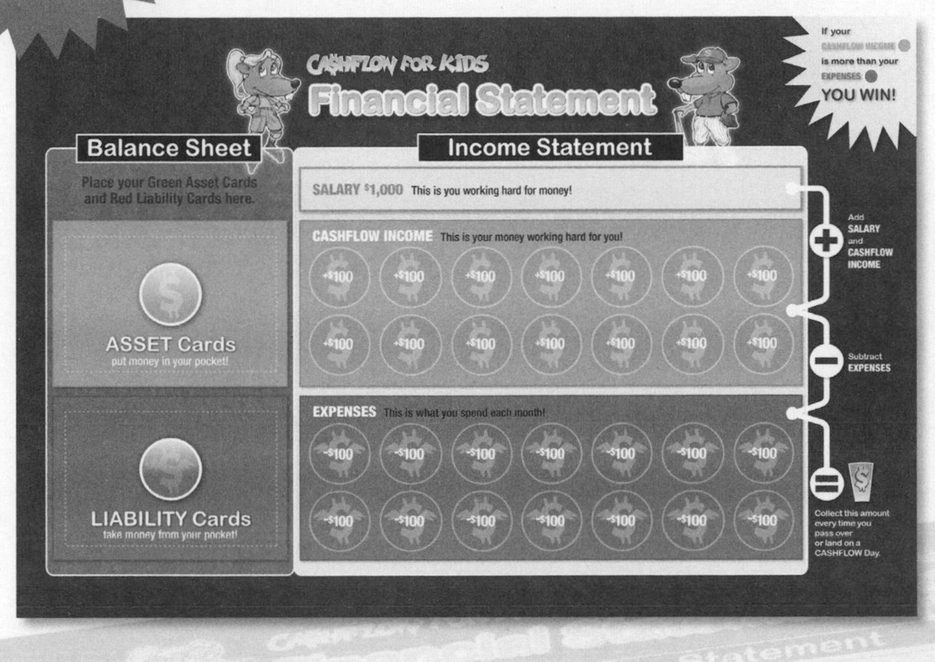

Financial Statement

A Financial Statement is your report card in the real world – it's a snapshot of your finances.

This financial statement is found in the board game, CASHFLOW for Kids.

NOTES

Best-selling Books
by Robert T. Kiyosaki

Rich Dad Poor Dad
What the Rich Teach Their Kids About Money –
That the Poor and Middle Class Do Not

Rich Dad's CASHFLOW Quadrant
Guide to Financial Freedom

Rich Dad's Guide to Investing
What the Rich Invest in That the Poor and Middle Class Do Not

Rich Dad's Rich Kid Smart Kid
Give Your Child a Financial Head Start

Rich Dad's Retire Young Retire Rich
How to Get Rich and Stay Rich

Rich Dad's Prophecy
Why the Biggest Stock Market Crash in History Is Still Coming...
And How You Can Prepare Yourself and Profit from It!

Rich Dad's Success Stories
Real-Life Success Stories from Real-Life People
Who Followed the Rich Dad Lessons

Rich Dad's Guide to Becoming Rich
Without Cutting Up Your Credit Cards
Turn Bad Debt into Good Debt

Rich Dad's Who Took My Money?
Why Slow Investors Lose and Fast Money Wins!

Rich Dad Poor Dad for Teens
The Secrets About Money – That You Don't Learn In School!

Escape the Rat Race
Learn How Money Works and Become a Rich Kid

Rich Dad's Before You Quit Your Job
Ten Real-Life Lessons Every Entrepreneur Should Know
About Building a Multimillion-Dollar Business

Rich Dad's Increase Your Financial IQ
Get Smarter with Your Money

Conspiracy of the Rich
The 8 New Rules of Money

Unfair Advantage
The Power of Financial Education

NOTES

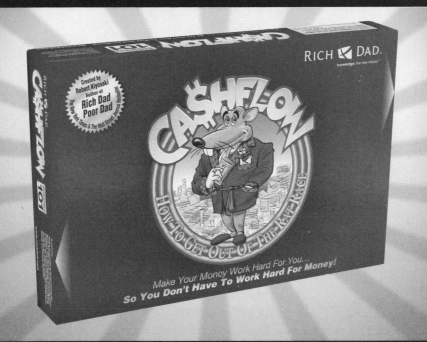

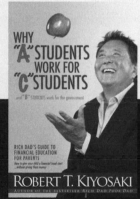

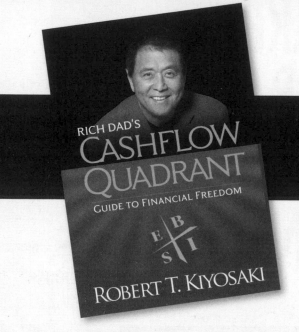